THE GRAND
FAILURE

THE GRAND FAILURE

FAILURE

*The Birth and Death of Communism
in the Twentieth Century*

Zbigniew Brzezinski

Charles Scribner's Sons
New York

Charles Scribner's Sons
Macmillan Publishing Company
866 Third Avenue, New York, NY 10022
Collier Macmillan Canada, Inc.

Library of Congress Cataloging-in-Publication Data
Brzezinski, Zbigniew K., 1928–
     The grand failure : the birth and death of communism in the twentieth century /
Zbigniew Brzezinski.
          p.   cm.
     Includes index.
     ISBN 0-684-19034-6
     1. Communism—History—20th century.   2. Communism.   I. Title.
HX40.B76   1989   88-38050   CIP
335.43—dc19

Macmillan books are available at special discounts for bulk purchases for sales pro-
motions, premiums, fund-raising, or educational use. For details, contact:

     Special Sales Director
     Macmillan Publishing Company
     866 Third Avenue
     New York, NY 10022

10 9 8 7 6 5 4 3 2 1

Printed in the United States of America

For Mrs. Emilie Beneš

Contents

Author's Note and Acknowledgments   ix

Introduction   1

I   The Grand Failure   13

1   The Leninist Legacy   17
2   The Stalinist Catastrophe   22
3   Stagnant Stalinism   33
4   The Paradox of Reform   41

II   The Soviet Disunion   51

5   From Vision to Revisionism   55
6   The Ten Dynamics of Disunion   65
7   An Evolving or Decaying Communism?   95

III   Organic Rejection   103

8   Ideological Transplantation and Transmutation   107
9   Polish Society's Self-Emancipation   114
10   From Social Solidarity to Political Pluralism   120
11   The Emerging Regional Unrest   129
12   Imperial Retrenchment   140

IV   Commercial Communism   145

13   China's Double Three Tries   150
14   Political Conflict and the Birth of Reform   157
15   Reform Strategy and Ideological Flexibility   164
16   The Real Cultural Revolution   175

V   Discredited Praxis   187

17   From Revolutionary Comintern to Annual Convention   192

18   Political Irrelevance in the Developed World   200
19   Socioeconomic Failure in the Developing Countries   210
20   Global Ideological Disintegration   225

VI   The Agony of Communism   229

21   The General Crisis   232
22   The Historical Record   236
23   Future Prospects   243
24   Post-Communism   252

     Appendix: Tables   259

     Index   271

Author's Note
and Acknowledgments

This book was completed in August 1988. Given the accelerating velocity of communism's historical disintegration, it is likely that further important events will transpire before the book reaches its readers. The resurgence of nationalism in Eastern Europe and within the Soviet Union poses a particularly dynamic challenge to the communist system as we have known it. Nonetheless, I believe that the framework developed in this volume will stand the test of time and will give its readers a useful tool for understanding what is happening within the increasingly turbulent Communist world.

The book represents in some respects a return to some of the issues that I addressed almost thirty years ago in my *The Soviet Bloc: Unity and Conflict*. In that major volume, I argued—at the time, contrary to the prevailing wisdom—that the forces of conflict were beginning to assert themselves over the elements of unity in the Soviet-dominated world. About a decade later, in a work entitled *Between Two Ages*, I made the case that the United States was plunging into the new technetronic age and that the Soviet Union would lag behind, ideologically and systemically mired down in the industrial phase of its development. This thesis was then also controversial. In this book, I anticipate the eventual demise—within a historically foreseeable period—of communism as this century has come to know it.

In this effort, I have benefited from the help of several key associates. As in the case of my two most recent books, Trudy Werner, my executive assistant—by skillfully managing my affairs and by imposing order on the various demands on my time—has made it possible for me to concentrate my efforts on the completion of this volume. Mr. Marin Strmecki, my research associate, directed the supportive research and made an invaluable contribution in criticizing and editing my drafts. To both of them I owe a very major debt, which I am pleased to acknowledge. Moreover, Marin was helped by several research assistants (Cecilia Pulido, Cindy Arends, Beth Smith, and Courtney Nemroff), and I thank them also.

Mr. Robert Stewart of Scribners encouraged me in this undertaking, skillfully edited the volume, and helped me in shaping its final organizational structure. Mrs. Leona Schecter, my agent, brought me together with Scribners and most effectively negotiated the arrangements that made this outcome possible.

Finally, there are two special debts that I must acknowledge. As always, my best and fiercest critic was my wife, Muška. More importantly, she encouraged me to write this book—and my writing of it was facilitated by my conversion to the Macintosh SE, which suddenly transformed the pain of writing into a technologically delightful adventure.

Zbigniew Brzezinski
Northeast Harbor, Maine
August 31, 1988

Introduction

This is a book about the terminal crisis of communism. It describes and analyzes the progressive decay and the deepening agony both of its system and of its dogma. It concludes that by the next century communism's irreversible historical decline will have made its practice and its dogma largely irrelevant to the human condition. Prospering only where it abandons its internal substance even if still retaining some of its external labels, communism will be remembered largely as the twentieth century's most extraordinary political and intellectual aberration.

The argument of the book is developed in six parts. The first argues that the key to communism's historic tragedy is the political and socioeconomic failure of the Soviet system. The second examines in more depth the current Soviet attempts to reform and revitalize that system and concludes that success is less likely than continuing internal decay or turmoil. The third reviews the social and political consequences of the imposition of communism on Eastern Europe and argues that the region, spearheaded by the self-emancipation of Polish society, has begun the process of repudiating its Soviet-imposed communist systems. The fourth reviews the Chinese experience with its own homegrown variety of communism and concludes that the chances for the success of China's reforms are growing as its leaders abjure established doctrines. The fifth spotlights the ideological and political decline of international Communist appeal. The sixth and final part looks more broadly at communism's final agony and at the likely post-Communist phenomenon.

Communism's domination of much of the history of the twentieth century was largely rooted in its role as the timely "grand oversimplification." Locating the origins of all evil in the institution of private property, it postulated that the abolition of property would permit

1

the attainment of true justice and of the perfection of human nature. This promise captivated the commitment and energized the hopes of hundreds of millions of people. It was thus psychologically well suited to the feelings of the newly politically awakened masses. In that sense it had some similarities to the appeal of the great religions, each of which provided an over-arching explanation of what life is all about. It was the totality and the simultaneous simplicity of the interpretation that was so captivating, so reassuring, and so firm a guidepost to zealous action.

Like the great religions, the communist doctrine offered several layers of analysis, ranging from the simplest explanation to rather more complex philosophical concepts. To the semi-literate, it sufficed to learn that all life is defined by the class struggle and that a state of social bliss will be achieved by the communist society. Especially gratifying from a psychological point of view to the disadvantaged was the justification of brutal violence against "enemies of the people," those previously endowed with greater material wealth, who could now be pleasurably humbled, oppressed, and destroyed.

But communism was not only a passionate response to deeply felt concerns or just a self-righteous creed of social hate. It was also a readily understandable system of thought, seemingly providing a unique insight into the future as well as the past. It satisfied the yearning of the newly literate segments of society for a deeper understanding of the world around them. Thus, to the intellectually more discriminating, Marxist theory seemed to provide the key to understanding human history, an analytical tool for assessing the dynamics of social and political change, a sophisticated interpretation of economic life, and a set of insights into social motivation. The concept of the "historical dialectic" appeared to be an especially valuable means for coping with the contradictions of reality. At the same time, the emphasis placed on political action to promote a redemptive "revolution," and on all-embracing state control to achieve a rationally planned just society, appealed especially to the intellectual's craving for action seemingly based on reason.

Communism thus appealed to the simpletons and to the sophisticates alike: It gave each a sense of direction, a satisfactory explanation, and a moral justification. It made its subscribers feel self-righteous, correct, and confident all at once. It left nothing uncertain. It claimed to be simultaneously a philosophy and a science. On whatever personal level of intellectual sophistication, or lack thereof, it provided timely guidance, historical comfort, and—above all—a grand oversimplification of what can be achieved through direct political action.

Moreover, by combining passion with reason, the communist doctrine was in a position to influence decisively the two central sources of human conduct. Political passion can be translated into enormous political power. Reason is attracted by the notion of social engineering, and social engineering is the point of departure for the mobilization of political power. Together, they produced the enormity of concentrated state power that came to be the most manifest characteristic of communism.

The twentieth century thus became the century of the State. This was largely an unexpected development. Indeed, no one of high public visibility predicted that the views elaborated by an émigré German-Jewish librarian, and by the turn of the century so enthusiastically embraced by an obscure Russian political pamphleteer, would become the century's compelling doctrine. Neither in America nor in Europe was much thought given to the likelihood of any serious ideological challenge to the nature of the existing system. The philosophical moorings of the status quo were generally seen as firm, indeed even immutable.

As was to be expected, January 1, 1900, was greeted everywhere by the usual spate of predictions regarding the prospects for the last century of the second millennium. Naturally, predictions varied. By and large the dominant note sounded on the occasion of the turn of the century in the leading journals of the Western world, and among Western statesmen, was self-congratulatory. The pervasive tone was of complacent satisfaction with the status quo, of almost intoxicated praise for the prosperity that was said to be increasingly widespread and—in the case of America—of great expectations for enhanced economic and political power. *The New York Times*, in its "Business Outlook" dated January 1, 1900, proclaimed that "prosperity has entered into every line of industry in the United States. The producer from the soil has had unusual prosperity, as have the workers in mines, mills, and workshops." It concluded its diagnosis by asserting, "in America, unbounded prosperity may be looked forward to during our forward march, making us the foremost Nation of the world."

Much the same theme dominated the State of the Union addresses by President William McKinley on December 3, 1900, and Theodore Roosevelt on December 2, 1902. But Roosevelt also noted that "there are many problems for us to face at the outset of the twentieth century—grave problems abroad and still graver at home." But he, too, reiterated the theme that "never before has material well-being been so widely diffused among our people. . . . Of course, when the conditions have favored the growth of so much that was good, they have also favored somewhat the growth of what was evil. . . . The evils are real and some of them are menacing, but they are the outgrowth, not of misery or decadence, but of prosperity."

Press editorials echoed this mood. Faith in democracy and confidence in America were seen as one. *The North American Review*, in an article entitled "The Burden of the Twentieth Century," focused on the question of the future of democracy and confidently asserted, "It is to America, and to America alone, that we must look. . . . It is a question the importance of which, to the future of humanity, cannot be exaggerated. Would that in the year 1999 or 2000 one could come back to earth, in order to hear the answer. May it be favorable to democracy. And may it be final!" And *The Washington Post* greeted the new century on January 1, 1900, with a triumphant reaffirmation of the American mission in its overseas imperial possessions, adding exultantly, "they are ours, and all talk of anti-expansion is as idle as the chatter of magpies."

On the European continent, the mood was no less confident, the view of the future similarly benign. In Great Britain, optimistic jingoism characterized the assessment offered by the *London Times* (welcoming the new century more correctly on January 1, 1901): "We have a reasonable trust that England and her sons will emerge triumphant from that ordeal at the end of the Twentieth Century as at the end of the Nineteenth, and that then and for ages to come they will live and prosper one united and Imperial people, to be 'a bulwark for the cause of men'." More serious judgments, however, focused on the longer-range threat to British primacy posed by the rise of American industrial prowess, with *The New York Times* on December

31, 1900, citing the aforementioned London paper as expressing concern that "it is useless to disguise the fact that Great Britain is being outdistanced."

In France and Germany, cultural and national optimism were also the major themes of the day. Faith in the inevitability of democracy pervaded the central message of *Le Journal des Debats*, which on January 5, 1901, asserted, "Today, one third of all human beings have rights recognized and guaranteed by the law." On the same day, the promise of science even in the realm of politics dominated *Le Figaro*'s comment that "science will teach man tolerance, by reflecting in front of him the images of his own mistakes."

In Germany, perhaps because of its central geopolitical location in Europe, the popular press reflected an appreciation of the continuity of conflict in international affairs and a preoccupation with Germany's emerging power. On January 1, 1900, the Berlin daily, *Tagliche Rundschau*, editorialized, "It will be a healthy lesson for the British when they recognize that the vulnerable times of compliances have ended. Then we will face England differently, being more respected." Only the Social Democratic paper, *Vorwarts*, injected an ideological note, greeting the New Year and the new century with a reaffirmation of capitalism's inevitable demise, but with the admonition that "we all know that the liquidation of modern bourgeois society will not proceed as quickly as the class conscious proletariat or even the prominent thinkers of socialism thought a generation ago."

Strikingly absent in these visions of the future designed for mass consumption was any preoccupation with ideological matters or systemic doctrines. Only in France and in Germany, with socialists already present in parliamentary institutions, was socialism taken more seriously, but even there on the level of the public discourse any possibility of an ideological upheaval, not to speak of ideological conflicts, was discounted. On the contrary, the prevailing view was well expressed by a Parisian commentator in *Le Figaro* who welcomed the new century with the prediction that it would be a century of reason rather than of passion: "What the twentieth century will probably bring us will be the penetration into social and private life of science which will give us rules for our conduct. And it will be a magnificent spectacle, of which I should like to see the beginning.

Let us hope that the nineteenth century which cradled us, will carry away with it into the abyss of the centuries the idiotic hatreds, stupid recriminations, and foolish calumnies which have saddened its last days, and which are unworthy of reasoning men."

Yet, as it turned out, much of the twentieth century came to be dominated not only by ideological passions but, more specifically, by a passion masquerading as scientific reason, namely communism. Indeed, by the middle of this century communism had come to prevail over the world's largest continent from the river Elbe to the Kamchatka peninsula and Shanghai, dominating the lives of more than a billion people. In Western Europe, communist parties were reaching for power. In Latin America, communist ferment was fusing with anti-American nationalism. Among the intellectuals in the Western world, and in the anti-colonial movements, Marxism was both the mode and on the march.

The State, by harnessing political power and by employing the newly available tools of social engineering made possible by the onset of industrialism, now became the central focus of social life, of social obedience, and of personal loyalty. Though this development was worldwide, it emerged in the most acute form first in the Soviet Union, in a state of total power dedicated, ironically, to the concept of the eventual "withering away" of the State.

The appearance of communism as the major political manifestation of the twentieth century has to be seen in tandem with the rise of fascism and nazism. In fact communism, fascism, and nazism were generically related, historically linked, and politically quite similar. They were all responses to the traumas of the industrial age, to the appearance of millions of rootless, first-generation industrial workers, to the iniquities of early capitalism, and to the newly acute sense of class hatred bred by these conditions. World War I brought about the collapse of existing values and of the political order in Tsarist Russia and in Imperial Germany. It generated acute social tensions as well in newly industrialized Italy. All these gave rise to movements that wrapped the concept of social justice around a message of social hatred and that proclaimed organized state violence as the instrument of social redemption.

The titanic war later waged between Hitler's Nazi Germany and Stalin's Soviet Russia has made many forget that the struggle between them was a fratricidal war between two strands of a common faith. To be sure, one proclaimed itself to be unalterably opposed to Marxism and preached unprecedented racial hatred; and the other saw itself as the only true offspring of Marxism in practicing unprecedented class hatred. But both elevated the State into the highest organ of collective action, both used brutal terror as the means of exacting social obedience, and both engaged in mass murders without parallel in human history. Both also organized their social control by similar means, ranging from youth groups to neighborhood informers to centralized and totally censored means of mass communications. And, finally, both asserted that they were engaged in constructing all-powerful "socialist" states.

It is relevant to note here that Hitler was an avid student of the political practices initiated both by Lenin and by Mussolini. These two men were his precursors, especially in regard to the use of new means of communications in energizing and then in mobilizing the newly politically awakened masses. But all three were pioneers in the quest for total power, and they were extraordinarily skillful in blending the exploitation of political passion with disciplined political organization. The way they seized power was the point of departure for the way they wielded power—and thus emerged in the totalitarian state a new type of political order.

Philosophically, Lenin and Hitler were both advocates of ideologies that called for social engineering on a vast scale, that arrogated to themselves the role of arbiters of truth, and that subordinated society to an ideological morality, one based on class warfare and the other on racial supremacy, and that justified any action that advanced their chosen historical missions. Hitler was a careful student of the Bolshevik concept of the militarized vanguard party and of the Leninist concept of tactical accommodation in the service of ultimate strategic victory, both in seizing power and in remolding society. Institutionally, Hitler learned from Lenin how to construct a state based on terror, complete with its elaborate secret police apparatus, its reliance on the concept of group culpability in dispensing justice, and its orchestrated show trials.

Moreover, with the passage of time each side came to embrace the other's major themes and even symbols. During World War II, Stalin increasingly legitimized his new ruling class with nationalist slogans, by pretentious uniforms even for his civilian bureaucrats, and through an exaltation of Great Power ambitions highly reminiscent of Nazi practices. Hitler at times remarked that while Stalin was a "beast," the Soviet dictator was at least a beast "on a grand scale," that Stalin was a "fellow of genius" for whom one had to have "unreserved respect," and that with another ten to fifteen years in power he would make the Soviet Union "the greatest power in the world." After the abortive coup against Hitler in 1944, the Nazi regime justified the extermination of the German aristocracy in a language of class hatred indistinguishable from the Soviet Union's. Hitler even exhibited a perverse envy of Stalin, who had taken Leninism to its logical conclusion. "I have often bitterly regretted," he said, "that I did not purge my officer corps in the way Stalin did."

In fact, it is no exaggeration to assert that Hitler was as much a Leninist as Stalin was a Nazi. Generically, and historically, the two totalitarian leaders were congenial to each other. Both tyrants justified the imposition of total control by the State by the openly proclaimed objective of reconstructing society from top to bottom, in keeping with a dogmatic but otherwise vague notion of a new utopian order. That reconstruction was to be achieved through the direct use of state power, crushing traditional social forms and eliminating any manifestations of social spontaneity. Totalitarianism thus became synonymous with quintessential statism.

World War II ended with the defeat of one major proponent of the new exaltation of the State as the supreme agent of history. But it resulted, also, in the enormous spread of influence and power of the other. The communist system, confined since 1917 to most of the earlier Tsarist empire, now dramatically expanded. Central Europe became de facto a Soviet province by 1947. China initially proclaimed its fidelity to the Soviet model after the Communist victory in 1949, and Communist regimes appeared in half of Korea in 1945 and in half of Vietnam in 1954. Within a decade after the end of World War II, more than a billion people were living under communist systems. Almost all of Eurasia had become communist, with only its far eastern and far western peripheries sheltered by American power. Communism seemed on the march, perhaps only temporarily halted by the injection of U.S. money and military power into large parts of the world.

Even more important was the indirect spread of the essence of the communist idea. Over the last four decades, almost everywhere the inclination to rely on state action to cope with economic or social ills had become quite prevalent. To be sure, in societies with more entrenched democratic traditions special efforts were made to prevent an excessive and abusive concentration of political power. Freedom of choice was preserved by open political competition and by constitutional safeguards. Nonetheless, even in highly democratic societies the notion of state action as the best means for promoting economic well-being and social justice became the dominant outlook.

This is not to say that democratic socialism, or the welfare state, were insidious manifestations of the spread of communism; indeed, both often represented the most effective means of combating the appeal of the communist doctrine and of creating a democratic alternative to the communist model. But the reliance on the state as the principal instrument of social salvation indirectly enhanced the status of the Soviet system as the most extreme example of state-planned and state-directed social innovation.

Inevitably, this tendency contributed to the initial inclination of the scores of newly created post-colonial states to embrace various varieties of state socialism. It also reinforced the initial inclination of many of them to look to the Soviet experience for inspiration and for an example to imitate. During the 1950s and the 1960s, much of the Third World was uncritically acclaiming the Soviet model as providing the best and the fastest road to modernity and social justice. Soviet leaders, in their trips abroad, were basking in uncritical adulation and freely dispensing advice on how best to adopt the Soviet path to socialism.

In the advanced world, the same intellectual fashions were much in vogue. As Paul Hollander has cataloged in his book, *Political Pilgrims*, many Western intellectuals who traveled to the Soviet Union in the 1920s and 1930s swallowed wholesale the grand oversimplification offered by communism. Lion Feuchtwanger, a German novelist, wrote, "I sympathized inevitably with the experiment of basing the construction of a gigantic state on reason alone." Like many activist religious leaders, American Quaker Henry Hodgkin embraced the collectivist rhetoric of the Soviet regime, proclaiming, "As we look at Russia's great experiment in brotherhood, it may seem to us that some dim perception of Jesus' way, all unbeknown, is inspiring it." Edmund Wilson perceived a more secular utopia: "You feel in the Soviet Union that you are at the moral top of the world where the light never really goes out."

Among these intellectuals, Soviet-style "democracy" was accepted as being as legitimate, if not more so, as Western democracy. Stalin's totalitarianism was seldom even noted, much less condemned. Sidney and Beatrice Webb insisted that Stalin did not rule as a despot: "He has not even the extensive power which the Congress of the United States has temporarily conferred upon President Roosevelt, or that which the American Constitution entrusts for four years every successive president."

This unqualified admiration of the Soviet system under Stalin extended even to the GULAG. Dr. J. L. Gillin, a one-time president of the American Sociological Society, wrote, "It is clear that the system is devised to correct the offender and return him to society." Harold Laski, the British political economist, concurred, writing that he detected in the Soviet system an "insistence that the prisoner must live, so far as conditions make it possible, a full and self-respecting life." A longtime journalist on Soviet affairs, Maurice Hindus, took this acclaim a step further: "Vindictiveness, punishment, torture, severity, humiliation, have no place in this system." George Bernard Shaw even noted an element of voluntarism in Stalin's system of labor camps, writing, "in England a delinquent enters [jail] as an ordinary man and comes out a criminal type whereas in Russia he enters as a criminal type and would come out an ordinary man but for the difficulty of inducing him to come out at all. As far as I could make out they could stay as long as they liked."

The initial fascination with the Soviet effort to build a new society during the 1930s, reflected in these blissfully misguided views, gained an enormous boost with Stalin's defeat of Hitler. Even the ensuing Cold War could not disabuse many Western intellectuals of their romance with the Communist reconstruction of society. Throughout the 1950s, and even into the 1960s, in many Western universities, the predominant social outlook was some form of "leftism," with the Soviet Union often obtaining the benefit of the doubt because of the attraction to the intellectuals of its domestic state-led social experimentation.

More generally, the new orthodoxy tended to stress the primacy of politically directed social planning. Largely in reaction to the chaos produced both by the Great Depression and then World War II, the globe was now moving into an era in which social behavior was to be increasingly channeled through political means and in which economic activity was responsive to planned political direction. Even though many advocates of the new orthodoxy were conscious of the fact that Soviet reality diverged dramatically from the ideal, they believed the potential for achieving the ideal was implicit in the Soviet system and thus held the way to the future.

The cumulative effect of the seeming success of the Soviet system was to make the twentieth century into an era dominated by the rise and the appeal of communism. Though America emerged during that century as the dominant global power, and though the American way of life exuded incomparably greater tangible attraction, America was widely—and unfairly—perceived as engaging in a defensive holding action, futilely seeking to stem history's inevitable tide. It was the spread of communism to Central Europe and to China that so fundamentally transformed global politics, that dominated intellectual discourse, and that seemed to represent the augury of history.

Yet, within a mere hundred years of its inception, communism is fading. The ideas and practices associated with communism have been discredited, as much so within the Communist world as outside of it. By the late 1980s, to spur their lagging economies into greater productivity and to motivate their workers into greater efforts, Communist leaders in the Soviet Union, in China, and in Eastern Europe were routinely making assertions that would not have been out of place at the annual meeting of the American Association of Manufacturers. Thus, as *Pravda* reported on August 11, 1988, Soviet workers heard Aleksandr Yakovlev, the Politburo member then responsible for Marxist-Leninist doctrine, proclaim that nowadays "the ideology of the owner must be paramount," adding that "instilling a sense of ownership was a good thing, for when a worker has a stake in something, a person will move mountains; if he does not, he will be indifferent." Almost at the same time, Polish workers were reminded by Stanisław Ciosek, a Politburo member, that "it is not possible for everyone to have his living standard improved to an equal degree. Surely those should be favored who serve the national economy well, and they should be better paid." To drive the message home, Ciosek added, "such are the brutal laws of economics." And only a few months earlier, at the far eastern extremity of the Communist world, Chinese workers were being ideologically enlightened by a new Politburo member, Hu Qili, who stated "whatever benefits the development of the productive forces is required or permitted by socialism."

On the eve of the last decade of the century, almost every communist system was thus groping for reforms that, in effect, were tantamount to a repudiation of the Marxist-Leninist experience. Most important was the associated philosophical rejection of communism's root premises. The exaltation of the State was giving way almost everywhere to the elevation of the individual, of human rights, of personal initiative, and even of private enterprise.

The resulting flight from statism, the growing primacy of human rights, and the belated turn to economic pragmatism represent an enormous revolution in attitudes and in the fundamental philosophy of life. It is a turnaround that is likely to have far-reaching and long-lasting effects. It is already affecting both politics and economics worldwide. And it portends the growing likelihood that by January 1, 2000, the social forecasters may assign to the communist doctrine—this time with genuine justification—as little importance for the future of the twenty-first century as was the case—much less justifiably—with their predecessors a hundred years earlier.

The terminal crisis of contemporary communism is thus all the more historically dramatic for the very suddenness of its onset. It is, therefore, timely to ask what befell the doctrine and the practice that for so much of this century seemed to be the wave of the future. What produced the disappointment, the failure, and especially the crimes that cumulatively so discredited an ideology, a political movement, and a social experiment that were originally perceived as leading the way to temporal redemption?

PART I

The Grand Failure

The precipitating cause of the agony of communism is the failure of the Soviet experience. Indeed, as we approach the end of the twentieth century it seems incredible that the Soviet model was once viewed as attractive and worthy of imitation. That is a measure of how much the Soviet experience has sunk in global public esteem. Yet there were times, and not so distant, when the Soviet model was acclaimed, admired, and even emulated. It is appropriate, therefore, to ask, What went wrong and why?

In reflecting on the Soviet failure, it is instructive to note very briefly the historical route followed by the Marxist experiment in Russia. It was a strange growth, that transplant of an essentially Western European doctrine, conceived in the public reading room of the British Museum by an émigré German-Jewish intellectual, to the quasi-oriental despotic tradition of a somewhat remote Euro-Asian empire, with a pamphleteering Russian revolutionary acting as history's surgeon.

By the time of the Russian Revolution, however, Marxism was no longer just a pedantic librarian's theory. It was already a major European political-social movement, playing an important role in several West European countries and possessing a defined political profile. That profile was distinctly one of social participation. The words *social democracy*—which was the self-designation of almost all Marxists of the time—symbolized that commitment of the relatively young socialist movement. Socialism, and hence Marxism, was thus seen in the West as predominantly democratic in spirit.

To be sure, by the time of World War I a smaller Marxist offshoot was actively preaching the concept of a violent revolution, to be followed by the imposition of the dictatorship of the proletariat. Those who feared the rise of socialism under any guise trembled at the

15

bloody memories of the Paris Commune of 1871. The word *communist* to many was already the antithesis of a democrat. The fall of Tsardom thus evoked mixed reactions in the West, ranging from initially hopeful enthusiasm for democracy to fearful anticipation of a communist dictatorship.

CHAPTER 1

The Leninist Legacy

What transpired in Russia following the Bolshevik Revolution should have come as no surprise to careful readers of Vladimir Ilyich Lenin. The Bolshevik leader of the more radical faction of the Russian Marxists made no bones about his intentions. In pamphlet after pamphlet and in speech after speech, he heaped scorn on those of his fellow Marxists who subscribed to the democratic process. He made it amply clear that in his view Russia was not ripe for a socialist democracy and that socialism would be constructed in Russia "from above," so to speak, by the dictatorship of the proletariat.

That dictatorship, in turn, was to be held by the proletariat only in name. In Lenin's view, the new ruling class was politically no more ready for actually ruling than Russia itself was historically ripe for socialism. The new dictatorship thus required a purposeful and historically conscious delegate to act on the proletariat's behalf. Precisely because of the backward conditions of Russia, neither society, nor the relatively meager industrial working class, were seen as ready for socialism. History was hence to be accelerated by a regimented "vanguard" party of committed revolutionaries who knew exactly what history's mandate was and who were prepared to be its self-ordained custodians. Lenin's concept of the vanguard party was his creative answer to the doctrinal dilemma of the unreadiness of Russia and of its proletariat for a Marxist revolution.

Lenin's contribution, and his personal determination in forging a disciplined organization of professional revolutionaries, was decisive in shaping the political character of the first state ever to come under the sway of a movement dedicated to the principles of socialism. There is no point in arguing here whether his commitment was doctrinally pure and hence whether it is appropriate to invoke the name of socialism in connection with Lenin and his adherents. To those deeply committed to democratic socialism, any such connection is anathema. But the point to register here is that Lenin and his followers considered themselves to be Marxists, that they saw themselves as embarking on the road toward first socialism and then communism, and that both subjectively and objectively they were thus part of the new phenomenon of socialism.

Moreover, to the extent that the new Bolshevik rulers were able to identify themselves with socialism, it helped enormously in gaining a sympathetic hearing in the West. The identification, whether genuine or merely tactical, was certainly beneficial. It captivated the imagination of many in the West who hoped for the victory of democratic socialism, but who despaired of it soon occurring within the entrenched capitalist system. For all of its shortcomings, the red star over the Kremlin seemed to symbolize the dawn of socialism, even if initially in an imperfect form.

The fact that within Russia the Leninist phase was marked by major ambiguities was also helpful in gaining Western sympathies. Though far from a democracy, and though embarking almost from the start on the brutal suppression of all opposition, the Leninist era (which continued for a few years after Lenin's death in 1923) witnessed a great deal of social and cultural experimentation. In the arts, in architecture, in literature, and more generally in intellectual life, the predominant mood was that of innovation, of creative iconoclasm, and of the opening of new scientific frontiers. Intellectual dynamism ran parallel to Lenin's willingness on the socioeconomic plane to compromise with the preponderant reality both of Russia's backwardness and of its early capitalist economy. The famous New Economic Policy (NEP)—which in essence relied on the market mechanism and private initiative to stimulate economic recovery— was an act of historical accommodation, postponing into the future the immediate construction of socialism by the new proletarian dictatorship.

Without idealizing this brief interlude, it is probably correct to describe the period as the most open and intellectually innovative phase in twentieth-century Russian history. (The democratic interlude in 1917 under the social democrat Aleksandr Kerensky lasted too briefly to have made a lasting impact.) Indeed, the NEP has become a shorthand term for a period of experimentation, flexibility, and moderation. For many Russians, even more than sixty years later, these were the best years of the era ushered in by the revolution of 1917.

But in fact there is too much idealization of the past—largely in reaction to later Stalinist history—in this idyllic view of the 1920s. More important than the phenomena of social and cultural innovation that dominated the surface of life in Moscow, in Leningrad, and in a few other large cities were the nationwide consolidation of the new system of one-party rule, the institutionalization of large-scale social violence, the imposition of doctrinal orthodoxy, and the enduring adoption of the practice that the ideological ends justify any political means, including the most tyrannical.

The two most catalytic features of the catastrophic legacy of Lenin were his concentration of political power in just a few hands and his reliance on terror. The former resulted in the centralization of all political power in an increasingly bureaucratized vanguard party, controlling the entire structure of society through its pervasive *nomenklatura*, i.e., a system of tightly layered top-down political control over all appointments. The willingness to use terror against real or imagined opponents, including Lenin's deliberate use of collective guilt as the justification for large-scale social persecution, made organized violence into the central means for resolving first political, then economic, and finally social or cultural problems.

Reliance on terror also prompted the growing symbiosis between the ruling party and the secret police (which Lenin established almost immediately after seizing power). It is neither accidental nor irrelevant to subsequent Soviet history that more than sixty years after Lenin's death the head of the Soviet secret police, Viktor M. Chebrikov, speaking in a September 1987 commemorative service in honor of the first head of that police, approvingly quoted Lenin's justification for terror against Russian peasants on the grounds that "the kulak violently despises Soviet power and is prepared to smother and slaughter hundreds of thousands of workers."

Both before and after seizing power, Lenin explicitly advocated the use of violence and mass terror to achieve his ends. As early as 1901, he said, "In principle we have never renounced terror and cannot renounce it." On the eve of the Bolshevik Revolution, he wrote in *State and Revolution* that when he called for democracy what he meant by the term was "an organization for the systematic use of *force* by one class against another, by one section of the population against another." In other writings and speeches included in his *Collected Works*, he remained consistent on this point. He openly proclaimed that for him democracy involved the dictatorship of the proletariat: "When we are reproached for exercising the dictatorship of a party . . . we say, 'Yes, the dictatorship of a party! We stand by it and cannot do without it.' " He also wrote, "The scientific definition of dictatorship is a power that is not limited by any laws, not bound by any rules, and based directly on force."

As soon as he took power, Lenin wasted no time putting his views into practice. Before long, he came to rely on the use of indiscriminate violence not only to terrorize society as a whole but even to eliminate the smallest of bureaucratic nuisances. In a decree issued in January 1918, which sought to define policy on handling those who in any way opposed Bolshevik rule, Lenin's regime called on state agencies to "purge the Russian land of all kinds of harmful insects." Lenin himself urged party leaders in one district to carry out "ruthless mass terror against the kulaks, priests, and White Guards" and to "confine all suspicious elements in a concentration camp outside the city." As for political opposition, Lenin would not tolerate any, arguing it was "a great deal better to 'discuss with rifles' than with the theses of the opposition."

Mass terror thus soon became an administrative device to solve all problems. For lazy workers, Lenin advocated "shooting on the spot one out of every ten found guilty of idling." For unruly workers, he said that "such disturbers of discipline should be shot." For a poor telephone connection, he gave Stalin explicit instructions: "Threaten to shoot the idiot who is in charge of telecommunications and who does not know how to give you a better amplifier and how to make a working telephone connection." For any disobedience, however small, among the rural masses, Lenin's regime passed a resolution that insisted that "hostages must be taken among the peasantry, so that if the snow is not cleared away, they will be shot."

This paranoiac vision helped to produce a system of rule that stood apart from society, essentially *a conspiracy in power*, even if in the early 1920s that society's continued spontaneity in the nonpolitical realm was temporarily tolerated. However, the central fact is that Lenin's political system was poised psychologically, as well as politically, for an all-out confrontation with society. Its new rulers could only justify themselves historically by eventually assaulting that society in order to re-create it in the image of the political system itself. A Leninist-type political system could not coexist indefinitely with a society operating largely on the basis of dynamic spontaneity. Such a coexistence would have either corrupted the political system or prompted a collision between them.

Lenin's unique solution was the promotion of a supreme party, endowed with the power to prompt the forcible *withering away* not of the state but *of the society* as an autonomous entity. Society had to be crushed lest it should co-opt, dilute, and eventually absorb the superficial political veneer of Communist rule. To Lenin, the logic of power dictated the conclusion that to accomplish the dissolution of traditional social ties the centrality of the State had to be enhanced, making the State into history's ordained instrument.

Many decades later, in 1987, in the course of the debates precipitated by Mikhail Gorbachev's efforts at reform, a leading Soviet intellectual dared to pose publicly the question, "Did Stalin create his system, or did the system create Stalin?" But if it was the system—as the question implies—that spawned Stalin, then whose system had it been? It was Lenin who created the system that created Stalin, and it was Stalin who then created the system that made the crimes of Stalin possible. Moreover, not only did Lenin make Stalin possible, but Lenin's ideological dogmatism and his political intolerance largely precluded any other alternative from arising. In essence, the enduring legacy of Leninism was Stalinism, and that is the strongest historical indictment of Lenin's role in the construction of socialism within Russia.

CHAPTER 2

The Stalinist Catastrophe

The genius of Joseph Stalin was that he understood well the inner meaning of the Leninist legacy. His principal rival, Leon Trotsky, made the basic error of trying to link the internal revolution with the simultaneous quest for a global upheaval. Trotsky subscribed to the notion that the Western capitalist system was ripe for a revolutionary upheaval and that the survival of Communist power in Russia depended on the prompt success of such a revolution. However, by preaching the concept of the permanent revolution, Trotsky offended the instinct for self-preservation of the newly entrenched party bureaucrats, who were not prepared to risk all on the altar of a premature world revolution. In contrast, Stalin exploited well their instinct for self-preservation by launching a domestic revolution designed to avoid the risk of seeing the Communist regime swallowed by the increasingly vital society. He thereby gratified their ideological zeal while appealing to their self-interest.

"Socialism in one country" was Stalin's doctrinal catch phrase for the unprecedented pulverization of society by the state machinery. A conspiratorially minded cluster of leaders, operating literally by night in a few rooms of the Kremlin, took upon itself the task of reconstructing society from top to bottom, of destroying much of its peasantry and middle class, of resettling forcibly millions of people, while in the process expanding the scope of state power to a degree never before matched in history. "Socialism in one country" thereby became a country totally subordinated to a supreme state.

Under Stalin the exaltation of the State, and the use of state violence as a tool of social reconstruction, reached its apogee. Everything was subordinated to the person of the dictator and to the state that he commanded. Extolled in poetry, hailed by music, idolized by thousands of monuments, Stalin was everywhere, and he dominated everything. But though a personal tyrant with few peers in all of history, his rule was exercised through a complex structure of state power, both highly bureaucratized and institutionalized. As society was ploughed over in keeping with Stalin's goal of constructing socialism in one country, the state machinery grew in status and opulence, in power and in privilege.

The pyramid of power was supported by a system of terror that left no individual secure, not even among Stalin's closest comrades. No one was spared the dictator's caprice. Stalin's favorite Politburo member one day could be the victim of a trial and shot on another. That was the sudden fate in the late 1940s, for example, of A. A. Voznesensky, viewed by many as being groomed by Stalin for the very top governmental position. Total loyalty to Stalin and even enthusiastic complicity in his crimes offered little protection from persecution or indignity. Molotov and Kalinin, both directly involved in drawing up lists of their comrades to be executed, continued to sit around the Politburo table though their wives had been carted off on Stalin's orders to forced labor camps.

It is no exaggeration to state that the ultimate power of life and death in the Soviet state for about a quarter of a century was in the hands of a small band of totally ruthless conspirators, for whom the infliction of death on countless thousands of alleged "enemies of the people" was a minor bureaucratic act. Even if Soviet archives are someday fully opened (and the dissident Moscow magazine *Glasnost* reported in August 1987 that, to cover up the past, the KGB was destroying dossiers on victims from the 1930s and 1940s at a rate of five thousand per month), one will never know the full measure of Stalin's killings. Extermination by direct execution or by lingering death was the fate of entire categories of people: political opponents, ideological rivals, suspect party members, accused military officers, kulaks, members of the deposed classes, former aristocrats, national groups viewed as potentially disloyal, ethnic groups labeled as hostile, religious preachers as well as the more active believers, and even the relatives and (in many cases) the entire families of the chosen victims.

It is simply impossible to evoke in words the full measure of the individual and collective human suffering that Stalin inflicted. In the name of socialism, several million peasant families were deported under the most primitive of conditions, with the survivors resettled in distant Siberia. Stalin was also responsible for the mass starvation of several million Ukrainian peasants during the Great Famine of the early 1930s—a famine deliberately exploited to accelerate the process of collectivization, but to a significant degree also generated by that same brutal collectivization itself. During the purges, the party itself was decimated, with most of its top leaders executed and with their families cruelly persecuted. Arrests and executions cut across the entire Soviet society and ran into the millions. According to Soviet data, in the military sector alone no less than thirty-seven thousand army officers and three thousand navy officers were shot in the years 1937 and 1938, more than actually perished during the first two years of the Nazi–Soviet war.

The GULAG kept swelling under Stalin. Individual and group arrests were a massive and continuous occurrence. Even entire ethnic groups were targeted for genocidal extinction. Just before the outbreak of the war in 1939, the entire Polish population living on the Soviet side of the then Soviet–Polish border, numbering several hundred thousand, suddenly disappeared, with only the women and children resettled in Kazakhstan. The men simply perished. In the last stages of the war, the Tatars of Crimea and the Chechen-Ingush of northern Caucasus, numbering also in the hundreds of thousands, were uprooted and deported to Siberia. After the war, and despite the revelations of the Nazi Holocaust of the Jews, the Jewish community in Moscow and Leningrad was suddenly targeted, and its leadership was decimated. In 1949, mass deportations to Siberia were inflicted on hundreds of thousands of Balts. According to scrupulously kept Soviet accounting, cited by Radio Vilnius on September 22, 1988, the victims included 108,362 from Lithuania alone. On the eve of Stalin's death, preparations were in progress for new show trials of the "Jewish doctors' plot," with the victims accused of having conspired to kill the top Kremlin leadership.

Literally millions of lives were thereby shattered. The suffering was inflicted on the lowly as well as on the socially prominent. When the exposure of Stalinism finally developed momentum in 1987, the Soviet press was swamped with personal recollections and accounts. The one that follows appeared in *Literaturnaia Gazeta* on December 23, 1987—the paper noted that it had received some 10,000 comparable letters—and was written by a simple woman. It was especially powerful because it was so prosaic. It is typical of the experiences of millions of others:

I am an attentive reader of yours. I have been reading your paper with interest for a long time. Recently a lot has been written about things which had been forgotten; I read some articles and my heart bleeds. I remember my life and my husband's life. Our generation lived through the difficult 1930s, then the war years, then also the difficult postwar years. Now the deaths of Kirov, Tukhachevskiy, Yakir, and other innocent victims are written about openly. This is understandable: The fate of great people is in public view. But if even great people did not survive, what can be said about ordinary people?

My husband, A. I. Bogomolov, was just such an ordinary person. He was arrested after the end of the Finnish war, sentenced to be shot, then given 10 years, plus 5 years deprivation of rights. He spent 4 years in a camp in the north in appalling conditions. Then came another arrest, another accusation, 15 months of *tridsatka* [allusion unknown], in an underground cell. In both cases he did not sign the accusation. He served his time there in the north, 12 years in total. His health was ruined forever, and his lungs were frostbitten. After the camp he lived in Syktyvkar.

I met my husband after 42 years' separation, the last time I had seen him had been in 1940, when I brought my newborn son to visit him at a Leningrad transit prison. We met. . . . My impression was appalling, but we decided not to part. His wife had died, my husband had died, and our children had grown up. So for 5 years I have been doctor, sister, nurse, and friend. My husband's health is completely ruined, he worked until he was 74 years old. We live in my room in a communal apartment, next door there is a mentally ill person. There are brawls, shouting matches, and the woman next door gets into fist fights. We have been refused a separate apartment—we have more than 6 meters per person.

But this is what I want to tell you. In 1955 my husband was rehabilitated with regard to his second conviction, while we received rehabilitation for the first conviction only in 1985, when I myself started to pursue the matter, and the Leningrad Military District military tribunal reconsidered his 1940 case and also quashed the verdict "for lack of corpus delicti." My husband was given R 270 only after his rehabilitation—2 months' salary for the post he held before the Finnish war. For all the 12 years in northern camps, for the interrogations, for the exhausting work in mines and felling timber— a total of R 270! Every time I inquired I was told that this is the law and referred to the 1955 statute.

My husband's rights as a participant in the war were restored only after the last rehabilitation. He is now a category one invalid, he is blind, I read him the articles and he cries. He gets a pension of R 113—this includes R 15 which he is given as a category one invalid "for nursing." But I have written and shall continue to write to all the official bodies because I think the whole thing is unjust. So long as he lives and I have the strength, I shall write about how people like my husband were given no benefits to compensate, however little, for everything they have suffered. They have not wronged their country, but their lives have been wrecked, their families' lives have been wrecked, they were deprived of society's respect, and they were not even given the right to fight, to become honored invalids or war veterans and receive festive congratulations!

I am not asking you to help me get an apartment. We are elderly people and even if you help us get a separate apartment, it will be too late for us. My husband is 82 years old. Recently he suffered a stroke. But I beg you to help all those who also suffered innocently and were unable to defend themselves since "the verdict was not subject to appeal."

Today they broadcast on the radio Tvardovskiy's poem "Right of Remembrance." I shook, and tears flowed from my husband's blind eyes. He was always a worker, a Komsomol member, he worked on the Kuznetskstroy, in Balkhash, and he always had callused hands. Now he cannot do anything, of course, but he senses the new time and believes that it is really revolutionary. Today a lot is changing, and it will be unjust if people who have suffered so terribly disappear from view when so much attention is being paid to war and labor veterans. Why not review the 1955 statute? Why don't the people who have suffered humiliation and shock enjoy any benefits—either material or moral? Are they to blame for the fact that they were unable to earn them?

I beg you to help me and to help those who can still be helped. Even now you sometimes hear people say of such-and-such a person that he was an enemy of the people and it is not for nothing that he was behind bars. It is not a question of money—the point is that society should be aware of its duty to these people.

Valentina Zinovevna Gromova, Leningrad

Though the total number of Stalin's victims will never be known, it is absolutely safe to estimate the number at no less than twenty million and perhaps as high as forty million. In his book *The Great Terror* (1968), the English historian Robert Conquest assembled the best and most complete estimates, and his careful calculations favor the upper end of this range. All in all, Stalin was probably the biggest mass murderer in human history, statistically overshadowing even Hitler.

These mass murders were part and parcel of the construction of the Soviet system. That system emerged, took shape institutionally, congealed bureaucratically, and developed its own sense of status as these mass killings took place. But the remarkable aspect of this process was that despite these atrocities Stalin succeeded in generating a real sense of accomplishment within the Soviet elite and in a large part of the new Soviet urban population. He did so by identifying his policies, and himself, with a reconstruction of Soviet society that involved massive industrialization and urbanization, all labeled as the construction of socialism. Thus, for many Soviet citizens, the Stalinist era was one of some social advancement, of a great historical leap forward, and even of a genuinely proud sense of patriotic accomplishment.

One could not otherwise explain the reactions of many average Soviet citizens first to the efforts of Nikita Khrushchev in the late 1950s and early 1960s and then of Mikhail Gorbachev in the late 1980s to expose Stalin's crimes. Apart from intellectuals and the relatives of victims, the popular reactions were far from enthusiastic. They ranged from the somewhat typically Russian xenophobic concern that Russia's enemies would exploit any public exposure of the ugly past, to the frequent assertion that the Stalinist era involved great accomplishment and should not be besmirched. Some citizens, in letters to papers like *Pravda* or *Izvestia*, even opposed the posthumous rehabilitation of Stalin's victims, on the grounds that this would be both unfair to the past and damaging to Soviet prestige.

Both typical and revealing was the account provided by the July 23, 1987, issue of *Pravda*, entitled "Reading the Mail." It reported that the party newspaper had received many letters expressing dismay at the anti-Stalinist turn in contemporary Soviet historical writings. As an example of an apparently widely held point of view, the paper quoted a reader, seventy-four-year-old Vasiliy Petrovich Peshketov (who consequently was twenty-four at the time of Stalin's worst terror), as proudly proclaiming that he went into battle against the Nazis with the words "For the motherland, for Stalin" on his lips. He went on to add: "How is it possible to have the slightest doubt about the sincerity of these words." The old, and apparently unreconstructed, veteran concluded his letter by charging the anti-Stalin campaign with being based on deception and half-truths and asked: "So why are such deceptions allowed to appear in the pages of reputable press organs?"

Pravda's own commentary confirmed that the cited letter expressed a more widely shared point of view:

> Maybe the veteran is exaggerating and overgeneralizing? Judging by the mail, no—he is not exaggerating at all. A big bundle of letters lies on the editorial office desk, and their authors ask roughly the same questions, but in a broader context. . . . How is it possible to reduce ambiguous, heterogeneous, contradictory, and disparate phenomena, events, episodes, and facts to a common denominator and to forcibly squeeze them into a single formula—the "personality cult"? How is it possible to decry the industrialization of the country, the collectivization of the agriculture, the cultural revolution, the Great Patriotic War, and the postwar restoration of the national economy in the same breath as the errors, negative phenomena, crimes, and violations of socialist legality and Leninist norms of party life? . . . And what about our daring, our enthusiasm, our youth, our songs? Are they to be discarded as well?

Such reactions on the part of some Soviet citizens to the renewed repudiation of Stalinism, more than thirty years after the dictator's death and after many public revelations of the scale and brutality of his crimes, are a testimony to his continued hold on the minds of at least a segment of the Soviet public.

Stalin was also quite successful abroad in justifying his methods and in gaining some approval for what he had wrought. In somewhat different terminology, many Western commentators were for years more inclined to give him credit for industrializing Russia than to condemn him for terrorizing it. The Stalinist era was thus widely interpreted as one of great social change, of rapid upward mobility, of a basic shift from a rural to an urban economy. And some of that, in a sense, was true. Under Stalin, the Soviet Union did become a major industrial power. Its population did shift from the countryside. A full-scale central-command socialist system was institutionalized. And the Soviet economy sustained a relatively high rate of growth. According to official statistics, Soviet national income rose fourfold during the first five-year plans, with annual growth rates running at almost 15 percent. This required a massive population shift, with the number of people living in urban areas doubling within thirteen years. Between 1928 and 1940, annual production of electricity rose from 5 billion to 48.3 billion kilowatt-hours; steel from 4.3 million to 18.3 million tons; machine tools from 2,000 to 58,400; and motor vehicles from 8,000 to 145,000. On the eve of the war, industry came to represent 84.7 percent of the Soviet economy. Even if exaggerated in official reports, these were undeniably major accomplishments.

The economic momentum of the early Stalin years explains in part the surprise of quite a few people in the West at the intensity of the Soviet anti-Stalin campaign, which surfaced so dramatically only three years after the tyrant's death. That campaign brought to the fore the pent-up frustrations, the unsettled scores, the limitless human suffering, and the pointless spilling of blood, all of which were the intangible costs of Stalin's "successes." Khrushchev's famous speech in 1956, and then the even more comprehensive documentation provided by the second wave of anti-Stalinist speeches at the Twenty-second Party Congress in 1961, represented a staggering indictment of the social costs of the Stalinist experience.

Even more damning is the fact that—despite the initial pace of Soviet industrialization—the social price of the Stalin era simply cannot be justified by the assertion that the Soviet model of socioeconomic change and modernization achieved higher rates of development than had been the case elsewhere. Leaving aside the moral impropriety of any such calculus, the claim does not stand up factually. To the extent that cross-national comparisons are possible, it is evident, for example, that Japan did better, both after the Meiji Restoration during the nineteenth century and after World War II, but without exacting a comparable human toll. Similarly, the overall record of Italian modernization in this century—and Italy and Russia were generally closely matched in terms of socioeconomic indices at the start of the century—is noticeably better. Last, but by no means least, Tsarist Russia maintained a higher rate of growth from 1890 to 1914 than Stalin achieved at such an unbelievably high human cost.

Not surprisingly, more recent Soviet leaders—even Mikhail Gorbachev—have sought to justify the social costs of Stalinist industrialization and collectivization as an imperative dictated by the rise of Hitler in Germany. "Industrialization in the twenties and thirties really was a very hard trial," the current Soviet leader wrote in his book, *Perestroika*. "But let's now, with hindsight, try to answer the question: Was it necessary? Could such a vast country as ours have lived in the twentieth century without being an industrially developed state? There was another reason that also very soon made it clear that we had no option but to speed up industrialization. As early as 1933 the threat of fascism began to grow swiftly. And where would the world now be if the Soviet Union had not blocked the road for Hitler's war machine? Our people routed fascism with the might created by them in the twenties and thirties. Had there been no industrialization, we would have been unarmed before fascism."

But the decision to convulse Soviet society was initiated not in 1933 but in 1928, when the threat of a militarized Germany was not yet on the horizon, when Stalin intoned gravely against the "war danger" from *Britain*, and when Moscow engaged in active military and political collusion with Germany. In fact, as late as the summer of 1932, Stalin was publicly assuring the Germans—through a highly publicized interview with Emil Ludwig, published prominently also in the Soviet press—that the Soviet Union was not prepared to guarantee the borders of Poland against German aspirations.

Clearly, it is no exaggeration to say that never before had so much human sacrifice been exacted for relatively so little social benefit. As Cyril Black, the Princeton historian, put it at the conclusion of his paper entitled "Soviet Society: A Comparative View," which was a comprehensive assessment of the Soviet modernization process:

> In the perspective of fifty years, the comparative ranking of the USSR in composite economic and social indices per capita has probably not changed significantly. So far as the rather limited available evidence permits a judgment, the USSR has not overtaken or surpassed any country on a per capita basis since 1917. . . . and the nineteen or twenty countries that rank higher than Russia today in this regard also ranked higher in 1900 and 1919.

Yet in the West the notion persisted even into the 1950s and 1960s that Stalinism was historically an ambivalent development, with much good offsetting the bad. It was not only the Western Communist parties that had a hard time coming to terms with the reality of the Stalinist history. In some ways, their predicament was understandable. Stalinism represented the only living example of "socialism" constructed by a communist party in power. Moreover, given Soviet control over these parties, they did not have much choice in the matter. More revealing of the attraction to the twentieth-century mind of Stalin's experiment in social engineering was the fact that much of Western scholarship was influenced by the view—propagated, for example, by the widely read and much cited historian Isaac Deutscher—that Stalinism had been a form of historical necessity, induced by the imperatives of rapid, politically imposed industrialization of a highly primitive society.

The Khrushchev-sponsored disclosures did much to shatter that perspective, and the final nail into the coffin of the myth of the "historically positive" Stalin was driven in by Aleksandr Solzhenitsyn's *Gulag Archipelago*. Even Western Communist parties came to realize that Stalinism had been a needless historic crime and represented for them a contemporary political liability. The Italian Communist party went the furthest in denouncing that phase of Soviet history, but the shock effects of the revelations were also felt more widely among the Marxist-leaning West European intellectuals. Stalinism thus came to be perceived as a monstrous error in the communist experience, an aberration to be regretted and averted.

But the roots of the catastrophic legacy of Stalin go back to Lenin—to his twin legacies of the dogmatic party and of the terroristic secret police. Stalin's bureaucratic behemoth was built on the foundations of the vanguard party to which everything must be subordinated. Once that party undertook the reconstruction of society, the power of the state had to grow and expand. Stalin's own legacy was the exaltation of state-sponsored violence against one's own society, the emergence of a police state stifling social creativity, nipping in the bud any display of intellectual innovation, the creation of a system of hierarchical privilege, all subject to centralized political control. Much of that legacy endured beyond Stalin, even surviving the onslaughts launched by Khrushchev. It thus not only served to discredit the Soviet model in the world at large, but also made possible after Khrushchev the subsequent twenty years of political and social stagnation under Leonid Brezhnev.

CHAPTER 3

Stagnant Stalinism

The ambivalence of many average Soviet people toward efforts at de-Stalinization explains why the Brezhnev era endured so long and why it assumed the forms that it did. Though it started as a modernizing regime, attempting to introduce rationality into Khrushchev's tempestuous reforms, the Brezhnev regime before too long became tantamount to a quasi-Stalinist restoration. The basic outlines of the Stalinist system, especially its centralized and stifling controls, its privileged *nomenklatura*, and the supremacy of the state bureaucracy, were perpetuated—but in a setting of gradually spreading social, economic, and even political decay. Only Stalin's massive terror gave way to a more discriminating but still arbitrary use of political coercion, largely because the ruling elite had learned through bitter experience that terror had a dynamic of its own, eventually consuming even its sponsors.

Stalinism, but without the state-induced social change from above and without the massive manifestations of terror, thus continued for another quarter of a century. In effect, Stalinism came to characterize two-thirds of the Soviet Communist era, leaving a decisive imprint on what communism has come to mean historically. But the Stalinist system endured not only because Brezhnev and his immediate comrades benefited from it and remained loyal to it. It survived because it had become a vast structure of overlapping privileges, controls, rewards, and vested interests. It also endured because the newly urbanized Soviet masses could not conceive of any other alternative, having been for half a century inculcated with the notion that their experience represented for them a giant step forward.

Most important, Stalinism both endured and stagnated because it was a political system without real political life within it. As the Soviet

33

historian Leonid Batkin put it, in *Nedelya*, no. 26, 1988, in the course
of the public debates that eventually erupted in reaction to the Stalinist legacy,

> ... politics had disappeared from our society's life since the late
> twenties. . . . Politics disappeared as a *specific* contemporary sphere of
> human activity where the differences in class and group interests are
> displayed and clash with each other, where there is direct public
> comparison of positions, and where methods are sought to bring them
> to some dynamic compromise. Politics disappeared—and thus *every-*
> *thing became "political."* (italics in the original)

The society as a whole was politicized from the top down, but real
politics was confined only to the very top. The system was thereby
protected from the challenge of change, but stagnation was the inevitable price of the system's coercive self-perpetuation.

That stagnation could not be forever ignored. Already by the
latter years of the Brezhnev era, a sense of malaise was developing
within a portion of the upper Soviet elite. An awareness of decay,
of ideological rot, of cultural sterility was setting in. It began not
only to permeate the intellectual circles but also to infect some
members of the political elite. That elite became increasingly aware
of the growing distance between the lagging Soviet Union and its
designated rival, the United States. In the words of the previously
cited historian, "while the Stalin system was exterminating people in the millions, people like Bohr, Wiener, Watson, and Crick
were at work. While the Brezhnev system was reducing our country
to a state of mediocrity, the world was developing lasers and personal computers and witnessing the explosion of the postindustrial
revolution."

The emerging historical pessimism within the Soviet elite stood
in sharp contrast to the boastful optimism of the Khrushchev era.
Only two decades earlier, starting in 1958, First Secretary Nikita
Khrushchev had begun to claim in public that the Soviet Union would
soon "bury" America in economic competition. Probably intoxicated
by the public relations triumph of putting the Soviet *sputnik* into space
ahead of the U.S. space program, and relying on official Soviet statistics for projected rates of growth, the Soviet leader asserted on
numerous occasions that by the early 1970s "the USSR will take

first place in the world" in economic output and that this "will secure our peoples the highest living standards in the world."

To make matters even more embarrassing, these public boasts could not be ascribed exclusively to the personal idiosyncrasy of the top Soviet leader because they became enshrined in the official ideological program of the ruling Communist party adopted in 1961. In other words, the following prognostication became an integral part of the allegedly scientific and infallible Marxist-Leninist doctrine: "In the current decade—1961–1970—the Soviet Union, while creating a material-technical base for communism, will surpass in per capita production the most powerful and richest capitalist country— the United States."

As if this were not enough, the party program went on to proclaim that in the subsequent decade "an abundance of material and cultural wealth will be ensured for the entire population. . . . And so in essence a communist society will be built in the USSR." Entering into the stage of genuine communism was to mark the ultimate historical triumph of the Soviet system. Soviet society was to be richer than America's, its economy to be more productive, and "the majestic edifice of communism" was to permit the implementation of "the principle of distribution according to need."

In reality, by the mid-1960s these boasts were already merely a mask for the painful reality of increasing stagnation. Perhaps for a while Brezhnev still had reason to entertain some lingering hopes of eventually closing the gap. By 1970, the Soviet economy had climbed to more than half the size of the United States', was still growing somewhat more rapidly, and had a considerable lead on any other rival. It accounted for 15.3 percent of the world's GNP, while the United States' stood for 27.7 percent. But during the 1970s, Soviet growth rates lost momentum, and the economy atrophied. By 1985, the Soviet percentage of global GNP had dropped to 14.7 percent, while the United States' had increased to 28.5 percent. Much worse, by the late 1980s, the Soviet Union no longer occupied an unquestioned second place in the global economic hierarchy. The country that saw itself destined to become the world's premier economic power by the early 1970s was about to be passed by Japan, whose economy was not only growing more rapidly than the Soviet Union's but was also technologically far more advanced.

Indeed, the dramatically widening technological gap was doubtless an even greater source of concern to the more discerning members of the Soviet elite. That elite realized that further economic progress required scientific-technological innovation and that the Soviet Union was now lagging badly, particularly in the socioeconomic application of the new technology. The data was widely known and told a dramatic story. The country that so ostentatiously claimed to be on the cutting edge of innovation was becoming mired in the mid-phases of the industrial age, unable to go beyond them. Just a few examples, as in the table below, speak volumes.

	USA	EEC	JAPAN	USSR
Large/medium computers	96,500	23,400	16,900	3,040
[per mill. pop. in 1983]	412	135	142	11
Small computers	1,000,000	240,000	70,000	22,000
[per mill. pop. in 1983]	4,273	1,387	588	80
Industrial robots	44,700	51,877	67,435	3,000
[per mill. pop. in 1981]	196	201	571	11

The Soviet economy was not only falling behind in the technological race. It had also become incredibly wasteful. With no internalized incentive to compete, to rationalize, and to innovate, not only the Soviet industrial sector but also its copies in Central Europe had become monuments to bureaucratic inefficiency and counter-productive resource extravagance. According to data meticulously compiled by a Polish economist, Professor Jan Winiecki, in his *Economic Prospects, East and West* (London, 1987), the Soviet-type economies consume two to three times as much energy per unit of production as the market-based economies of Western Europe.

SOVIET BLOC	ENERGY P/$1000 GDP	STEEL P/$1000 GDP
Soviet Union	1490	135
Poland	1515	135
East Germany	1356	88
Hungary	1058	88
WESTERN EUROPE		
France	502	42
West Germany	565	52
Britain	820	38

The ideological irrationality of the Stalinist economic legacy was even more destructive in the agricultural sector. By the 1970s, chronic inefficiency of its collectivized system, compounded by occasionally poor weather conditions, compelled the Soviet leaders to annually spend billions of dollars in hard currency for the import of grain. As a result, the government also felt compelled to subsidize food prices, lest the prohibitive costs for the Soviet consumer prompt civil unrest. Yet, at the same time, the private plots that were tolerated in agriculture were being limited to only 4 percent of arable land, even though they were producing—thanks to individual initiative—25 percent of the Soviet food supplies.

The resulting economic waste and the associated industrial and technological backwardness also had an adverse impact on the Soviet ability to participate in world trade. Increasingly, the Soviet Union was becoming an exporter mainly of commodities and minerals, like much of the Third World, but was unable to compete with the world's leading exporters of manufactured goods. According to the annual GATT report, the Soviet Union dropped from eleventh place in 1973 down to fifteenth in 1985 in the export of manufactured goods, having been passed in the intervening years by Taiwan, South Korea, Hong Kong, and Switzerland.

More generally, some forty years after the end of World War II, Soviet society was still subject to partial rationing of food and suffered from continued shortages of consumer goods. Standing in line for hours every single day was the normal routine for the overwhelming majority of Soviet urban housewives. Alcoholism continued to spread, while hospital care for the average Soviet citizen generally deteriorated. In March 1987, the newly appointed Soviet Minister of Health revealed that a large percentage of Soviet hospitals had no hot water, inadequate sewage, and lacked basic sanitation. It was no wonder that male life expectancy dramatically declined during the Brezhnev years from 66 to 62 years, compared to 71.5 years in the United States, and that infant mortality rose to a level 2.5 times higher than that of the United States, thus placing the Soviet Union fiftieth in global rankings—behind Barbados. The only group truly exempted from social hardship was the ruling party officialdom and the upper military and managerial elite. Benefiting from special closed shops, good hospitals, and special vacation centers, it enjoyed the benefits of socialism for one class.

The reality of socialism for one class not only collided head-on with the official myth of social egalitarianism, but, in time, bred growing social resentment. A remarkable public opinion poll, published by *Moscow News* on July 3, 1988, showed that about half of the Soviet public did not feel they were living in "a society of social justice." The strongest grievance was directed at the system of special privileges for the senior officialdom. These included—in order of resentment—"food packages, goods from exclusive stores"; "free availability of any books or seats in theatres, movies, etc."; "flats in superior housing in highly prestigious areas"; and "state-owned dachas." Such social resentment was intensified by the fact that the quality of life for the masses was clearly not improving at a satisfactory pace and in some significant aspects was even deteriorating.

Compounding the problem was the fact that a growing number of Soviet citizens, especially among the professional elite, now knew that conditions abroad were considerably better, including even in communized Eastern Europe. Among the intellectuals, the awareness of Soviet backwardness, and of its debilitating effects, became quite widespread during the 1970s. It was no longer possible to claim and pretend, as was done for years under Stalin, that life in the Soviet Union was better than elsewhere. Many Soviet citizens, long isolated from the world, had believed Soviet propaganda even as late as the mid-1960s.

In 1987, a leading member of the Soviet academic establishment, Yevgeniy Afanasyev, candidly explained to a Hungarian audience on Radio Budapest, on November 7, 1987, the intellectual price paid for this state of affairs:

> It is certain that national consciousness, in as much as it developed at all in the Soviet society, developed amid totally abnormal conditions. In other words, it developed in a one-sided manner, as did historical and social consciousness. . . . Soviet society lived in a state of voluntary [*sic!*] intellectual isolation, that is, that it knew nothing about the West . . . we did not concern ourselves with Max Weber or Durkheim, or Freud, or Toynbee, or Spengler. These are not just names, they are names which have worlds, world systems behind them. If a society fails to acquaint itself with these worlds, it simply falls out of the 20th century, it finds itself on the periphery of the most important discoveries of the century.

To the world at large, the spectacle of an ideologically self-isolated and bureaucratically centralized system hardly offered an example of economic or social dynamism. It literally took a political decision on the level of the ruling Politburo to produce a single quality consumer item, and in the seventy years of Soviet rule not a single such item capable of competing on the world market has yet been produced. That was the legacy that Stalin bequeathed and Brezhnev perpetuated. In that economic system, the state bureaucracy set the quotas and prices for millions of items, while the managers supervised production without any incentives to be innovative. The workers produced without any motivation to increase productivity or to enhance quality. Moreover, both the managers and the workers shared an interest in distorting upward the reporting of their performance. As a result, in recent years Soviet state statistics, by official admission, became increasingly unreliable and thus unhelpful to any rational planning process.

Despite official boasting, the truth could no longer be hidden: Both quantitatively and qualitatively the Soviet Union was stagnating. Instead of outracing the United States, it was at best holding its own as the most developed of the developing countries—and even in that category it was beginning to face the potential threat of eventually being surpassed in some critical areas by the more ambitiously innovative of the developing countries, especially China. This was without a doubt a galling and worrisome prospect for the more informed members of the ruling Soviet elite. The Soviet military command, acutely conscious that modern warfare was becoming increasingly dependent on the ability to adapt quickly the latest technological innovations, had to be especially concerned.

To the more historically minded members of the Russian elite, the Soviet Union's current condition must have evoked some disturbing analogies with Russia's decay during the last decades of the preceding century. In 1815, having played the central role in the defeat of Napoleon and with Tsar Alexander I having ridden in triumph into Paris, Russia was militarily the most powerful nation in the world. Russia's economy grew rapidly for the next several decades, and there was also hope for political change. Yet gradually stagnation set in. Between 1870 and 1890, the country's GNP actually declined, with both Great Britain and Germany surpassing Russia, and with

France and the Hapsburg Empire closing in. Two costly and inconclusive local wars—the Crimean War and the Bulgarian and Caucasian campaign—and the crushing of the Polish rebellion contributed to a drastic decline in Russia's international standing. Before long, revolutionary ferment was surfacing, reflecting growing political and social discontent.

All of that has contemporary parallels. In 1945, Stalin conquered Berlin and the Red Army was the largest military force in the world. By the 1960s, the Soviet leaders had become convinced that soon the Soviet Union would also be the world's leading economic power. Yet during the 1970s the economy stagnated. By 1990, the Soviet Union will have fallen further behind not only the United States but also Western Europe and Japan. The failed nine-year-long war in Afghanistan, growing unrest in Eastern Europe, and the economic effects of prohibitively high expenditures on military power were all contributing to a widespread sense of social malaise at home and to the loss of prestige abroad.

While the mounting evidence that the Soviet Union was losing in the economic race with the United States was bad enough, it was only half the story. Even more galling, and compounding Soviet geostrategic concerns, was the grim projection made in 1988 by the U.S. Commission on Integrated Long-Range Strategy that by the year 2010 the global economic hierarchy would likely find the Soviet Union only in fifth place. The United States would still be first. Then would come Western Europe (which probably still would not be a fully integrated political-military power), China, and Japan. The Soviet Union would tail behind—with its GNP by then much less than one half of the United States'.

Moreover, the four top powers will likely be enjoying a better relationship with one another than with the Soviet Union. The Kremlin is thus facing the prospect of geopolitical encirclement by potentially hostile and economically stronger states. The strategic, as well as the ideological, implications of that prospect have to be appalling to any Soviet leader, especially to those who based their power on the claim that the communist ideology contained the key to a utopian future.

CHAPTER 4

The Paradox of Reform

Awareness of needed change, reform, and greater innovation finally surfaced on a politically significant scale after Brezhnev's death in 1982. But more than two decades had been wasted. As a result, the legacies to be overcome had become cumulative and massive. The existing Soviet system was by then the ossified product of three closely linked and overlapping formative phases:

1. under Lenin, that of a totalitarian party aiming at the total reconstruction of society;
2. under Stalin, that of a totalitarian state which had totally subordinated society;
3. and under Brezhnev, that of a totally stagnant state dominated by a corrupt totalitarian party.

To reform the existing system, it was necessary to attack all three historical layers. Yet to do so was to run the risk of alienating the critical institutions of power and of arousing the hostility of the mentally Stalinized segments of the Soviet masses. Any reform, to succeed, therefore, had to be quite gradual. It had to move layer by layer, consolidating its progress, careful not to antagonize simultaneously all of the existing subjective and objective vested interests.

The easiest to assault was the Brezhnev legacy, with its personal corruption, social stagnation, and increasingly visible economic backwardness. More difficult to take on was the Stalinist legacy, given its bureaucratic vested interests and the residual loyalty of some older Soviet citizens. Most difficult to challenge was the Leninist legacy, which combined the fond memories of NEP with the self-serving assertion of a unique historical role for an elitist vanguard party, and which provided the ruling elite with its historical legitimacy.

The initial assault was launched, but only for a very brief time, by

Brezhnev's immediate successor, Yuri Andropov. By then the re-
vulsion against the prevailing stagnation and corruption had become
so widespread that those who remained devoted to the two earlier
layers of the Soviet experience, the Leninist and the Stalinist, could
unite with the anti-Brezhnev reformers in a common front. Unfortunately for the reformers, the Andropov phase came to a quick end
with the sudden death of the innovative leader in 1984. For a brief
moment, the moribund system gained a respite under Konstantin
Chernenko, whom Brezhnev initially preferred as his successor. But
by then the pent-up pressures for a renewal—one that at least would
strip away the most recent layer of the Soviet experience—were so
strong that Chernenko's death in 1985 pushed to the forefront a new
and much more dynamic personality, one clearly identified with the
brief Andropov interlude of aborted reforms.

Mikhail Gorbachev came to power with a vague mandate to get
the Soviet system moving again. What was even less clear was how
far the needed reforms were to go and what was to serve as their
historical model. More specifically, was Stalinism to be repudiated
as well? And in the name of what? If Leninism was to be the revered
antidote to Stalinism, what central aspect of that Leninist experience
was to be evoked? Was it to be the NEP or was it to be a revitalized,
militant, and ideologically motivated party? And, as a practical matter,
could Stalinism be repudiated not only historically but also in terms
of current reality without in some fashion assaulting the real essence
and the true legacy of Leninism?

Nonetheless, it must be explicitly stated—and the point is
important—that Gorbachev's emergence was not a freak event. His
coming to power represented the surfacing of a new reality in the
Soviet Union, both on the objective and the subjective levels. In other
words, if not he then some other Soviet reformer would have in all
probability emerged as the leader in the mid-1980s. The Soviet
population, for all of its physical deprivations and sustained indoctrination, was by the early 1980s a relatively educated one, with many
of its upper echelons quite familiar with conditions in the world at
large and less gullible to deceptive ideological claims. Particularly
among the upper professional economists, specialists on world affairs,
and their colleagues in some of the more internationally oriented
sectors of the party *nomenklatura*, a pervasive awareness emerged of

a growing crisis that called for reforms which, in turn, might also provide answers to the questions posed above.

Gorbachev's celebrated campaign of *glasnost*, or overtness, did not, and probably could not, provide all at once an overall strategic response to the above questions. Rather, the *glasnost* campaign seemed to progress through several tactical stages. At first, when launched in 1985, it largely involved exposés of ongoing abuses by the state bureaucracy, including even the hitherto untouchable police, and of waste and mismanagement in the economic sector. Before too long, the scope of *glasnost* expanded to include the beginnings of a critical reappraisal of the past, concentrating on some of the more self-evident abuses of the Stalinist era. It did not, however, include an all-out assault on the systemic legacy of that dark period, for that might have entailed potentially destabilizing consequences for the structure of the political system as a whole.

Nonetheless, even the somewhat initially confined scope of the *glasnost* campaign unleashed powerful impulses for reform within the key Soviet urban centers. That enabled Gorbachev and his associates to widen the scope of the campaign to include, by 1987, an increasingly ambitious program of changes focused primarily on the management and planning of the state economy. Labeled *perestroika*, or restructuring, the campaign sought to exploit the momentum unleashed by *glasnost* to energize and streamline the stagnating economic bureaucracy and to revive economic growth. But that also brought to the surface the question of whether genuine reform of the Soviet economy was possible without significantly tampering with the political system and without opening more generally the doors to intellectual freedom.

Where to draw the boundaries of reform thus remained the key unanswered question. Even Gorbachev probably did not know the precise answer, though some of his comments hinted at an inclination to go quite far. His informal and spontaneous remarks delivered to various Soviet publics tended to be more far-reaching in their implications than formally prepared speeches delivered to leading Communist party bodies. In addressing an assembly of the leaders of the mass media and the so-called creative unions in mid-July 1987, Gorbachev called for a new Soviet "political culture" and the use of these two words, borrowed from Western political sociology, was quite striking. In urging increased democratization, Gorbachev observed, "We are now, as it were, going through the school of democracy afresh. We are learning. Our political culture is still inadequate. Our standard of debate is inadequate; our ability to respect the point of view of even our friends and comrades—even that is inadequate."

Gorbachev's goal of shaping a new political culture was all the more forbidding because the "inadequacies" that he deplored were not only a legacy of Leninism-Stalinism. They were deeply rooted in Russian history. Marquis Astolphe de Custine's *Letters from Russia*, published in 1839 after a lengthy visit to that country, suggests a striking continuity between the politics of nineteenth century Russia and the Soviet Union of today. De Custine was struck by the pervasive role of the state bureaucracy which "is based on minutiae, sloppiness, and corruption" and in which "secrecy presides over everything." He charged that the "only domain in which the tyranny shows invention is in the means of perpetuating its power" and that "[d]espotism is the worst when allegedly it is doing good, because it then justifies through its intentions the most outrageous acts, and the evil which is viewed as the medicine knows no bounds." His evaluation of the regime's performance could be easily applied to the Soviet experience: "I do not say that their political system has created nothing good, but merely affirm that too high a price has been paid for its accomplishments."

De Custine was also struck by the restraints placed on free thought and by the misuse of history by those in power. He observed that history is "the possession of the tsar," who "presents to the people such historical truths as are in keeping with the currently dominant fiction." Perhaps most significantly, he commented, "The political system of Russia could not withstand twenty years of free communication with Western Europe."

No wonder, then, that shaping a new political culture in the Soviet Union, after fifty years of direct and indirect state Stalinism and after seventy years of party Leninism, would necessarily require a major political upheaval. Gorbachev hinted as much in a private conversation held in May 1987 with a top Hungarian party leader (who recounted it the next day to this author), stating that in his view the totality of Soviet experience since 1929 had been wrong. In effect, according to the top Soviet leader, no less than three-quarters of the

Soviet practice was discredited and should somehow be repudiated or corrected.

It is very doubtful that even Gorbachev's colleagues on the Politburo fully agreed. Probably most of them instinctively sensed that Leninism was not only the basis of their legitimacy but that much of the Stalinist experience provided the basis for their power. Partial tinkering with the Stalinist system was both acceptable and even viewed as necessary, but a general repudiation, they feared, could destabilize the Soviet system as a whole. The consensus regarding reforms was thus relatively thin. It was vulnerable to splits on the question of how much of the Stalinist legacy could safely be undone, while the pernicious Leninist tradition remained an untouchable sacred cow.

Indeed, Leninism and not reform was thus the ultimate—but hidden—issue of contention among the top Soviet leaders. For example, much has been made in the West over the alleged conflict between the reformer, Gorbachev, and his allegedly conservative and anti-reformist rival, Yegor Ligachev, who until the fall of 1988 was the number-two man in the Politburo and also party secretary. Though to this day, and despite *glasnost*, almost nothing is known about the internal debates within the top leadership, it does appear quite clear that Ligachev has been speaking on behalf of those Soviet leaders who are not against reform as such but who would prefer that it be undertaken in "a Leninist manner," from above and in a more disciplined fashion so as not to jeopardize effective party control over the process.

The difference between the two approaches was best summarized by Aleksandr Gelman, an active member of the Soviet cinematographers' party organization, himself an enthusiastic supporter of Gorbachev, who drew a sharp distinction between the concepts of "democratization" and "liberalization." In his powerful words (as quoted by *Sovetskaia Kultura*, April 9, 1988):

Democratization provides for the redistribution of power, rights, and freedoms, the creation of a number of independent structures of management and information. And liberalization is the conservation of all the foundations of the administrative system but in a milder form. Liberalization is an unclenched fist, but the hand is the same and at any moment it could be clenched again into a fist. Only outwardly is liberalization sometimes reminiscent of democratization, but in actual fact it is a fundamental and intolerable usurpation.

Even if overdrawn, the implied contrast between a "democratizing" and a merely "liberalizing" leader was in essence correct. To succeed in the setting of the Stalinist legacy, the former favors a sharper break with the past whereas the latter is more inclined to stress elements of continuity. Thus Ligachev, who went out of his way in a celebrated interview with the French daily *Le Monde* on December 4, 1987, to stress that "I chair the Central Committee Secretariat's meetings and . . . I organize its work" and that "Gorbachev chairs the Politburo meetings," has not been shy in providing a more positive assessment of the Soviet past than offered by Gorbachev himself. While always stressing the need for reforms and fully endorsing the program of *perestroika*, Ligachev has publicly stated that for him even the Brezhnev era was one of "impressive" accomplishments. As he put it, according to *Pravda* on August 27, 1987, "it was an unforgettable time, it was really living life to the full. . . . It was there, in difficult conditions, that true Communists were forged." He also emphasized that "we will never leave the Leninist path," which he pointedly associated with the entire "glorious seventy-year history of Soviet power."

The consensus on the need for reform thus represented a compromise regarding the present, obscuring an important disagreement regarding much of the past. That compromise had a double effect. On the one hand, it permitted criticisms of the Stalinist era to surface and be propagated. The Soviet experience and the Soviet model were thereby even further discredited in the world at large. On the other hand, by perpetuating the fundamentally totalitarian character of the system through the retention not only of the Leninist-type totalitarian party, with its claim of unique insight into the laws of history, but also of the principal institutions of the Stalinist-type behemoth state, with its crushing subordination of society, the scope of potential reforms was severely circumscribed. The Soviet Union thereby paid a double price. It continued to lose its ideological appeal, but it did not gain domestically the wide-ranging freedom to recoup through a genuinely systemic reform.

Retardation as a systemic condition, prompting a widening lag behind the Western world, was thus the most likely prospect for the Soviet Union, Gorbachev's efforts and his international popularity notwithstanding. To avoid that grim prospect required not only a revolution in political culture but a truly fundamental and far-reaching institutional repudiation of the twin sources of the current Soviet dilemma: both Stalinism and Leninism. Unless Stalinism was undone and Leninism grossly diluted, the Soviet state would still remain a behemoth without constructive social content and without idealism or historic vision. As such, it would continue to be in conflict with the global tendency to enhance the rights of the individual and would continue to lack the necessary preconditions for genuine social and technological creativity.

Yet the practical political fact is that the dismantling of Stalinism and the diluting of Leninism could be pursued, at best, only in stages and, particularly in the case of the Leninist tradition, with great caution. The genuine dismantling of Stalinism would require, above all, the breakup of the all-powerful state bureaucracy both in the economic and social realms and some significant decollectivization in agriculture. These are monumental tasks, given the ruling elite's vested interests, not to speak of the enduring Russian tradition of supremacy of the state over the society. Moreover, the multinational character of the Soviet state posed a special complication, for any genuine de-Stalinization raised the specter of increasingly self-assertive nationalist aspirations among the non-Russian peoples, threatening the very survival of the Soviet Union.

Leninism is even more difficult to tackle. First of all, the attack on the Stalinist legacy is easier to launch from a purportedly Leninist basis. The invocation of the "good Lenin" provided the needed ideological legitimacy for the denigration of Stalin. The more the Stalinist era was denounced, the more the Leninist period had to be idealized. Thus, even for good tactical reasons, the attack on Stalinism had to be separated from any effort to revise or dilute the Leninist legacy. That legacy, after all, provided a most convenient springboard for justifying the anti-Stalinist reforms and for countering the charge that such actions represented a revisionist deviation. The effect, however, was to fortify the hold of Leninism on Soviet politics.

Leninism thus remains central to the sense of historical legitimacy of the ruling elite, rationalizing its claim to power. Any rejection of it would be tantamount to collective psychological suicide. After so many decades, the Soviet Communist elite could not suddenly re-define itself as some Russian variant of Western social democracy, a resuscitated version of the earlier Mensheviks (whom Lenin had crushed). That this is not an easy task is shown by the experience of some Western European Communists. For example, to this day, the French Communists, who would have much political cause to do so, have been unable to effect such a change, even though they operate in an environment in which democratic traditions prevail.

Hence, in fairness to Gorbachev it must be said that he did not have much choice in the matter. Even with a partial repudiation of Stalinism, Leninism was all that was left of the communist experi-ence in the Soviet Union. To reject both Stalinism and Leninism would mean the repudiation of the entirety of the Communist era. Gorbachev could hardly be expected to base his legitimacy on the pre-Bolshevik history, or to reach out for some social-democratic antecedent. He thus had no choice but to assert that *perestroika* was based on Leninism, rooted in Leninism, and represented the genuine revival of Leninism. But in doing so, Gorbachev was also revitalizing the ruling elite's propensity toward the dogmatic grand oversimpli-fication inherent in the Communist claim to a unique grasp of all truth and in the Communist quest for a total monopoly of power. That, after all, was the essence of Leninism, and that essence made Stalinism inevitable.

The political obstacles to a real *perestroika* are thus not only for-midable but probably insurmountable. A break with the Leninist legacy would require nothing short of a basic redefinition of the nature of the ruling party, of its historical role, and of its legitimacy. In fact, a real break would require a repudiation of the grand oversimplifi-cation's central premise, namely that a perfect social system can be shaped by political fiat through which society is subordinated to the supreme state acting as history's all-knowing agent. It would require an acceptance of the notion that much of social change is contingent, ambiguous, and often spontaneous, with the result that social com-plexity cannot be fitted into an ideological straitjacket.

To truly break with the past and to unleash social creativity, the Leninist legacy at some point will have to be confronted. Some of Gorbachev's supporters were willing to go that far. In the heady atmosphere of mid-1988 *glasnost*, the respected monthly *Novy Mir* published in May an article in which the author, V. Selyunin, quite explicitly charged Lenin with having initiated mass repressions as a would-be solution first to political and then to economic problems. Another Soviet publication, *Nash Sovremennik*, went even further, asserting in April 1988 that more people were killed in Lenin's days than under Stalin.

However, these were still isolated views. The top leaders, including Gorbachev, realized that to repudiate Leninism entirely and openly would mean delegitimizing the Soviet system itself. The Soviet reformers thus confront a historical vicious circle: By having to assault Stalinism from the basis of a revitalized Leninism, they are also reenergizing, relegitimizing, and thus perpetuating the very ideological-political forces that directly led to Stalinism.

The more practical path that someday could be taken by a boldly revisionist Soviet leader would be to redefine the *meaning* of Leninism so that it begins to resemble social democracy more than bolshevism. Some of Gorbachev's statements, linking Lenin with democracy, indicated that he leaned in that direction, and some of his most fervent supporters seemed to be paving the way by arguing publicly that the contemporary Soviet understanding of Marxism-Leninism had been distorted by the Stalinist era. In the pointed words of Fedor Burlatskiy in *Literaturnaia Gazeta*, on April 20, 1988:

> . . . it is very important to study Stalin's concepts which justified the deformation of socialism. Our ideas of Marxism and Leninism, of socialism itself, were handed down to us by Stalin himself. From the early thirties, the system of tuition and education was based on Stalin's work *Problems of Leninism*, the *Short Course in the History of the All-Union Communist Party (Bolsheviks)*, which he edited, and the work *Economic Problems of Socialism in the USSR*. In one way or another, all current textbooks on party history, political economy, scientific communism, and philosophy, as well as most theoretical studies in the social sciences, hark back to these sources.

But such a basic intellectual realignment, redefining Lenin as a social democrat, contains obvious dangers for the ruling party's monopoly of power. The party officialdom is thus certain to resist any such redefinition of its roots. That, in turn, means that the Soviet Union will remain subject to the rule of a dogmatic and socially stifling organization that insists on a monopoly of political power in an age in which creativity and pluralism have become interdependent. It will remain under the domain of a party committed to the Leninist notion of a central truth that it alone perceives and that it has the right and the power to impose on society.

In essence, an intractable historical paradox confronts the Soviet leadership: To restore the global prestige of communism, the Soviet Union has to repudiate most of its own communist past, both in terms of doctrine and practice. In the 1920s, to much of the world at large, the communist experiment in the Soviet Union seemed to be promising the future. In the 1930s, it appeared to be building that future. After the war and even into the 1960s, it looked like the wave of the future. Yet by the waning years of this century the Soviet Union has come to be seen as an ideologically unattractive example of arrested social and economic development.

For the world at large, the Soviet experience, an icon no more, is henceforth not to be imitated but avoided. As a result, communism no longer has a practical model for others to emulate.

PART II

The Soviet Disunion

"Perestroika is our last chance," said a grim Mikhail Gorbachev on January 8, 1988. "If we stop, it will be our death." His foreboding words, spoken at a meeting with Soviet mass media leaders, were then circulated with special emphasis by *Moscow News* and widely quoted within the Soviet elite.

What a contrast to the ebullient optimism of his predecessor, Nikita Khrushchev, who thirty years earlier had also been addressing the subject of the Soviet future. Over and over again, Khrushchev had projected the vision of a triumphant socialist Soviet Union on the verge of entering the age of communism as the number-one economic power of the world: "Within a period of, say, five years following 1965, the level of U.S. production per capita should be equaled and over-taken. Thus, by that time, perhaps even sooner, the USSR will have captured first place in the world both in absolute volume of production and per capita production, which will ensure the world's highest standard of living." This was Khrushchev's boast on November 14, 1958, to the graduating class of the Soviet military academies.

This was no idle boast or solitary slip. The grandiose claim was continually reiterated amid frequent references to the "majestic program of economic construction" that would ensure for the Soviet Union global economic leadership in the relatively near future. Indeed, as previously noted, the forecast was even made part of the official program of the Soviet Communist party, adopted in 1961, which also promised that the current Soviet generation would actually live in the hallowed phase of full communism.

Thirty years later, historical anxiety dominated the outlook of the new Soviet General Secretary and of his immediate associates. They could not evade the depressing reality that the gap with the capitalist archrival had not only widened to the Soviet Union's disadvantage, but that other powers were likely to surpass the Soviet Union over the next two or three decades. Japan was already doing so. It was bad enough for the Soviet Union's global prestige that the whole world knew of its slippage. No wonder that Gorbachev evoked the specter of communism's death in attempting to spur the Soviet elite into a desperate renewal of their system.

Contrary to widespread Western speculation that the Soviet Politburo was split between "reformers" in favor of change and "reactionaries" wedded to the status quo, most top Soviet leaders accepted by the mid-1980s the need for renewal—for a *perestroika* of the Soviet system—as a necessity. Genuine opposition was centered more among various republican and provincial first secretaries entrenched in their privileged fiefdoms and lacking the wider and even global perspectives of the men in the Kremlin. At the top, the debates focused on how to effect the reform, how to define its scope, and how much to mobilize the Soviet public's direct involvement in the process through deliberate press campaigns. Some top Soviet leaders clearly favored a more carefully managed process, dominated from the top down, in which control over socioeconomic renewal would remain firmly in the grasp of the ruling party. But they also agreed that drastic changes were needed to avoid a catastrophic decline in Soviet prospects. To use the terminology cited in the previous chapter, they were "liberals" but not "democrats."

Gorbachev advocated a different tactic, publicly spearheading the drive for reform and in doing so deliberately seeking to generate social pressures from below on its behalf. That was the tactical significance of the *glasnost* campaign, which stimulated nothing short of a nationwide debate over the Soviet present and the past. In the course of that debate, things once held to be sacred were publicly profaned; matters long ago swept under the rug, openly exposed; the seeming unanimity of the country shattered; and in some eyes even the future of the system placed in doubt. Many participants in that debate—which culminated in the Nineteenth Special Party Conference in June 1988—began speaking in terms that a few years earlier would have been condemned as rank revisionism, an ideological offense of great magnitude in a ruling party dominated during its entire life span by rigid orthodoxy. The country's apparent consensus was split asunder by public rancor over a large number of interlocking issues that collectively threatened to escalate into a severe political conflict. As a result, the totalitarian Soviet Union increasingly was becoming a volatile Soviet disunion.

CHAPTER 5

From Vision
to Revisionism

Nothing demonstrated this new and dynamic reality more dramatically than the startling fact that in the process the new Soviet leader, Mikhail Gorbachev, became somewhat of a convert to revisionism. In the short span of three years, his rhetoric and conduct had changed from that of an advocate of a revitalizing reform of the economy to that of a propagator of more basic revisions, not only in the economic structure, but also of the system's ideological foundations and to some extent even of its political processes. This transformation was testimony both to his growing appreciation of the depths of the Soviet crisis and to his intellectual boldness. But it also portended the likelihood of a protracted and truly divisive political conflict over the Communist party's management of the Soviet Union's future. It even posed the possibility that the monopolistic control over society might some day slip from the party's grasp.

The notion of "revisionism" has had a long and painful history in the Soviet Marxist-Leninist movement. In the Soviet political lexicon, the term has acquired a particularly pejorative meaning. It has been applied over the years to those who have allegedly strayed from the fundamentals of party doctrine, notably in the direction of the much maligned social democracy that Lenin had so hated and that Stalin did so much to extirpate. The Leninist legacy showed particular hostility toward social democratic notions, with their emphasis on genuine democracy, openness, popular participation in decision making, tolerance for opposing views, and even formal competition for power within the social democratic movement itself. Lenin and his disciples rejected these notions as manifestations of "petty bourgeois" leanings, which were said to have nothing in common with the proletariat's need for a disciplined party of professional revolutionaries. After 1917, this party became not only the professional but also the permanent rulers of that proletariat.

Lenin's bolshevism was nurtured in the struggle against the social democracy of the Mensheviks, and the latter were physically destroyed immediately after the Bolshevik seizure of power. Stalin continued the struggle, labeling as social democratic revisionists some of his principal rivals for power and using that doctrinal excommunication as the justification for their physical liquidation. After World War II, with the Soviet sphere of influence expanded to Eastern Europe, Stalin stigmatized social democracy as nothing less than the willing tool of Western imperialism and made it the object of his special vengeance. Indeed, throughout Soviet history, the challenge from the social democratic left has been viewed with particular gravity, not only because the partially shared Marxist antecedents inherently tended to transform disagreement into heresy but also because of the Soviet leaders' awareness that the social democratic platform spoke with a language and used symbolism of potentially great appeal to the masses subject to communist political control.

Soviet hostility has been especially strong to any manifestations of revisionism within the leaderships of the ruling Communist parties. The defection of Yugoslavia, and especially Tito's experimentation with various forms of workers' councils, was labeled as a particularly hostile manifestation of revisionism, alien to the spirit of Marxism-Leninism. That condemnation precipitated in the late 1940s and early 1950s a number of show trials in Eastern Europe, with the victims invariably lumped together as revisionists, traitors, and spies for the West.

Later, following the nationalist and anti-Stalinist upheavals of 1956 in both Poland and Hungary, Moscow leveled the charge of revisionism against Imre Nagy, the Hungarian leader executed in 1958 for his attempt to create a neutral and essentially social democratic Hungary, and for a while against Władysław Gomułka, the nationalistically inclined Polish Communist leader. The Kremlin viewed the latter with special suspicion because, to consolidate a somewhat more autonomous Polish Communist regime, Gomułka was prepared to compromise with the peasantry, by abolishing the hated system of collectivization, and with the Catholic church, thereby inevitably diluting the party's control over ideological indoctrination. Though eventually the Kremlin came to terms with Gomułka personally and extended grudging support to his regime, it continued to view with considerable concern internal developments in Poland. Throughout the late 1950s, the Soviet press waged a sustained campaign against all manifestations of revisionism in Poland, seeing in it a potentially dangerous rebirth of the hated social democracy.

The Soviet obsession with revisionism reached a high-water mark during the Prague Spring of 1968. The ideas advocated by the new Czechoslovak Communist leadership, notably by First Secretary Alexander Dubček, and expressed in the party's historically important "Action Program," were denounced with extraordinary vigor by the Soviet leadership. The program's call for the democratization of Czechoslovak political life, for the decentralization of the economy, for ideological openness, as well as for the full exposure of Stalinist crimes, was condemned by Moscow as "right-wing revisionism" paving the way to a "return to capitalism and a detachment from the Warsaw Pact." Brezhnev's military intervention, which removed Dubček and his associates from power, was the logical conclusion.

Yet the parallels between some of Gorbachev's views of the late 1980s and those advocated by the revisionists so damningly condemned by his own predecessors in the Kremlin were striking. To be sure, they did not emerge all at once. While assuming power at a time when he and his Politburo colleagues shared the realization that reforms in the Soviet system were long overdue, Gorbachev focused initially on the rationalization and modernization of the Soviet economy. Either out of caution or perhaps because he felt that economic performance could be upgraded largely by improvements in economic management and planning, he directed the early thrust of his public advocacy at eliminating the problems of waste, poor management, inadequate quality control, loose labor discipline, alcoholism, and general sloppiness. One had the impression that initially his model for the Soviet Union was East Germany, with its efficient, disciplined, and technologically advanced Communist system.

Doubtless to his chagrin, Gorbachev soon learned that Russians were not Prussians, that his vision of the Soviet Union as an East Germany writ large was not to be. He had to face the fact that the problems he was confronting were more deep-seated culturally and more deep-rooted systemically. In effect, Gorbachev's learning process, concentrated into a relatively short span of two years, drove him to the realization that any effective reform in the Soviet Union would also require far-reaching changes in the public outlook—"the political culture" of society—and even in the character of the political system itself.

The turning point came in June 1988 at the Nineteenth Special Party Conference. In his opening address, Gorbachev elevated the importance of political reform above that of economic restructuring: "We are facing many intricate questions. But which one of them is the crucial one? As the [Central Committee of the Soviet Communist Party] sees it, the crucial one is that of reforming our political system." Only after political reforms could the economic reforms produce "success" in the sense that the Soviet Union could genuinely aspire to a standard of living comparable to the world's more advanced societies, to a technological level sufficient to enable the Soviet Union to compete politically and militarily with the West, and to a quality of life that would justify the ideological claims for many years so grandiosely made on behalf of Soviet "socialism." One had the sense that by mid-1988 Gorbachev was looking toward Hungary for inspiration.

In shifting his emphasis from economics to politics, Gorbachev had by 1987 embraced an approach in which comprehensive reform from above—the *perestroika*—was to be reinforced and even driven by deliberately released social pressures from below—the famous *glasnost*. The latter in turn was meant to stimulate a more wide-ranging democratization—*demokratizatsiia*—of the Soviet system in general. It is important to note that in a significant departure from the traditional Leninist emphasis on total control from above, *glasnost* and *demokratizatsiia* were to drive the reconstruction forward, transforming in the process the very nature of the system itself. As he put it in his speech at the Special Party Conference, chiding those who awaited top-down reforms and encouraging those who sought to initiate bottom-up pressure: "It is being said and written by people in various localities that *perestroika* has not reached them; they ask when this will happen. But *perestroika* is not manna from the skies—instead of waiting for it to be brought in from somewhere, it has to be brought about by the people themselves in their town or village, in their work collective." In other words, not just "liberalization" of the system but its "democratization" was needed to spur the reform drive.

In doing so, Gorbachev doubtless subjectively felt that he was acting as a true Leninist, returning his party to its true doctrinal foundations and releasing it from the pernicious hold of Stalinist traditions. But Gorbachev apparently was driven to the articulation and propagation of this more ambitious, comprehensive, and socially dynamic approach by his increasing awareness that nothing less would do. He must have sensed that continued reliance on the traditional Leninist tenet, that only control from above should produce social change below, would condemn him to defeat by the still resilient Stalinist structures of power and of privilege. That drove him to embrace an approach that in the orthodox Soviet perspective could stamp him as a revisionist.

It is noteworthy that revisionist overtones were more marked in his spontaneous public utterances than in his formal speeches, which were presumably collectively approved by the Politburo. That provides a suggestive clue to Gorbachev's personal feelings on the matter. In any case, the themes that Gorbachev came to emphasize both spontaneously and formally were in some sensitive respects reminiscent of those stressed in earlier years by Dubček, not to mention the doctrinally much more cautious revisions of Gomułka or Tito. These came to be voiced with a desperation hardly in keeping with the officially prescribed optimism about socialism's "inevitable" triumph. On more than one occasion, Gorbachev spoke in almost apocalyptic terms. He warned his own Central Committee on February 18, 1988, that "the main thing, comrades, is democratization. . . . During the new stage of restructuring the party can ensure its leading, vanguard role and inspire the masses only by using democratic methods. . . . Without exaggeration, everything hinges on it today."

The note of urgency became a frequent refrain. Over and over again Gorbachev would remind his audiences that time was running out, that change must come now, and that it must be comprehensive. To people on the street in Leningrad, he called out, in October 1987, "it is two years since we, together with you, consulted, spoke, argued, and thought of how to find a correct answer to those problems that life itself had posed. What must be done? Now we will finish this path. Now the whole of society must change over to these principles: democracy, in the running of the economy, and in the entire moral atmosphere of the life of our society. Everything must change!" To his Central Committee, he complained that "in practice a negative reaction to initiative, a rejection of initiative, can often be encountered. Furthermore, in many cases no effort is made to understand what is being proposed, and pretexts for snubbing the author of an initiative are deliberately sought. This is still quite a widespread phenomenon." And impatiently he warned, "we can no longer tolerate such a state of affairs. Otherwise restructuring will fail."

Again in Leningrad, a city with a special Bolshevik mystique, Gorbachev called for popular support for the second—and more ambitious—political stage of *perestroika* that would involve some institutional democratization. He told his audience that "a second stage is necessary, a decisive stage, so that we really do not get bogged down in words and decisions. This has been the case, this has been the case in the past, comrades. This is a lesson, a bitter lesson from the past. We started a lot and started correctly, but then it snapped. If it snaps now, losses in the country will be enormous. We should not permit that and we will not, I am sure. This is the mood the people are in. We are not playing at restructuring. The country's fate and the life of the people are behind restructuring."

But the reception was mixed. The enthusiasm of his supporters, notably in the various institutes and the intelligentsia of Moscow, was offset by marked coolness among the bureaucracy and the party's *nomenklatura*. Indicative of the widespread skepticism among the party's entrenched officialdom was the fact that Gorbachev had to quote and then to attack head-on the traditional argument of the elite: "Let us hope democracy does not lead to chaos." He countered that criticism with the potentially irritating allegation that party officials expressing such fears "are fussing about their own selfish interests."

Even more significantly, as reported by *Pravda* on February 19, 1988, Gorbachev had to admit in the course of debating with his critics that his program was prompting charges of the deadly sin, of nothing less than revisionism propagated by the party's General Secretary himself! His own rebuttal showed this was no minor charge: "We can see that some people are confused, wondering whether we are backsliding from socialist positions . . . and whether we are not *revising* Marxist-Leninist teaching itself. It is no wonder that 'defenders' of Marxism-Leninism have already appeared along with the mourners of socialism, who believe that both Marxism-Leninism and socialism *are under threat*." (emphasis added)

The instinctive fear of democracy among the party bureaucrats was intensified by widespread suspicions that Gorbachev, in his campaigns for public support for a wide-ranging *perestroika*, was either deliberately or unintentionally stimulating anti-bureaucratic sentiments among the masses. To some extent, the charge was true. To overcome resistance to change, the Soviet leader had no choice but to argue that institutional inertia and unwillingness to experiment were impeding the process of restructuring. Moreover, to propagate the merits of genuine democratization, Gorbachev had to invoke populist slogans, emphasizing the need for the people to assume responsibility for their own well-being, to become more active participants in the country's social and political life. All of that inevitably raised the specter of the General Secretary agitating among the masses against his own party cadres!

Gorbachev showed sensitivity to these fears as well, thereby also confirming their existence. On more than one occasion, he went out of his way to try to be reassuring, to erase the horrifying specter of even something like a Soviet version of the Chinese Cultural Revolution devouring the party cadres at the instigation of the top leader himself. For example, on October 13, 1987, he said: "The restructuring process and developing socialism need talented, highly moral cadres which are seized completely by the idea of the revolutionary renewal of society and which are close to the people. . . . When I put the matter this way, I do not at all want it to be understood as an appeal—as once was the case during the years of *the Cultural Revolution in China*—to open fire on the functionaries. No, no, comrades . . ." (emphasis added). On another occasion, when speaking of the need to replace indifferent officials, Gorbachev hastily added: "Such an approach does not mean at all a disrespectful attitude toward the cadres, for our cadres, our intelligentsia, are talented people and should be pampered."

These reassurances notwithstanding, it is also noteworthy that Gorbachev did normally couple his praise of the party cadres with reminders that they were expendable if they were unwilling to change in keeping with the spirit of the new times. On almost every occasion, his praise for the special and even unique role of "Leninist cadres" was linked to warnings that passivity and lack of innovation would not be tolerated. As he put it himself in one of his spontaneous comments to a street crowd: "There are some people in our country who will either have to alter their attitude to matters and to people or they will have to stand aside for others."

While Gorbachev sought to cloak himself in the mantle of Leninism, he was indeed staking out a position that was bound to be troubling to the orthodox. His calls for a public debate could hardly be reassuring to the party officialdom, steeped in the Leninist view that the party is the only guardian of doctrinal truth. His more elaborate prescriptions were just as unsettling, though less explicitly revisionist doctrinally. His book, *Perestroika*, a compendium presumably prepared by his like-minded supporters but apparently also involving a serious input by Gorbachev himself, provided nothing short of an indictment of current and past Soviet reality. Although Gorbachev was careful to reiterate standard Leninist tenets, his case was occasionally reminiscent of the arguments made earlier by several East European Communist leaders and theorists who were subsequently condemned by the Kremlin as revisionists.

The more orthodox Soviet leaders must have been particularly disturbed by some overlap between Gorbachev's book and Dubček's Czechoslovak "Action Program" of 1968. To be sure, the Soviet leader protected his ideological flanks by stressing throughout that his intention was to return to true Leninist principles and that he was not prepared in any way to dilute the party's leading role or the related principle of democratic centralism. The differences between Gorbachev's and Dubček's programs were especially marked when it came to defining what democracy was to mean in practice: Dubček was ready to accept the ballot box whereas Gorbachev's version was confined essentially to that of the suggestion box. Dubček's democratization involved breaking up the Communist monopoly over political power, while Gorbachev's called for a party more responsive to the wishes of the people. Nonetheless, both documents basically denounced recent Stalinist practices and economic priorities, including its overemphasis on extensive development. They decried the resulting social stagnation and moral corruption. Both also called for social renewal through greater democratization and more open debate.

Without quite saying so directly, Gorbachev—like the earlier Eastern European revisionists—was in effect challenging the very concept of the party's doctrinal infallibility. The notion that correct policies were to be derived from both debate and practice, with the debate open to wider participation than just to party members, struck directly at the claim that doctrine, only as defined from above, was the essential guide to action. The concept of *demokratizatsiia*, even if falling quite short of the Western democratic notion of genuine political choice, similarly threatened the Marxist-Leninist edifice of power. To repeat, in neither case was Gorbachev endorsing, or even hinting at, the adoption of Western-style democracy. But the gulf separating Soviet reality from such democracy had become so wide that even timid steps in the direction of the latter—much more timid than those advocated by the East European revisionists—represented a major deviation from established Soviet practices.

Gorbachev's progressive conversion to revisionism also touched on several other issues fundamental to the established Soviet doctrine. For the sake of efficiency and productivity, he was willing to attack the hallowed concept of egalitarianism. As he put it quite bluntly to the party's Central Committee in February 1988: "Basically, wage-leveling has a destructive impact not only on the economy but also on people's morality and their entire way of thinking and acting. It diminishes the prestige of conscientious, creative labor, weakens discipline, destroys interest in improving skills, and is detrimental to the competitive spirit in work. We must say bluntly that wage-leveling is a reflection of petty bourgeois views which have nothing in common with Marxism-Leninism or scientific socialism." In effect, Gorbachev was saying that henceforth wage differentials based on productivity were to be the true expression of genuine equality, a principle which many American industrialists of pre–trade union days would have heartily endorsed.

Last but not least, his direct linkage of institutional economic reforms from above to political democratization generating social pressures from below inescapably posed the danger of diluting the party's monopoly over the management of social change. The effort to create a new political culture in the Soviet Union, one in which the people would help the party to govern more effectively, at the very least opened the doors to public disputations—as in the televised arguments at the Special Party Conference in June 1988—totally out of keeping with the established norms of Soviet public life, even to some manifestations of open political dissent, and eventually to unanticipated social turmoil. And all that, to use Marxist terminology, was "objectively" revisionism.

The implications of a revisionist General Secretary in the Kremlin were momentous. It was not only bound to fuel a bitter and intense debate within the Soviet Union over almost all aspects of Soviet life. It was also bound to revive and intensify the more far-reaching East European revisionism, while depriving the Kremlin of the ideological cathedra from which to excommunicate the heretics. It posed the particularly grave danger of dissolving the common core of Marxist-Leninist tenets of world communism. In brief, even modest revisionism in Moscow had to accelerate the political disintegration and the doctrinal eclipse of communism as a distinctive historical phenomenon.

CHAPTER 6

The Ten Dynamics
of Disunion

It is unlikely that Gorbachev has ever read Marquis de Custine's remarkably perceptive *Letters from Russia*, describing a visit to that country in 1839, a century and a half ago. If he had, he might have well pondered the Frenchman's incisiveness when de Custine observed, "When the gagged Russian nation finally recovers [its] freedom of speech, one will hear so much contestation that the amazed world will think that the times of the Tower of Babel are back."

Indeed, the Soviet Union of the late 1980s was beginning to sound like the mythical tower. On almost every major issue, and in many parts of the country, wide-ranging and even potentially explosive debates were in progress. Some were taking place in the officially controlled mass media; some were surfacing in the newly emerging and still very limited quasi-underground organs of dissent; and some were occurring literally on the streets, through lively public encounters or even violent protest demonstrations.

The scope and substance of the internal Soviet debates unleashed in the quest for *perestroika* involved ten major and interlocking issues. Collectively, they were dynamically fracturing the long-established façade of Soviet unity. Each of the major subjects under debate tended to overlap with others, thereby widening the range and intensifying the vigor of the disputation among the politically or socially conscious groups of the Soviet society. The ten central areas of public debate included the following: (1) economic reform; (2) social priorities; (3) political democratization; (4) role of the party; (5) ideology, religion, and culture; (6) history (or Stalinism); (7) internal national problems; (8) domestic concerns over the war in Afghanistan; (9)

65

foreign and defense policy; (10) the Soviet bloc and the world Communist movement.

Economic reform. Although the most tangible actions in implementing *perestroika* were actually taken in the economic sector, those efforts actually intensified the debate over the country's economic future. In the process, new issues and old wounds were being opened up in a widening debate.

By January 1988, some 60 percent of Soviet industrial enterprises had been shifted to the new system of enhanced responsibility for setting their own production plans, choosing their suppliers, and even to some extent setting their own prices and retaining some of their profits. Small-scale cooperatives were also now permitted, especially in the service sector. By mid-1988, thirteen thousand such cooperatives employing three hundred thousand people were said to exist. Collective farmers were also permitted to lease land for individual exploitation to enhance the supply of agricultural products to the cities. Gorbachev also had in the works more ambitious plans for further structural reforms, for the elimination of redundant bureaucracy and useless jobs, the latter estimated by his favorite economist, Abel Aganbegyan, to number as many as sixteen million.

Given the scale of the centralized Soviet economy, the steps actually implemented were only a modest beginning at best. Gorbachev's reforms left, for the time being at least, the system of collectivized agriculture, the most benighted sector of the Soviet economy, still basically untouched. That, by itself, tended to drag down the country's economic prospects. Moreover, the initial reforms actually produced dislocations, with *Pravda* reporting on October 29, 1987, instances of panic buying in anticipation of higher prices and blaming "ideological ill-wishers" of reform for deliberately promoting public anxiety. The specter of unemployment also contributed to a rising sense of unease, while the sudden decentralization of the Soviet foreign trade apparatus generated confusion, with many foreign businessmen complaining over the resulting chaos in decision making. After a brief spurt of economic growth following Gorbachev's initial calls for reform, the economy again slowed down and the growth in labor productivity dropped in 1987 and 1988.

In the frank words of a leading Soviet economist, L. I. Abalkin, head of the USSR Academy of Sciences Economics Institute, addressing on June 30, 1988, the Special Party Conference, "it is important to make it emphatically clear that there has been no radical breakthrough in the economy and it has not emerged from a state of stagnation. In the past two years the national income . . . has grown at a slower rate than in the stagnation years [of the Brezhnev era]."

The evident public anxiety over the uncertain consequences of reform was paralleled by a wide-ranging debate over its direction and scope. Research and academic economists supporting Gorbachev were arguing that the initial steps had to be followed by a more dramatic, truly comprehensive dismantling of the centralized planning apparatus which they said was overwhelmed by the task of coordinating annual targets for over twenty-four million production items. Central planning, they argued, had to be replaced with a modified market-mechanism, which implied willingness to accept the reality of some structural unemployment and to confront head-on the abysmal failure of the ideologically induced collectivization of agriculture. As Nikolai Shmelyov, another of Gorbachev's economic advisers, put it in *Novy Mir* in June 1987: "At one time we proclaimed the slogan of 'liquidating the kulaks,' but essentially we ended up eliminating the peasantry. . . . We must call things by their proper names: foolishness as foolishness, incompetence as incompetence, Stalinism in action as Stalinism in action. . . . Perhaps we will lose our ideological virginity, but it now exists only in the fairy-tale editorials of newspapers. There is more theft and graft than ever under this virginity."

Yet, not surprisingly, the established bureaucratic managers did not share this enthusiasm for reforms. Some publicly warned in *Pravda* on November 16, 1987, that such changes were likely to induce "all-permissiveness, anarchy, and chaos" and repudiated such "playing at democracy." Unaccustomed to individual responsibility, they preferred the security of a highly centralized system, with predictable rewards for steady but mediocre performance. The massive Soviet bureaucracy was doubtless also resentful of assertions by Gorbachev's supporters that it was overblown and in need of drastic reductions. As *Izvestia* menacingly noted on November 2, 1987, "our management apparatus is indeed vast: about 18 million people are involved! . . . They account for 15 percent of the country's labor resources. There is a management representative for every six to seven people."

At the Special Party Conference in June 1988, Gorbachev took note of the bureaucratic opposition to his economic reforms: "We are running into undisguised attempts at perverting the essence of the reform, at filling the new managerial forms with old content. All too often, ministries and departments depart from the letter and the spirit of the law on enterprises, with the result, as many economists admit, that it is not being fully carried out." He also observed that through state orders enterprises were being compelled to produce unwanted goods "for the simple reason that they want to attain the notorious 'gross output' targets"—a deformation of his reforms that Gorbachev condemned as a "dead end."

Thus, on the agenda for the future, there remained the difficult questions of whether—and, if so, how—to dismantle the collectivized and state farms, of how to cope with the potentially disruptive problem of structural unemployment, and of how to overcome the institutional opposition of the bureaucracy to any far-reaching decentralization. Each of these questions posed truly agonizing economic dilemmas, the gravity of which was compounded by their ideological sensitivity. In the background lurked the even more difficult practical problem of how to replace the existing system of artificial and arbitrary prices, based on fundamentally unreliable statistical methods, with some self-regulative market-mechanism. These issues, enormously complex in themselves, inevitably were also politically and ideologically very divisive. No quick resolution was in sight.

Social priorities. The debate over the economic future of the country inherently led to a collision over social priorities. For years, the heavy industrial sector was the favorite child of the Soviet system. The key indicator of the construction of socialism was the growth of heavy industrial production. Investment through social deprivation was justified as the necessary sacrifice for attaining full communism. Capitalist encirclement of the Soviet Union was cited also as the justification for the massive commitment of national resources—at least 20 percent of GNP throughout the postwar period—to building up its armed forces and to projecting Soviet power beyond its borders.

The economic debate quite naturally prompted the question of whether Soviet priorities should change. Moreover, by the mid-1980s too many members of Soviet society had a reasonably accurate knowledge of living conditions in the West to permit the ruling party to continue claiming that life in the Soviet Union was fundamentally better than elsewhere. Greater emphasis had to be put on the urgent improvement in the Soviet standard of living, and hence on consumption, rather than on investments in heavy industry or even in technological innovation. Even senior officials publicly conceded in *Trud* on March 13, 1988, that "the demand for consumer goods is rising rapidly and we are unable to fully meet it today," with the problem made acute by the fact that "approximately 15 percent of consumer goods . . . do not 'survive' to be sold owing to their poor quality."

The Soviet leadership was in a bind on this issue. Popular demands could no longer be ignored. Yet the Soviet leaders evidently feared that shifting the investment priority to satisfying consumer demands posed the risk that the Soviet Union might fall even further behind the United States, Western Europe, and Japan in overall economic growth, with serious international and ideological consequences for the Kremlin. Moscow's preferred solution was to obtain Western credits, both for financing the acquisition of Western technology and for improvements in consumption, while concentrating domestic resources on the somewhat downgraded but still central traditional priorities. To obtain those credits, however, not only would some compromises in foreign policy be required but also adjustments in domestic economic practices regarding foreign ventures, foreign ownership, and the repatriation by foreign capitalists of profits would be necessary. These issues immediately raised doctrinal concerns, especially because in the past any steps in that direction initiated by the East Europeans had been condemned by Moscow as revisionism pointing toward "the restoration of capitalism."

Two additional factors compounded the doctrinal dilemma. The first were the emerging demands within the Soviet Union for a more truly egalitarian distribution of services and for the elimination of established privileges. These led to the highly publicized clashes within the Moscow Party Committee over the existing system of special privileges for the party elite, ranging from restricted stores through special holiday resorts, free meals, exclusive schools, chauffeured cars, private dachas, and special hospitals. The abrupt political demise of the one-time Gorbachev protégé, Boris Yeltsin, removed in the fall of 1987 from his post as Moscow's party first secretary, was in large measure the product of the rage of the party *apparatchiki* over the fact that he had dared to raise publicly the possibility of terminating such privileges in the name of social egalitarianism.

The second was the widespread recognition of the imperative need for greater initiative and productivity. Despite the modest scale of the steps taken in the introduction of some private initiative in the service sector, envious charges of excessive self-enrichment soon arose. As one writer bitterly complained in *Pravda* on March 7, 1988, "No one imagined that Soviet 'millionaires' would appear in our society, which is building communism . . . certain individuals have managed to amass huge fortunes, they live in luxury." Indeed, the one area in which the prolonged ideological indoctrination of the masses seems to have scored some success has been the propagation of egalitarianism—with the result that this now impeded efforts to reward the individual initiative so necessary to *perestroika*'s success.

The surfacing debates over economic policy or social priorities could not be confined to the economic or social spheres alone. They ultimately raised basic political questions regarding the proper role of the state in economic and social matters. They were thus directly related to the mushrooming debate in the Soviet Union over the desirable forms of the political framework itself.

Political democratization. Neither a more self-regulating and less centralized economic system, which would place greater emphasis on the fulfillment of the society's material aspirations, nor a society more imbued with genuinely innovative values could be attained within the still largely enduring Stalinist political system. That system, created in the process of asserting total social regimentation, was simply incompatible with these contemplated changes and with the mounting aspirations for ever more far-reaching reforms in the economic and social spheres. That is why the Special Party Conference in mid-1988 had to recognize the preeminent need for political reform.

At the core of the resulting political debate, therefore, were the questions of what Gorbachev really meant when he invoked the word *demokratizatsiia* and to what extent would the "democratizing" process tolerate true political spontaneity from below. Indeed, could democratization be genuine if it were limited to initiatives graciously granted only from above, however politically generous they may in fact be? Thus, the two central issues in the surfacing political dialogue pertained to the forms and scope of institutional reform initiated by the existing political leadership and to the degree to which a revival of even modest manifestations of autonomous political life (which Stalin had rendered extinct) would now be tolerated.

That thoughts of more genuine democracy were beginning to percolate within the Soviet society was reflected in some of the letters from readers published in the Soviet press. *Izvestia*, for example, published on May 14, 1988, complaints about the working of the nominal Soviet parliament, the Supreme Soviet, about "the phenomenon of an almost unanimous vote, which is unknown in other countries," and about the fact that "our legislative organs have become law-approving organs which simply approve everything that they are instructed to." Other readers criticized the mechanical and non-representative character of the deliberations conducted by party organizations.

These matters raised painful dilemmas for the ruling elite, long accustomed to asserting a total control over the country's political life. Even limited democratization from above meant concessions that were bound to be repugnant to an elite steeped in the self-serving Marxist-Leninist notions that it alone was the repository of historical truth and thus the only source of political wisdom. Yet the practical consequences of *glasnost* had to be reduced political censorship over the mass media and in literature, thereby opening the gates to ideological pluralism. Greater emphasis on legality automatically confined the arbitrary powers of the KGB, in turn reducing its potential for political intimidation. Talk of greater popular access to the process of nominating candidates for local government, including the possibility of permitting genuine electoral contests, inherently reduced the political control exercised by local or regional party committees.

No wonder, therefore, that those with a vested interest in the political status quo found some of these proposals quite repugnant. On November 16, 1987, the official organ of the party, *Pravda*, expressed the views of much of the party's officialdom when it bristled at those who seek "to debar party organs from participating in the selection of leaders," denouncing such unnamed proponents as worshipers of democracy "as a blind elemental force." It pointedly reminded its readers that the party remains "a ruling party" and as such should continue to exercise direct control over the selection process of would-be participants in local or national government.

The then head of the KGB, Viktor M. Chebrikov, himself a Politburo member and thus presumably a direct participant in the top-level discussions of the permissible scope of democratization, was probably troubled by the increasingly frequent press accounts of illegality and corruption within the police apparatus, all of them doubtless inspired by greater *glasnost*. According to *Komsomolskaia Pravda* of July 24, 1988, between 1985 and 1987 no less than forty thousand police officials were dismissed for various illegal acts, including the fabrication of cases and collusion in corruption. In one instance, reported by Radio Moscow on January 20, 1988, a corrupt republic official was even helped in maintaining his own "secret underground prison . . . where protesters were put."

Such accounts, coupled with calls in Soviet legal journals for the supremacy of law over arbitrary police actions, tended both to discredit and dilute the authority of the police, with obviously potentially significant political consequences. Thus, on September 11, 1987, Chebrikov used an occasion honoring the founder of the Soviet secret police and the initial implementor of Soviet terror, Feliks Dzerzhinskiy, to proclaim publicly that the quest for stricter observance of socialist legality should not be reduced to an interpretation that "narrows and impoverishes the profound substance of the principle of socialist legality," which he then defined in effect as total obedience. To drive the point home, he went on to warn that:

> . . . we have people who hold ideas and views which are alien and even frankly hostile to socialism. Some of them embark on the path of committing antistate and antisocial actions. Among them are people who pursue selfish interests and hope to gain political capital through demagogic talk and through flirting with Western reactionary circles. . . .
>
> All strata of our country's population are the targets of the imperialist special services. . . . Realizing this, our opponents are trying to push individual representatives of the artistic intelligentsia into positions of carping, demagogy, nihilism, the blackening of certain stages of our society's historical development, and the abandonment of the main purpose of socialist culture—the elevation of the working person.

His warning was quite explicit. The chief of the Soviet secret police postulated that the calls for more *glasnost* and for enhanced legality could be a political provocation inspired by hostile foreign sources. Traditional socialist vigilance was thus in order. It was all the more needed, at least in the eyes of the Soviet police apparatus, because the talk of democratization from above was generating spontaneous democratization from below, with the latter not subject to central control.

The most remarkable manifestation of democratization from below was the blossoming of a large number of self-organized informal groups, dedicated either to the promotion of special causes or to the discussion of a variety of current issues. Their very emergence defied the established tradition that social initiative was derived from and controlled by the party. Their appearance signaled the beginnings, but so far only the beginnings, of something that eventually could perhaps become authentic and autonomous political participation, thereby challenging the Communist party's monopoly over all forms of organized social and political activity.

By one account in *Pravda* on February 1, 1988, some thirty thousand "informal groups"—neither created nor even sanctioned by the state—had sprung up throughout the Soviet Union. These groups represented society's response to a variety of concerns, ranging from ecology, urban renewal, social activities, youth music groups, and the preservation of historical and religious monuments, to more politically sensitive matters such as historical debates, issues pertaining to legality, philosophy, national linguistic concerns, religious activities, chronicling political arrests, and political-ideological dissent. Although the largest number were concentrated in Moscow, in Leningrad, and in the major national capitals of the Soviet republics, smaller towns—despite inevitably tighter political control—also saw such manifestations of social spontaneity.

The ruling party reacted ambivalently to this novel development. Those most committed to Gorbachev's concept of restructuring, including also his emphasis on releasing spontaneous social pressures from below, tended to be positive and even supportive. Thus, on Radio Moscow's "Top Priority" program of February 13, 1988, leading Soviet commentators endorsed the appearance of such groups as evidence of the democratization of Soviet life and as a natural reaction

to the stultifying stagnation of the Brezhnev era. An even stronger
endorsement appeared in the official party organ for Soviet youth,
Komsomolskaia Pravda, on December 11, 1987. In a detailed statistical
analysis, it made the point that most of these initiatives were constructive, dedicated to the enhancement of Soviet life, and reflected
a positive reaction on the part of the younger generation to the progressive decay and bureaucratization of the official and monopolistic
youth organization, the Komsomol. Even more startling were some
of the statistics cited to the effect that these new groups command
relatively stable and extensive participation.

But from the ruling party's point of view not all of the new informal
groups were so benign. A number of them focused on directly political
themes, and as such were beginning to pose a political and ideological
challenge. Moreover, some groups undertook to publish quasi-underground magazines to advance either specific human rights or religious and national causes. This collided even more directly with
the party's Leninist concept of its political monopoly over all mass
media.

In addition to the political and ideological challenge from what
might be called the democratic left, a challenge to the party also arose
from the nationalist right. Another new and extremely active group,
Pamyat (or memory), which was ostensibly dedicated to the recovery
of genuine Russian history, took the lead on this front. With its young
members dressed in black shirts (!), emblazoned with the seal of the
historic Kremlin bell, the group staged public demonstrations, organized lectures, and generally proclaimed that Russian history had
been deflected from its true course by the "Masonic-Zionist" influences which had permeated Marxism. With the appeal of the official
ideology waning, *Pamyat* was catering directly, and from the party's
standpoint dangerously, to the rising nationalist sentiments of the
Great Russian masses.

In this context, Gorbachev and the Soviet leadership faced the
dilemma of finding a way to capitalize on the intensifying social
activism in order to advance the cause of *perestroika*, but without
jeopardizing their effective political control. This called for some
ideological gymnastics as well as for political compromise. A Soviet
academician tackled the first task in *Pravda* on March 3, 1988. He
wrote that "it was not so long ago that our society's sociopolitical and

ideological unity was treated in an oversimplified fashion. It was held that unity, and even identity, of interests would emerge almost automatically with the elimination of private property and exploitation. But everything is much more complex in reality. . . . contradictions and divergences of interests are not removed. Classes, social groups, and strata, and also nations and ethnic groups with their own traditions have their specific interests." He was arguing in effect that the party had to accept nonantagonistic group participation as normal and even desirable.

Enhanced grass-roots political participation, but not fundamental freedom of choice, was the solution that Gorbachev offered at the Special Party Conference. He thus proposed that the role of the largely formalistic local soviets be upgraded. These purportedly represent the Soviet peoples within the political system, but actually serve as a façade for the party's rule. He asserted that "not a single question concerning the state, the economy or the social fabric can be decided if the soviets are bypassed." He also proposed the creation of a new governmental structure, the Congress of the USSR People's Deputies, composed of delegates elected from territorial districts and from civil organizations. It would meet once a year and would elect by secret ballot a new bicameral parliament, which would, in turn, select the president and the presidium of the Soviet Union— offices that would also be given real power in the management of the economy, foreign policy, and national security of the country. At the same time, Gorbachev emphasized the need to strengthen the role of law within the Soviet system and to limit the exercise of arbitrary power.

Nonetheless, the question of where to draw the line between acceptable social spontaneity and intolerable political dissent remained unresolved. Drawing the line too tightly on the latter would stifle the former, thereby hurting the cause of restructuring; too much tolerance for the former would encourage the latter, to the detriment of the party's monopoly of power. Thus, ultimately, the underlying and central political question in the process of *demokratizatsiia* was the proper role of the party itself.

The role of the party. On this issue, two questions were critical. First, to what extent should the party itself be democratized? Second, to what degree should the democratization of society affect the party's role in directly exercising power? Inherent in the discussion—but without ever being explicitly raised—was not only the question of how far the party should go in de-Stalinizing itself, but also the far more sensitive issue of the extent to which even the Leninist notion of strict internal party regimentation and of complete subordination of society should be revised.

On the latter point, Gorbachev hinted at considerable flexibility. As he put it, "Too often socialism was understood as an *a priori* theoretical scheme, dividing society into those who give instructions and those who carry them out. I abhor that oversimplified, mechanically directive understanding of socialism. . . ." At the Special Party Conference, Gorbachev asserted that "there must be a strict demarcation of the functions of party and state bodies, in conformity with Lenin's conception of the Communist party as the political vanguard of society and the role of the Soviet state as an instrument of government by the people." It is doubtful, however, that the other top party leaders were prepared to go that far, and Ligachev particularly was emphatic in reaffirming the principle of the party's leading and central role.

Nonetheless, at the start of the reform process, a consensus seemed to exist within the leadership on the need to revive greater initiative within the party organizations and to stimulate enhanced competition through a carefully controlled process of competitive elections to subordinate posts. This led to the introduction of some limited electoral contests, even by secret ballot, for the posts of lower-level party secretaries, and to greater emphasis on the more frequent turnover in the party's bureaucratic cadres. At the Special Party Conference, with the acceptance of proposals made by Gorbachev that tenure at the very top be limited to a fixed number of years and that the roles of the party and the state be separated, the Soviets essentially caught up rhetorically with the actions taken by the Chinese one year earlier.

Even more radical and contentious in its implications was the fleeting appearance of a discussion among some Soviet academics of the possible utility of establishing some new political organizations in order to provide for more extensive social representation. They referred specifically in that context to the experience of the East European Communist states, where the so-called National or Popular Fronts have served as a coalition of Communist-dominated but nominally non-Communist parties allegedly representing the interests of the peasantry and of the intelligentsia. In a public briefing for foreign correspondents on the history of one-party rule in the Soviet Union, which was organized by the Soviet Foreign Ministry on February 25, 1988, two Soviet academicians were surprisingly nonhostile to the idea of experimenting with something similar to these national fronts, with one of them observing (according to TASS) that in the USSR "theoretically it was possible, though only on the condition that the other parties would have platforms expressing the interests of different sections of Soviet society."

The very fact that the issue of new political organizations was raised was itself remarkable. It reflected the fact that the efforts to infuse some life into the moribund structures of the Soviet political system were dynamic in nature and were bound to eventually affect the position and role of the party itself. Already, calls for political democratization led to appeals for more extensive intermingling of party members and nonmembers in joint meetings and in the discussion of national issues. Political exclusivity inherent in party membership was thereby being breached. To the entrenched officials of the party's *nomenklatura*, fuzzing the border line between membership and nonmembership, as well as opening of doors to new forms of political participation, inevitably posed the threat of a revisionist redefinition of the very special position in Soviet life that the party had sustained since 1917.

Ideology, religion, and culture. The party's dilemma was most visible in the area of beliefs. What was to be imposed from above and to what extent were personal values, esthetics, and convictions to be a private domain, not subject to party control? These issues, seemingly resolved once and for all by Lenin and Stalin, were now agitating the intellectual community and perplexing the party's ideologues.

The ideological edifice of the system was hence in deep trouble. Not only were practical developments in economics, society, and politics pointing away from long-asserted verities, but the party's ideological control over the society's value system was under threat. The dictatorship of the proletariat, exercised by a monopolistic party, in a doctrinally uniform society, with a highly centralized planning system, based on the highest priority for heavy industry, and with a collectivized agriculture, was being shaken by public discussions pointing in every case away from established, and ideologically sanctified, practices. To complicate matters, the country's cultural sector was openly rebelling against established doctrine and even religion was threatening to make a comeback.

Massive ferment in favor of *glasnost* surfaced quickly in the cultural sector, generating intense acrimony and even political showdowns in the various literary and cultural organizations around which Soviet intellectual life is structured. Open contests for the domination over editorial boards, over the executive committees of writers' or filmmakers' unions, and over the leading theaters broke out as early as 1987, in the initial phases of Gorbachev's restructuring. Long-suppressed writings were hailed and ordered republished, though *Sovetskaia kultura* revealed on March 22, 1988, that some six thousand titles of Soviet works were still on the banned list. In addition, earlier doctrinal condemnations were repudiated, and invitations were issued to leading cultural figures to return to the homeland from foreign exile.

In the initial burst of enthusiasm, proponents of truly wide-ranging, essentially uninhibited *glasnost* succeeded in taking over several key cultural journals and in gaining a dominant position in the dramatic arts. From these vantage points, they were able to launch campaigns and to produce works (such as the much acclaimed film *Repentance*) that discredited Stalinism and mobilized support for desired social and political changes. They were less successful in the centrally important USSR Union of Writers, long the special object of the party ideologues' attention, where the established leadership succeeded (with the encouragement of the central party apparatus) in rebuffing attempts to install a reformist slate. But even here, the very fact that such a contest could even occur generated outbursts of free expression damning in its criticisms of Soviet reality.

The creative intelligentsia was certainly the source of the most enthusiastic support for Gorbachev's reforms and embraced him as one of its own. That is also why the more cautiously reformist party leaders from quite early on strove to contain the ideological ferment in the intellectual community. They sponsored what in effect was a counterattack, in which Gorbachev's deputy, Yegor Ligachev, the then party secretary directly involved in ideological-cultural matters, took the lead. Ligachev publicly insisted that the creative community project greater "social optimism" and demanded on more than one occasion—in rather familiar language—that they project not "a one-sided truth" but "the full truth" about socialist accomplishments. His supporters went even further, comparing *glasnost*'s attack on orthodoxy to the German invasion of 1941 and charging, in *Litera-turnaia Rossiya* on March 17, 1987, that "speculators, mediocrities, and very shady people" were behind it.

An important aspect of these debates was their breach of the institutional uniformity of the Soviet system. As the campaign for restructuring gathered momentum, some Soviet press organs became themselves active protagonists, propagating and practicing *glasnost* to the hilt, while others reacted in a noticeably cool fashion. Such magazines as *Novy Mir* and *Ogonyok*, and such newspapers as *Moscow News* and even *Pravda* and *Literaturnaia Gazeta*, became quite outspoken in their support of extensive change, while such organs as the Moscow daily *Sovetskaia Rossiya* and the military paper *Krasnaia Zvezda* conveyed coolness and even defended to some degree the Stalinist past. A particularly notorious and very explicit breach in the customary unanimity of the Soviet mass media occurred in early 1988, when *Sovetskaia Rossiya* published on March 13 a spirited defense of Stalinism and *Pravda* denounced the tract on April 5 as an anti-*perestroika* manifesto. Such institutional diversity, shocking to Soviet traditionalists, was in itself a novel development and a sharp break with totalitarian norms.

This new diversity provoked bitter reactions from the more traditionally minded party officials. Ligachev expressed their feelings when he denounced, in an unusual public outburst at the Special Party Conference, a leading Moscow newspaper for its alleged distortions. Evoking much spontaneous applause from the assembled officials, he cried out, "we are feeding on ersatz from the newspaper, from such a well-known newspaper—I would like to call it something else—as *Moskovskiye Novosti*."

The massive ferment in the creative arts and in the mass media reflected the more basic crisis of the official ideology itself. That ideology could neither cope with the complexities of modern life nor provide a vessel for a creativity that was responsive to existing social conditions and to new social cravings. To make matters even more difficult for the guardians of official truth, the debates that had broken

out revealed the spiritual emptiness of the contemporary Soviet
Union. The official emphasis on material values, which the system
was actually incapable of gratifying but which it was claiming to have
fully satisfied, contributed to that emptiness and to widespread cyn-
icism. The moral landscape of the country thus came to be
defined—some Soviet writers now openly stated—by careerism as
well as by political and police ruthlessness, a spiritually depraved
condition.

This was a particularly grave accusation considering the degree to
which the party has for years asserted that its Marxist-Leninist tutelage of society had succeeded in producing a new Soviet man
characterized by the highest standards of socialist morality. In *Pravda*
on February 14, 1987, a remarkably pointed article appeared by
Chingiz Aitmatov, author of the much-discussed novel *The Execu-
tioner's Block*, which had been condemned as "God-seeking," or excessively religious, by the devotees of the party's orthodoxy. He flatly
stated that seventy years of Soviet power had, indeed, succeeded in
extirpating Christian values but had failed to replace them with anything positive. He charged that Soviet society was devoid of the
concept of "compassion" and was dominated by the view that "to
achieve success in life was possible thanks to ruthlessness, suckering,
dubious scams in [the] trade or in [the] service sector, or ultimately
in [the] foreign service. In this manner are being warped [our] concepts of social justice."

Another well-known Soviet writer, Daniil Granin, focused on the
same themes in *Literaturnaia Gazeta* on March 18, 1988. He noted
the ruthless character of Soviet society, the absence of any spirit of
mercy in its value system, and traced the origins of that condition to
the extraordinary brutality with which collectivization had been imposed on the Soviet rural masses. "Compassion was lacking not by
accident," he wrote. "In the difficult years of mass repressions, people
were not permitted to help their fellow-beings, their neighbors, the
families of the mistreated. Children of the accused and deported
could not be sheltered. People were forced to praise publicly severe
verdicts. Even sympathy for the imprisoned was forbidden. Feelings
akin to compassion were treated as suspect, even as criminal. . . .
Compassion could truly have interfered with illegality and cruelty,
interfered with imprisonment, denunciation, the violation of law,

beating, liquidation. In the years of the thirties and forties that conception disappeared from our vocabulary, and thereafter ceased to be used."

The guardians of the party's dogma—the professional doctrinarians in the Central Committee—various retired NKVD-KGB veterans, and officials of the party's *nomenklatura* must have been aghast at reading such words. To all of them, any discussion of the moral failure of communism had to pose not only an ideological challenge but also a potential threat to the existing structure of power. And in that respect their concerns were probably justified, for the dawning of this new and growing awareness of moral rot opened the doors to a revival of religion.

The existing moral vacuum and the reawakening sense of national history among the Great Russians helped to rekindle their interest in Russian Orthodoxy and in its role in national life. This was an important development inasmuch as the Russian Orthodox church had initially proven relatively easy for the Soviet leaders to suppress, largely because of its traditional submissiveness to state power. As a result, official atheism seemed to have made substantial progress, especially in the Russian urban centers, with organized religion restricted to only a few surviving churches and largely relegated to private family observances. In contrast, religious practices among the less numerous Soviet Catholics, who were concentrated predominantly in Lithuania and the western Ukraine, and among the Moslems of Soviet Central Asia, continued to endure. For them, such observance represented—beyond the spiritual aspect—a form of national resistance to Russian as well as Soviet domination.

At this stage, it would be premature to speak of a major resurgence of Russian Orthodox faith and incorrect to think of its church as in any way posing a challenge to the party (as has been most dramatically the case with the Roman Catholic church in neighboring Communist-dominated Poland). The Orthodox church as an institution remained firmly under the party's control, with effective political and even secret police penetration of its clergy. But Russian Orthodoxy as a generalized Christian belief was beginning to make a noticeable comeback as the only available source of moral inspiration and as the genuine national expression of more enduring cultural values. In that sense, it represented a deeply rooted response to the spiritual and cultural wasteland that Soviet communism had become.

The fact that 1988 was the one-thousandth anniversary of the conversion to Christianity of ancient Rus'—the geographical equivalent today of the Ukraine—invigorated this trend. The jubilee celebration reawakened public interest in religion and in its role in Russian history. Among the intelligentsia, it became increasingly fashionable to sport religious emblems and also to engage in the artistic restoration of long-abandoned and desecrated churches. For growing numbers of Russian intellectuals, religion was thus "in" and ideology was now "out."

It was not only members of the Russian intelligentsia who succumbed to the pull of religion. Symbolic of the spreading spiritual renewal was the remarkable conversion to the Russian Orthodox faith—little noticed abroad but much discussed in Moscow—of Georgyi Malenkov, one of Stalin's most loyal henchmen during the bloody years of the great purges. He spent his very last years in devoted participation in a religious choir, and he insisted upon and received a Christian burial upon his death in 1987. Whatever the enemies of Stalinism may have thought of Malenkov, this act by Stalin's chosen successor in itself dramatized the failure of the party's propagation of atheism.

At the Special Party Conference in 1988, Gorbachev recognized and seemingly accepted the renaissance of religion in the Soviet Union. He said, "We do not conceal our attitude to the religious outlook as being nonmaterialistic and unscientific. But this is no reason for a disrespectful attitude to the spiritual-mindedness of the believer, still less for applying administrative pressure to assert materialistic views." Thus, Gorbachev implicitly signaled the failure of the drive for atheism—the party's religion—and granted a more respectful status for genuine religion.

History (or Stalinism). At the heart of every one of these highly divisive issues was the question of Stalinism. Almost every debate ultimately led to politically sensitive questions regarding the contemporary relevance of the Stalinist system, to bitter debates over the extent to which the past should be fully ventilated, and to the still very embarrassing issue of individual culpability for Stalinism's (and not just Stalin's) worst crimes.

The issue of Stalinism created a serious dilemma for the leadership and its political system. On the one hand, to move reforms forward, it was necessary to overcome not only bureaucratic inertia but the resistance of Stalinist institutions and traditions. Restructuring implied the repudiation of long-established ways of doing things, and many of these had been institutionalized during the quarter of a century dominated by Stalin's brutal reconstruction of Soviet society. On the other hand, a complete rejection of so much of the past threatened to unleash pent-up emotions and long-suppressed memories, and thus to undermine the foundations on which the party's rule rested.

No wonder then that the leadership temporized and agonized. In the official assessment of Stalinism, delivered on the authority of the Politburo itself to the seventieth anniversary of the Bolshevik Revolution, Gorbachev condemned Stalin and Stalinism in unambiguous and sharp terms, but avoided any dramatic specificity, speaking impersonally of Stalin's "thousands" of victims. At the Special Party Conference, Gorbachev continued in this restrained approach, remarking only that "it is a fact—and we have to admit this today—that at a certain stage the political system established as a result of the October Revolution underwent serious deformation." Other top leaders, notably Ligachev, called for a balanced appraisal of the past, in which the exposure of past evil would not obliterate the memory of the alleged accomplishments. But once the doors to the rejection of that era had been opened, it was impossible to contain the outpouring of grief, the flood of memoirs, the recollections of unspeakable brutalities, and—most dangerously—the calls for some effort at restitution and even perhaps retribution.

The Soviet press and journals became saturated with accounts, often extraordinarily painful and gripping, of individual and collective suffering. Some dramatized the degradation that the massive and eventually mindless Stalinist terror inflicted on very simple and lowly people. Others provided highly personalized accounts of the circumstances surrounding the fall of the once-mighty, many of whom at the time simply disappeared without a trace, plunging their families into unexpected social ostracism or exile or even death. For example, both the wife and son of the executed Marshal Tukhachevskiy were also killed. Still others dealt with the larger dimensions and consequences of Stalinist tyranny, such as the physical destruction of literally several millions of Ukrainian peasants or of much of the Soviet officer corps (thereby contributing to the initial Soviet defeats in the 1941 Nazi invasion).

Strikingly, some issues still remained taboo. The official Soviet press avoided any thorough discussion of the Stalinist suppression of the non-Russian peoples. The crushing of the Ukrainian or Lithuanian national aspirations after World War II, as well as the massive deportations from the Baltic republics (following their annexation in 1940 and again after their reoccupation in 1944–45), were discussed only in generalities. This was also true of the expulsion and forcible resettlement in Siberia of some 1.5 million Poles, undertaken with extreme brutality in the dead of winter in 1940, from the half of Poland obtained by the Soviet Union in the 1939 Hitler–Stalin Pact. Soviet media remained silent regarding the 15,000 Polish officers, taken prisoner in 1939 and murdered one-by-one in total secrecy in the Katyń woods and elsewhere in the spring of 1940. Thus Stalinism as the assertion of Great Russian imperialism still enjoyed a certain indulgence.

Nonetheless, the exposure of Stalin's domestic crimes inevitably raised three more issues, each quite divisive. The first of these was posed openly and with increasing intensity; the second was debated mainly behind closed doors in the party's inner sanctum; and the third was never openly articulated but was inherent in the quest for historical truth.

The first pertained to individual culpability. Was Stalin alone responsible for his misdeeds? Was that credible, given their historically unprecedented scale? If not, then what about his accomplices and henchmen? To be sure, his immediate associates were all dead, but many of the executioners, tormentors, interrogators, concentration camp guards, and even commanders were certainly still alive. A young NKVD major, who may have been twenty-five years old when he tortured his prisoners during the Great Terror of the late 1930s, would now be seventy-five; the officers and men personally executing the Polish officers in the Katyń woods would now be in their late sixties or early seventies. The MVD tormentors of the victims arrested in the anti-Jewish purges, as well as in the broader terror-net of the late 1940s, would now be in their early sixties.

It was impossible to reveal the crimes of Stalin without the broader issue of culpability eventually surfacing. By 1987, it did. A number of Soviet writers raised explicitly the question of Stalin's accomplices. L. G. Ionin, writing in the Soviet sociological journal *Sotsiologicheskie Issledovaniia* (no. 3, 1987), not only utilized the Western concept of totalitarianism to analyze the nature of the Stalinist phenomenon but even drew a deliberate analogy to Nazism by using the German term *Schuldfrage* (i.e., the question of guilt) in posing the question of the guilt of others. The matter also arose in the mass press. On December 26, 1987, *Izvestia* cited a reader who wrote that many "persecutors must still be alive. . . . I cannot help thinking that they are laughing at your publications."

Soviet TV also addressed the issue. In a program on June 22, 1988, devoted to Stalin's misdeeds, it noted that some former torturers find themselves in "a good job," adding,

> And so a logical question arises: Why is there a statute of limitation for these terrible crimes, like for anyone who, say, steals a purse or beats up his neighbor in a drunken brawl? There is no statute of limitation for war criminals, or for high treason, so why is there one for traitors who shot their own people, who tortured honest Soviet people? How can the statute of limitation be kept for them? Are they not traitors of the homeland?

In an obvious attempt to strike a balance on this sensitive issue, the mass-circulation weekly magazine *Nedelya* published in early February 1988 a long article by a prominent Soviet scholar specifically focused on the question of culpability. He exonerated "many Chekists" as "irreproachably honest Leninist Communists," asserted that "an even larger number of people who served in NKVD-MGB units and subunits had absolutely no direct involvement with the repressions," but drew a contrast with individual investigators, interrogators, guards, and denouncers who partook of moral responsibility for Stalinism. But he was not prepared to go further than that, doubtless leaving many surviving victims with a sense of frustration.

While the issue remained open, it was not likely to be actively pursued. This was so, not only becuase the political leadership did not want to aggravate the divisions that the debate over Stalinism was surfacing and because a still significant number of Soviet officials and citizens were devoted to Stalin, but also because the society at large was confused over the actual facts and ambivalent in its attitude. One might have assumed that Soviet youth would be inclined to be the most critical of Stalin, yet a Soviet poll allegedly conducted among students within Soviet universities and higher party schools indicated, according to TASS on January 24, 1988, that only 8 percent felt they had sufficient knowledge of the past, while 72 percent gave Stalin personally a mixed assessment, 3 percent approved of him, and 18 percent condemned his policies.

Social ambivalence, and not only official reticence, indicated that the issue of Stalinism would continue to gnaw at the Soviet conscience but without a decisive resolution and a clear-cut, total rejection. That, in turn, was bound not only to complicate the process of restructuring but also to prevent communism from fully cleansing itself of the Stalinist moral stigma.

The second politically and ideologically sensitive question pertained to the implications of the rehabilitation of some of Stalin's most prominent Bolshevik victims. The purge trials of 1936 through 1938 resulted in the execution of the entire surviving Leninist leadership, most of whom Stalin distrusted and with some of whom he had ideologically disagreed. That these leading figures had been unjustly and even illegally killed was no longer contested. Their legal rehabilitation and historical restoration, in a gruesome and macabre ritual that can be described as the uniquely Soviet posthumous circulation of the elite, took place. But the rehabilitation of their views obviously troubled the party leadership since it could shatter the party's already strained ideological consensus. Accordingly, the Kremlin strove to draw a line between a complete legal and a partial doctrinal rehabilitation, thereby further frustrating efforts at full de-Stalinization and generating open resentments from the surviving relatives of the victims.

The third unspoken question regarding Stalinism had even further-reaching implications: the relationship between Leninism and Stalinism. Solzhenitsyn's *Gulag Archipelago* established conclusively that the roots of the Stalinist terror lay in Leninism and specifically in Lenin's approach toward forcible social reconstruction. Yet, to retain even a semblance of historical legitimacy, the Soviet leadership had to draw a sharp line between the bad Stalin and the faultless Lenin. While the question of Lenin's culpability for Stalinism was raised very timidly in the Soviet press before the Special Party Conference, it was clear that any official exploration of Stalinism had to be halted before the full repudiation of its crimes led to an equally full exploration of its real causes—thereby ensuring that the ghost of Stalinism will continue to perplex the Soviet future.

Internal national problems. Stalin seemed to have closed the national question once and for all—largely by killing off all independent-minded non-Russian leaders. Yet even the partial repudiation of Stalinism revealed that the question remained potentially the most unsettling of all domestic political dilemmas. Having crushed all manifestations of independence or even just of the desire for autonomy among the Soviet non-Russians, Stalin created a superficial semblance of ethnic harmony, dominated by ritualized proclamations of respect and affection for the Russian "big brother." Even most Western observers of the Soviet Union have tended to accept the notion that its "national" problem had been solved. Symptomatic of this inclination was the unwitting acceptance in the West of the Soviet terminology according to which only the Great Russians were described as a "nation," whereas all the non-Russians—who actually account for about 50 percent of the Soviet population—were designated merely as "nationalities."

The façade of Soviet national unity cracked quickly, once *glasnost* extended to the issue of Stalinism itself. Suppressed national aspirations and national antagonisms surfaced rapidly among the several truly historic nations of the Soviet Union, thereby belying the claim that these "nationalities" had become submerged in a larger sense of Soviet nationalism. Between January 1987 and mid-1988, some three hundred national disturbances—some of them on a massive scale—occurred in nine out of the fifteen non-Russian Soviet republics. They ranged from mass meetings, involving tens and even hundreds of thousands of aroused participants, to intercommunal bloodshed, resulting in scores of fatalities.

The grievances of the non-Russian nations were channeled in two major directions: (1) vertically, against centralized domination by the

Great Russians in Moscow; and (2) horizontally, through the more open expression of conflicts of interest between the non-Russian nations. Some of those who resented Great Russian control primarily sought a redressing of past injustice, as was the case with the Crimean Tatars who were forcibly resettled by Stalin in 1944–45 from their warm Black Sea peninsula to distant Central Asia and Siberia. Others, such as Ukrainian or Byelorussian intellectuals, spoke up against the Russification of their languages and culture. Still others, such as the Moslem Central Asians, became more assertive in their quest for increased religious as well as cultural autonomy. A few went even further, as in the case of the Lithuanians, Latvians, and Estonians, who—after four decades of suppression—erupted into massive street demonstrations against their forcible incorporation into the Soviet Union in 1940.

The outpouring of patriotic sentiment was especially explosive in the Baltic countries. Seemingly crushed by Stalinism, the Lithuanians, Latvians, and Estonians never lost their sense of distinctive identity, which has more in common with democratic Scandinavia than with Soviet Russia. Gorbachev's *glasnost* unleashed these feelings, and they first expressed themselves in the massive unfurling of long-forbidden national flags and in the mass singing of long-banned national anthems at large public demonstrations, at some of which even former anti-Soviet guerrilla fighters appeared as principal speakers. Some top Baltic party officials were also swept up by the euphoria, publicly advocating a new and upgraded political status for these "Soviet republics" and the transformation of their Moscow-controlled economies into "free economic zones" (an idea also endorsed by Gorbachev's economist, Abel Aganbegyan), much like the special Chinese coastal regions designated for free enterprise and foreign investment. The spontaneously emerging Baltic Popular Fronts, which have formulated ambitious plans for genuine autonomy and quasi-sovereignty for their countries, represent also the beginning of a political structure that could become a rival to the ruling Communist party. Formal demands for genuine national sovereignty were only a matter of time, if *glasnost* continued.

In the meantime, public denunciations of Stalinism served as a screen for direct anti-Russian sentiments still too dangerous to express openly. Thus, in *Literaturna Ukraina* on February 18, 1988, a

Ukrainian writer, Oleksa Musiyenko, could publicly denounce Stalin as "a monster" for murdering the Ukrainian political and intellectual elite during the purges and for precipitating deliberately the mass famine of the Ukrainian peasantry, without having to point the finger directly at the Great Russians. The Balts could rally both in the fall of 1987 and in the spring of 1988 to honor the victims of Stalinist deportations and to press for more rights without having to denounce directly Great Russian oppression. The Tatars could demonstrate for the right to return to their homes as a way of expressing their rejection of the exile imposed so forcibly upon them. The Central Asian Moslems could organize seemingly religious pilgrimages to the graves of their mullahs who had been killed while resisting Stalin's suppression of their regions and of fellow Moslems who had been shot for refusing to serve in the Red Army in World War II. Others could even seize upon Gorbachev's replacement of their own local non-Russian satrap by a Great Russian as an excuse for demonstrating against central control, as happened quite violently for several days in late 1986 in the Kazakhstan capital of Alma-Ata. All of these nationalist manifestations shared the common desire to loosen, perhaps eventually even to sever, the bonds imposed from above by Moscow's Great Russians.

Religion as the basis for national self-assertion was particularly important in the case of Central Asia, with its forty-five to fifty million Moslems. After years of proclaiming that the hold of "superstition" had been broken, the Soviet press confessed in 1987 and 1988 that Islam was staging a significant revival, that underground religious activities were on the upswing, and that the war in Afghanistan had rekindled a sense of Moslem identity. Even Communist officials in the Moslem regions were said to be quietly partaking in religious ceremonies and increasingly identifying themselves with local customs and national traditions. In *Literaturnaia Gazeta* on May 20, 1987, a writer complained that in Tashkent, "at the republic specialized communications center . . . where, incidentally, comparatively educated people work, 'strange' texts began to appear on the announcements board practically every day . . . inviting their colleagues to various religious events" and that the local Komsomol secretary invited people "for a memorial meeting with a prayer reading from the Koran."

Horizontal national conflicts posed a similarly grave threat of dis-
ruption. No love was lost among some of the non-Russian nations,
particularly in the Caucasus. The historically ancient Georgians,
Armenians, Azerbaijanis, and several other smaller peoples have
feuded for centuries over religious and territorial conflicts. With the
region representing a mosaic of Christian and Islamic religions and
sects—complicated by the intricate commingling of ethnic populations—violent hostility remained latent during the years of Stalinist
uniformity. It exploded brutally and lethally in the Armenian–Azeri
fighting in early 1988 over the allocation of the Armenian-populated
Nagorno-Karabakh Region to Azerbaijan, portending even wider national and religious conflicts in the future. Scores were killed, the
capital of Armenia, Yerevan, was for days dominated by surging
crowds numbering in the hundreds of thousands, and the Kremlin
was forced into the thankless task of mediating between the aroused
nationalist passions of the Armenians and Azerbaijanis.

Gorbachev's policies allowed all of these problems to surface. The
reason for this was quite simple. It was impossible to preach and
even modestly to practice *glasnost* and *demokratizatsiia* without open
expression of national grievances. The legacy of the Stalinist past
was too bitter, and the recollections of Great Russian abuse too fresh
for the intellectuals and students among the non-Russians not to
exploit the opportunities that *glasnost* now provided. Gorbachev himself admitted that even horizontal conflicts tended to become vertical
rejections of Great Russian rule, noting on July 19, 1988, that in the
Armenian–Azeri clash "passions are to some extent running out of
control. There appear slogans of anti-socialist, anti-Soviet, and anti-
Russian character." Moreover, even the modest economic decentralization also served to strengthen local pressures for more direct
control, thereby fusing but also complicating the quest for economic
reform with the far more explosive national issue.

Even well-meaning and moderate leaders in the Kremlin were
probably caught by surprise by these developments. Judging from the
analyses of the national problem published in Moscow after these
nationalist outbreaks, the center appeared to have been blinded by
its own propaganda and to have come truly to believe that the national
problem no longer existed. Reactions thus ranged from *Izvestia*'s
outraged denunciations on February 9, 1988, of "the ideological

saboteurs" in Lithuania who were said to view Communists as "traitors to the national interests," to Gorbachev's own more perplexed analysis, made in the wake of the Alma-Ata violence, urging that the national problem be no longer viewed in simplistic terms "reminiscent at times of complimentary toasts rather than of serious scientific studies." The national problem, politically dormant since the 1930s, had thus resurfaced—this time both as the major consequence of the quest for *perestroika* and potentially as the gravest challenge to it.

The remaining three dynamic sources of domestic disunion pertained to foreign affairs. They tended to involve a smaller circle of disputants, who were confined largely to the Soviet policy elite. Nonetheless, a debate over foreign policy issues was also a startling novelty in the Soviet system, testifying either to the remarkable spread of *demokratizatsiia* or, more likely, to the progressive loss of centralized control by the party's officialdom.

The war in Afghanistan. This foreign policy issue gradually produced the widest public debate. Although initially the goals of the war were not publicly questioned, mounting casualties generated growing resentment against the Kremlin's efforts to keep the war out of the public consciousness. Secret burials, innocuous references to "proletarian internationalist duty" on the gravestones of the fallen, no special treatment for returning veterans or even invalids—not to speak of quiet deferrals for the sons of senior officials—all bred a bitterness that could not be indefinitely ignored, especially in the context of the broader *glasnost* campaign.

Eventually, all these grievances were aired, even the most politically sensitive ones. For example, in *Pravda* on November 25, 1987, the party offered an explanation, albeit a lame one, for the preference given to the sons of the politically mighty: "We are sending the very best to Afghanistan, those in top condition. Strange as it may seem, the children of leadership officials are very often physically unfit for service in the army." While this must have simply enraged the parents of anyone maimed or killed in the war, it was significant that in 1987 all of these matters had broken into print, thereby making the war into yet another divisive public issue.

In time, such largely personal grievances led to a politically more significant public questioning of the actual wisdom of the decision by the Kremlin to launch the invasion. Rumor had it in Moscow that

Brezhnev and his key comrades had been actually drunk when issuing the final order to invade. Open criticism of an ongoing foreign policy had simply no precedent in recent Soviet history. Yet in *Literaturnaia Gazeta* on March 16, 1988, academician O. Bogomolov, a leading Soviet specialist on foreign affairs, made the remarkable revelation that three weeks after the attack the Institute of Economics of the World Socialist System of the USSR Academy of Sciences sent to the party leadership an analysis of "the futile and damaging nature of this action." Another Soviet specialist on foreign affairs, A. Bovin, argued on Radio Moscow on May 22, 1988, that henceforth "[t]he sending of Soviet armed forces abroad to take part in combat activities can only be done after discussion in the highest legislative organs of the country, and it must be with their agreement."

One can only surmise that the eventual decision to withdraw Soviet forces resulted in part from domestic pressures, although the Soviet army and the secret police quite likely were deeply troubled by the longer-range implications of such an implicit acknowledgment of defeat. Thus, the debate over Afghanistan is likely to linger on even after the termination of the more direct forms of Soviet involvement, particularly if the defeat stimulates further national self-assertion either in Eastern Europe or even inside the Soviet Union.

Foreign and defense policy. Although the debate on foreign policy took place largely within the various specialized institutes, the propensity was to question past assumptions and to call for "new thinking" (which the leading French Sovietologist Michel Tatu scornfully described as an alternative to the past's "no thinking"). The fullest statement of the revisionist approach was provided by one of Gorbachev's brain trusters, Ye. Primakov, who in a major article entitled "New Philosophy of Foreign Policy" in *Pravda* on July 9, 1987, called for the rejection of the notion that peaceful coexistence represented merely a breathing spell, urged the abandonment of the export of revolution as a facet of Soviet policy, and stressed the new reality of global interdependence. The same themes were subsequently more fully developed in Gorbachev's own book, while in the military realm Soviet strategists began to develop the theme of a "defensive doctrine" as the point of departure for a more stable strategic relationship with the West. On all these points, the contrast between these views and recent Soviet policies was striking.

The Soviet bloc and the world Communist movement. At the Moscow celebration of the seventieth anniversary of the Bolshevik Revolution, Gorbachev stressed the nominal equality of all Communist parties and explicitly rejected any claim for the Soviet party of a special leading role—a major doctrinal departure from Moscow's past claims that its interests should be the guide for all Communists worldwide. While the Brezhnev doctrine was not officially repudiated, Gorbachev intimated that it would not be applied to inhibit gradual changes in Eastern Europe, which in turn led some East Europeans to assert that the 1968 occupation of Czechoslovakia would have never occurred with Gorbachev in power. Though the validity of this assumption could never be tested, the effect was to encourage those East Europeans who were pressing for changes considerably ahead of the pace of the Soviet restructuring. For some Soviet leaders, Gorbachev's position was doubtless troublesome. Any major instability in Eastern Europe was thus likely to generate even sharper debates in the Kremlin over this foreign policy issue.

All these interlocking debates created a dynamic effect. The quest for economic renewal generated pressures for democratization, which in turn threatened the party's monopoly over power and formal beliefs, thereby opening the doors to competing appeals of religion and nationalism, and even posing the danger of protracted and perhaps even intensifying Soviet disunion. That these debates were actually occurring, and that they were no longer confined to the inner sanctums of the party, was particularly significant for three reasons:

First, it represented a remarkable break with established political norms. Soviet totalitarianism for several decades had involved the regimentation of society into a state of depoliticized orthodoxy and apparent political unanimity. The new reality of social and political disputation stood in sharp contrast to the silent conformity of Stalinism, dominant since at least 1928.

Second, it posed a danger to the integrity of the Marxist-Leninist doctrine and even potentially to the unity of the Soviet Union. An open-ended intellectual debate, based on the assimilation of new scientific insights and philosophical categories, was inherently incompatible with a doctrine that saw itself as a closed system containing scientifically correct answers to all social dilemmas. Moreover, unless the emerging debates on a large number of sensitive issues were either somehow channeled into a framework of institutionalized pluralism or repressed, they could generate a dynamic escalation threatening eventually the very integrity of the Soviet Union itself.

Third, it discredited Soviet communism specifically and, by inference, communism in general. The revelations regarding the crimes of the past, and the criticisms of current and past performance, confirmed almost everything that many Western scholars had previously written about Stalinism, for which they had been often maligned in the Soviet press as "inveterate anti-communist propagandists." Indeed, the detailed, poignant, and truly painful accounts of the sufferings inflicted on innocent human beings that appeared in the Soviet press were even more devastating in their ideological implications than much that had been written abroad. Similarly, the debates surfaced additional data regarding current and recent failures in the Soviet economy and society, confirming thereby the more critical Western assessments of the overall Communist performance.

CHAPTER 7

An Evolving
or Decaying Communism?

The real issue for the future is not whether Gorbachev will last or even whether he will succeed or fail. The real issue is whether Soviet communism is evolving into a significantly more permissive and economically innovative system or whether it is decaying or even fragmenting. After all, Gorbachev could be removed from power or die in somewhat ambiguous circumstances and yet some of his reforms could continue, albeit in a more cautious mode. Alternatively, he could remain nominally in power—given his popularity abroad, he could still be useful to the Kremlin in Gromyko's place as the head of state—but with his policies largely abandoned. Finally, he himself could slow down or even accelerate his policies to save his power even while dismissing his rivals—like Ligachev—from office.

The key question is whether the Soviet system can successfully evolve into a more pluralistic organism, one that generates greater social and economic creativity and thus makes the Soviet Union more truly competitive on the world scene. On that answer depend not only the fate of the Soviet Union as a major power but also the prospects for communism more generally. The current turmoil could perhaps be a signal of such change, but it could also be the first stage in the progressive fragmentation of the system itself.

That system over the years has come to be called totalitarian not only because the society was coercively subordinated to the political system, but also because that society was violently remolded according to an ideological blueprint. A condition of depoliticized orthodoxy was thereby created, genuine political life ceased to exist, and a silent consensus seemed to reflect total social unanimity. Politics became the preserve and the prerogative of the top leaders only.

An evolutionary abandonment of the system's totalitarian characteristics would, therefore, require the gradual institutionalization of a more pluralistic political framework, one that permits society to assume a more active role and even some genuine political life to become a facet of normal social existence. The ultimate answer to the question of the likelihood of such an evolution depends on whether two apparently irreconcilable dilemmas inherent in the current Soviet reality can be overcome: First, can economic revitalization be achieved without a truly basic redefinition of the Communist party's role in social management? Second, can economic decentralization, as well as the required concomitant contraction in the party's central governing role, be accomplished without a massive strengthening of the power of the non-Russians to the point that decentralization eventually could become equivalent to the gradual dismantling of the Soviet Union?

The Soviet party leadership acknowledged in mid-1988 the primacy of political over economic reform. The party's resolution explicitly stated "that top priority is to be given today to a fundamental reform of the political system." But, as *Pravda* conceded literally three days later, on July 7, "the processes of democratization—both at the center and at the local level—have so far been progressing slowly." The party's *nomenklatura* has suffered no retrenchment because of economic reforms, nor have Gorbachev's proposed political changes in the proper role of the party been institutionalized. The constant evocations of the centrality of the Leninist legacy seem to reaffirm the party's determination to retain its special place and its monopolistic hold on power, whether that is economically functional or not.

The question, therefore, becomes whether economic reform can succeed if the party is unwilling to retract. The answer seems to be negative. The genuine introduction of a market-mechanism, the emergence of a price structure based on supply and demand, the promotion of a free flow of labor, the appearance of a managerial class predisposed to risk taking and with access to venture capital, and the unfettering of agriculture are all necessary preconditions to genuine economic success. But they also require a significant diminution in the role of the party in exactly the kinds of ways the Soviet *apparatchiki* are unwilling to tolerate. The glaring gap between *glasnost* and *perestroika* is rooted in this condition. It is therefore bound to breed destructive disappointments.

Moreover, genuine social receptivity to the needed reforms is lacking. Old habits and inertia pose massive obstacles to change. The masses are at best skeptical and largely concerned with the immediate economic consequences of *perestroika*. Workers have internalized the worst features of egalitarianism and are suspicious of reforms designed to reward performance. The peasant tradition has been destroyed. Managers fear greater responsibility and lack the entrepreneurial impulse. Officials prefer centralism. Russian history and Soviet reality thus both conspire against restructuring.

Compounding the dilemmas of *perestroika* is the national problem. Population growth rates have been significantly higher among the non-Russians, especially among the Central Asians, whose numbers increased between 1959 and 1979 by almost 72 percent, in contrast to a growth rate of about 19 percent for the Soviet Slavs. Thus, before long the non-Russians will constitute the majority of the Soviet people. Yet, the dominant Great Russians wield, in effect, exclusive political power at the center, with largely symbolic representation for the non-Russians. The Russians generally enjoy better access to elite positions throughout the Soviet state, and the Politburo is currently thoroughly dominated by the Great Russians. The state's linguistic policy also favors the Russian language with, for example, 14 books published in Russian in 1986 for every Russian living in the Soviet Union but with only 2.4 in native languages for every non-Russian. Also, the Kremlin's economic policy favors capital investment and development in the Russian parts of the country.

Genuine decentralization would inevitably breed demands for the correction of these inequities. However, central Russian control is so deeply embedded in existing arrangements that the needed corrective would require a massive upheaval. A vicious circle in effect exists. Lack of reforms breeds national resentments, but reforms would probably nourish an even greater appetite among the non-Russians for more power. Separatist attitudes, especially among the Balts and the Soviet Moslems, the latter stimulated by the worldwide resurgence of Islam and encouraged by the Soviet military failure in Afghanistan, thus could eventually pose a real threat to the unity of the Soviet state.

A key point to watch will be the growing nationalism within the Soviet Ukraine, with its fifty million people and great natural resources. Both in Kiev and in Lvov quasi-underground Ukrainian political, religious, and cultural activity has increased, taking advantage of the openings created by *glasnost*. Its thrust has been to emphasize the damage inflicted on the Ukraine by past Soviet policies and the national imperative of resisting further Russification. Most Ukrainians, rightly or wrongly, blame Moscow—and thus inferentially the Russians—for the Chernobyl disaster, and view it as the second-worst calamity (after the famine of the 1930s) inflicted upon their nation by the rulers in the Kremlin. Should the linguistic and cultural resentments of the Ukrainian people, already openly and quite vehemently expressed even in the official Ukrainian media, develop into separatist aspirations supported by a significant portion of the Ukrainian population, the national problem will have become the Soviet Union's crisis of survival.

A foretaste of things to come was provided by the account in Moscow's *Komsomolskaia Pravda* on July 10, 1988, of a mass rally in the city of Lvov. Organized ostensibly to conserve historical monuments, the rally—"of many thousands of people"—quickly turned into a massive nationalist demonstration. Its leadership was taken over by nationalist activists and emotionally charged political demands dominated the evening. The Russian paper denounced the Ukrainian speakers at the rally as "descending to a frenzy unworthy of a man, citizen, and patriot."

The national problem is clearly the Achilles' heel of *perestroika*. By the spring of 1988, the Soviet mass media were finally conceding that the national problem was far from having been resolved. At the same time, the increasing Great Russian awareness of anti-Muscovite national sentiments has been further inhibiting the chances of genuine decentralization, one that could perhaps promote a constructive evolution of the system. It has been reinforcing the vested stake of the Great Russians in the continued exercise by them of central rule, even at the price of economic inefficiency.

To decentralize a state-owned economy, one has to decentralize the political system as well; but to decentralize the political system of a multinational empire means yielding power to previously subordinated nations. Accordingly, to be successful economically, *perestroika* must involve the restructuring of the Soviet "Union" into a genuine confederation, thereby ending the Muscovite rule. In effect, that is tantamount to the dissolution of the empire. It is doubtful that the Russian political elite would be prepared to trade the effective loss of their imperial power for the benefits of economic decentralization.

An emerging Great Russian backlash against *demokratizatsiia*, on the grounds that it was breeding non-Russian nationalisms, was noted with alarm by *Moscow News*, a paper outspokenly supportive of Gorbachev's reforms. It reported on April 3, 1988, that "many people believe that inter-national problems have become aggravated, suddenly, by the process of democratization of our society. Dark, conservative forces already reproach the forces of renewal with having 'loosened the screws,' painstakingly recording in their 'roll of wisdom' all that is brought to the surface by glasnost and which, in their opinion, 'undermines the system.'" According to the Italian Communist party's paper, *L'Unita*, on May 23, 1988, the original text of the violent attack on *perestroika* that had been published earlier that year in *Sovetskaia Rossiya* contained a passage which even that orthodox organ chose to omit: "The greatest danger . . . is constituted by the scandalous nationalism of insignificant nations such as the Tatars of the Crimea and Zionist-type Jews, whose actions are deliberately aimed at destroying friendship between the Soviet peoples."

Such Great Russian fears of growing nationalist conflicts, by impeding the needed reforms, enhance the likelihood that the real prospect for Soviet communism is debilitating decay and not constructive evolution. A truly renovating success—one that results in a creative, innovative, and self-energizing Soviet society—could only happen through the dilution of doctrine, the dispersal of the party's power, and the gradual emancipation of the non-Russians from Moscow's centralized control. It is highly improbable that the party leadership and the ruling elite, no matter how eager for an economic revival, will be prepared to risk going politically that far.

One is thus entitled to be doubtful that genuine success—which can be called Option 1—is in store for Gorbachev's *perestroika*. Other options must, therefore, be considered. These could include:

Option 2: Protracted but inconclusive turmoil.
Option 3: Renewed stagnation, as *perestroika* runs out of steam.
Option 4: A regressive and repressive political coup, in reaction to either Option 2 or 3.
Option 5: Fragmentation of the Soviet Union, as a consequence of some combination of the above.

Of these options, the most likely alternative for the next several years seems to be Option 2, but with a high probability that *perestroika* will gradually lose some of its momentum in the face of internal obstacles. Growing domestic turmoil or eventually renewed stagnation could in turn prompt some renewed efforts on behalf of heightened social and political discipline. The latter could even lead to a military dictatorship, especially if the party proves to be too complacent and incompetent either in the promotion of change or in the maintenance of order. Such a turn of events would damage badly communism's historic prospects. Economic and technological stagnation would further handicap the Soviet Union in its race with America. Repression would mean renewed international disrepute for a regime that has not quite yet come to terms with its recent Stalinist past.

In any case, it will be extremely difficult to put the genie of social assertiveness back into the totalitarian bottle, now that Soviet society has had a whiff of open debates and has become generally less immune to foreign communications and ideas. The Soviet intelligentsia, intoxicated with *glasnost*, would most certainly resent with intense bitterness any reactionary repression. Hence, inherent in the failure of the political system to evolve, or in any effort to repress society, is the further possibility of growing political unrest and even eventually of systemic fragmentation. To use some Marxist terminology, the bottom line is that a totalitarian political "superstructure" cannot long coexist with a social "base" that ceases to be subject to its total control.

Unintentionally—but "objectively," to use another Marxist term —Gorbachev's policies are thus contributing to the buildup of a potentially revolutionary situation. His reforms are creating constit-uencies for change. They are unleashing hopes that are almost fated to be disappointed. They are creating dislocations that, in the mean-time, are actually worsening the quality of life for the average person. They are also reducing the level of political fear—even as they are raising the level of social frustration. Such a combination is inherently explosive.

In response to surfacing difficulties further concessions and des-perate changes are likely—perhaps even dramatic reforms in agri-culture or symbolic acts, such as welcoming back Aleksandr Solzhenitsyn. However, institutional confusion and social disillu-sionment are not likely to be thereby relieved. On the contrary, such steps are likely to magnify the emerging political crisis. The fact that the failure of economic reform has compelled Gorbachev to assign the highest priority to political change has helped to underline the historically revolutionary proposition—which Gorbachev could not state explicitly—that the ultimate flaw of the Soviet system is its Leninist legacy.

Yet undoing that legacy—given that no doctrinal or organizational alternatives currently exist—could let loose powerful forces that are inherent in the rot, frustration, and accumulating antagonisms of contemporary Soviet life. The continued quest for *perestroika* might actually intensify these contradictions because the required reforms are likely to deprive the Soviet workers of the principal benefits that they have enjoyed under the existing Soviet system—namely, security of employment and stable wages regardless of performance—without granting them any corresponding advantages. The urban proletariat is the class likely to be the most adversely affected by the short-term social consequences of the restructuring—such as inflation, more costly housing (with rents frozen since 1928!), and probably also unemployment—and, at some point, it is almost certain to make its resentments felt. Consequently, sporadic and eventually revolutionary unrest might come from the politically more awakened Soviet work-ers, who will have come to take seriously the socialist slogans of workers' democracy and who could also become infected by the example of the Polish workers' Solidarity.

Intensifying national and religious conflicts or separatist aspirations among the non-Russians, bitter over Moscow's continued domina-

tion, are also likely to contribute to the potential for systemic fragmentation. The Soviet Union cannot evade the age of nationalism,
and inherent in the disunion that is now manifesting itself is the
surfacing of inherently conflicting national sentiments. The quest for
greater local economic autonomy is already inevitably escalating into
demands from at least some non-Russians for greater political autonomy, if not yet for genuine independence. Such demands are likely
to be cloaked initially in socialist and democratic slogans, but their
ultimate import for the Soviet Union will be lethal. It will not be easy
for the Kremlin to deal with such aspirations without some recourse
to coercion.

A progressive breakdown of order could lead eventually to a coup
at the center, undertaken by the military, with KGB backing. The
leadership for such a coup most likely would then come from a
coalition of disgruntled Great Russian officers, fearful central party
bureaucrats, and outraged KGB officials, determined to restore disciplined "national unity" more in the name of Russian nationalism
than of Soviet socialism. They might claim historical legitimacy for
such action by appealing to patriotism and by evoking the imperative
of discipline in the face of domestic chaos. Communism as an ideology would thereby be further discredited.

In brief, the fatal dilemma of the communist system in the Soviet
Union is that its economic success can only be purchased at the cost
of political stability, while its political stability can only be sustained
at the cost of economic failure.

PART III

Organic Rejection

A single crucial fact is the key to understanding the future of communism in Eastern Europe: Marxism-Leninism is an alien doctrine imposed on the region by an imperial power whose rule is culturally repugnant to the dominated peoples. As a result, a process of organic rejection of communism by East European societies—a phenomenon similar to the human body's rejection of a transplanted organ—is underway. This process is being played out in a contest between national forces seeking ways to free their societies from Moscow's dogma and Soviet attempts to develop new ways to retain ultimate control over the region's destiny.

Although Marxism was first conceived in Western Europe, its adaptation to Russia's oriental despotic political culture brutalized its initially humanistic orientation. When Stalin forcibly grafted Soviet-style communism upon the countries of Eastern Europe, he transplanted Marxism-Leninism-Stalinism to societies that identified themselves largely with Western Europe's cultural, religious, and intellectual heritage. As a result, the Soviet empire in Eastern Europe is almost unique in imperial history: The dominant nation is *not* viewed by the subject people as culturally superior.

Cultural superiority, even if reluctantly and secretly acknowledged by those dominated, was a critical factor in the ability of the Roman or British or French empires to endure for so long. In contrast, the Soviet empire is viewed in Eastern Europe—rightly or wrongly—as retrogressive subjugation by a culturally inferior nation. Thus, even forty years after Stalin's imposition of Soviet rule, the East European societies still chafe under their Communist regimes.

For a while, however, communist ideology managed to compensate for that condition. Even though most East Europeans viewed Russian domination as a cultural setback, many believed that the communist

105

doctrine had the potential for more rapid modernization and industrialization. Since the Soviet Union was at the time considered to be
the model of communism in practice, ideology served to justify not
only imitation of the Soviet Union but acceptance—as a positive
historical necessity—of domination by the Kremlin.

Thus, the failure of the Soviet model has potentially devastating
consequences for the Soviet imperial domain. It accelerates the attrition of the communist doctrine as the empire's unifying bond. It
also intensifies resentment against an external domination, increasingly viewed as the source of the region's growing social and cultural
retardation. It imposes on Moscow the need to buttress the empire
by new ties. These, in turn, are stimulating additional national hostility against the Kremlin's central control.

In recent years, the Kremlin has strived to forge new military and
economic links with Eastern Europe. It has reinforced its control
over the Warsaw Pact by the increased subordination of the various
national armies to the Soviet High Command. At the same time, to
further the renovation of the Soviet economy, Gorbachev has placed
a special premium on extracting capital, new technology, and even
specialized labor from Eastern Europe. These initiatives were also a
response to the growing recognition in Moscow that the binding force
of ideology was waning, that nationalism in Eastern Europe was on
the rise, and that the Soviet Union had lost much of its historical
prestige.

As a result, two conflicting pulls are straining the fabric of the
Soviet empire in Eastern Europe. On the one hand, a process of self-
emancipation from Soviet ideological control threatens to dilute—or
even break—the imperial bonds. On the other hand, Soviet-sponsored efforts to intensify military-economic integration seek to
counter these centrifugal dynamics. The first thus involves organic
rejection of communism by much of Eastern Europe. The second
entails efforts to enhance the dependence of Eastern Europe for its
economic well-being and for its territorial security on the goodwill
and decisions of the Kremlin.

CHAPTER 8

Ideological Transplantation and Transmutation

Czesław Miłosz, in his celebrated book, *The Captive Mind*, conveyed dramatically how initially gripping was the hold of the Marxist-Leninist doctrine even on non-Communist East Europeans, crushed by Hitler and then "liberated" by Stalin. A sense of irresistible power radiated from the Stalinist regime. At the same time, the democratic West conveyed a sense of indifference to the fate of Eastern Europe. Combined with the monumental scope of the social experiment undertaken in the Soviet Union, it cumulatively created a sense of historical inevitability to the sovietization of the region. Destiny seemed to dictate a posture of acceptance and even of conversion.

Fervent fanaticism among the true believers—the newly established Communist power elite—was at an even higher pitch. They saw themselves as riding the crest of history. An ecstatic exclamation to the Central Committee of the ruling Polish party in July 1948 by one of its most fervently Stalinist leaders, Mieczysław Moczar, captured perfectly the prevailing mood among the disciplined faithful: "For us, partymen, the Soviet Union is our Motherland, and our frontiers today I cannot define, today beyond Berlin, and tomorrow at Gibraltar."

Moreover, there were admittedly some positive tangibles for the region in the initial communist transformation. It was thus not all a matter of abstract ideological attraction. Eastern Europe emerged from the war devastated and acutely conscious of its relative lag in comparison with both the industrially more advanced Western Europe and the newly industrialized Stalinist Russia. The Soviet-imposed Communist elites made it their central goal to combine desirable social reforms, particularly the much needed redistribution of land to the

107

peasants, with rapid industrialization. They set the goal of matching within two decades and then surpassing in heavy industrial production the more advanced West European economies. In fact, rapid rates of industrial growth during the initial period were for a while achieved.

The first decade of Communist rule in Eastern Europe was also the time of rapid social promotion for the socially disadvantaged. This was especially so in the less advanced countries, such as Romania and Bulgaria, but also to a lesser extent Poland and Hungary. All had large numbers of rural poor, as well as some highly radicalized industrial workers, who were willing and even eager to identify with the new regime. For them, the onset of the Communist rule opened the doors to rapid advancement through greater educational opportunities, as well as in the new institutions of power, notably the police and the military. To a lesser extent, that was also true of Czechoslovakia and East Germany, although in these countries the industrial working class provided the more plentiful source of recruitment for the revolutionary regime.

In the initial period of communist construction, the new rulers were able to also exploit the enthusiasm of some segments of the intellectual community captivated by the notion of state-sponsored social engineering and by the pseudo-scientific vision of communism. The new order also mobilized in the early years the support of many of the young, drawn by the vision of a new age, by grandiose urban and industrial projects, and by the humanitarian goals of social reform. The notion of building a new and just social order on the ruins of the past was genuinely appealing to those traumatized by World War II and seeking some firm but idealistic sense of historical direction.

Though highly dependent on Soviet power, the new East European Communist regimes were not without some genuine social backing. As a broad generalization, it may be said that communism initially enjoyed the most domestic support in Czechoslovakia and in Bulgaria, and the least in Poland. In the former, strong Communist movements existed even before the advent of Soviet military power, along with considerable traditional affinity for the Russians. In the latter, national resistance to sovietization was strong and persistent.

While the Communists enjoyed some support, nowhere did they have majority support. In fact, during this initial phase the new rulers were preoccupied with crushing and altogether eliminating any domestic political alternative. The concept of the class struggle, reinforced by Stalin's "dialectical" doctrine that the struggle actually intensifies with growing success in the building of socialism, was used to justify the prolonged application of Stalinist-type terror throughout the region. Particularly violent were the years 1948–53, during which Eastern Europe was subjected to very intense sovietization. The Communist regimes executed tens of thousands, imprisoned hundreds of thousands, staged show-trials, and practiced mass intimidation.

Stalinist terror was not only cruel but also sometimes bizarre. In 1986, a German author, Hans-Henning Paetzke, published a book entitled *Andersdenkende in Ungarn*, containing interviews with various figures from the Hungarian dissident movement. One of these was Laszlo Rajk, the son of the Communist party leader of the same name who was arrested in mid-1949, tortured, forced to confess to having been a Zionist spy, and hanged later in that year. The son's account of his own fate dramatically illustrates the personal and bureaucratic perversions of terror as social policy.

The young Rajk was only four months old when his father was arrested. His mother and grandmother were also imprisoned, and the baby boy was "confiscated" by the state and placed in a foster home. It was full of other children of political prisoners. When the senior Rajk was hanged, his mother was sentenced to a long prison term, but her family was not informed of what happened to her. It was not known whether she was alive, and the authorities would not respond to any inquiries. The mother's sister continued to appeal on behalf of the boy, but there were no responses, despite long hours of waiting in various police offices. The appeals were met with hostility and silence.

One day, after Stalin's death, the aunt received word from the secret police that on a designated date and at a fixed hour she was to stand on a certain street corner in Budapest. An official car then pulled up, and a four-year-old boy was pushed out. The car then sped away. The aunt, still not knowing what befell the mother, adopted the boy as her own and discovered in the process that his name, the same as of the condemned father, had been changed to a totally different one. This had been done, according to official documents, "on his own request" at a time when he was only four months old. Indeed, the child had no idea of his identity, and learned of it only some years later when his real mother was finally released from prison.

Without dwelling at length on the immeasurable human suffering, a

few statistics help to convey the scale of the terror involved in the sovietization of Eastern Europe. In Hungary, with a population at the
time of about 6 million, between 1950 and 1953 some 387,000 alleged
political opponents—or more than 5 percent of all Hungarians—were
imprisoned, according to the careful accounting provided by Paul
Lendvai in *Das Eigenwillige Ungarn* (1987). Following the suppression
of the Hungarian uprising in 1956, the Soviet-installed Kádár regime
executed an estimated 2,000 to 4,000 political opponents. During the
Prague Spring of 1968, the Communist regime itself initiated an ex-
amination of its past, thereby surfacing some staggering statistics: In
1951, in the relatively compliant Czechoslovakia, more than 100,000
people (including more than 6,100 priests, monks, and nuns) were incarcerated in concentration camps, while bloody inner-party purges
resulted in the execution of the party's own 278 top leaders. In Poland,
the crushing of the armed resistance to Communist rule resulted in
about 45,000 deaths, followed by an estimated 5,000 executions of
various political opponents. To that must be added an unknown
number—but certainly in the tens of thousands—who were deported
to Soviet concentration camps and who never returned.

The Polish Communist regime was particularly determined to
stamp out all signs and symbols of independent political leadership.
With the active help of Soviet secret police advisers, the Polish regime
concentrated much of its violence on the surviving leaders of the anti-
Nazi underground, especially former commanders and officers of the
Home Army, the largest World War II underground organization.
They were subjected to special brutality, and their show trials were
designed to stigmatize them as Nazi "collaborators." During prolonged and often violent interrogations designed to exact confessions,
some were draped in newspaper cutouts of swastikas. Some were deliberately held in death-cells with condemned Nazi war criminals.

Through this massive and organized violence, the Communist
leaders succeeded in imposing the new Soviet-type totalitarian system on
Eastern Europe. They crushed the existing societies and thereby made
possible the creation of a new social and political order. But it would
be a mistake to see in organized terror the defining characteristic of
the mundane day-to-day realities of life under a totalitarian system.
Intense and widespread terror was used both as a means of social reconstruction and as the ultimate tool of perpetuating the system. But

once established, that system became characterized, above all, by a pervasive and petty bureaucratization of all aspects of normal life. This was the case to a degree and in a manner which a superficial observer from the pluralistic and democratic West could not comprehend.

In the *East European Reporter* (vol. 2, no. 3, 1987), a Czechoslovak political dissident, Vaclav Havel, conveyed better than most the essence of the communist system that emerged from the systematic and ruthless use of terror: "Totalitarianism is something that one has to experience at first hand. It is something that is invisible at a distance. . . . In our system, the violence is spiritual rather than physical. In other words, hidden, covert. Life here seems pretty normal to outsiders. You can see people walking the streets, chatting happily, going shopping—superficially nothing seems wrong, and there are no signs of massacres. The violence of our system will never be seen by a tourist or visitor."

Havel went on to point out that to experience the real oppression of the system Westerners would have to live under it, to be continuously "at the mercy of the all-powerful bureaucracy, so that for every little thing they have to approach some official or other. They would observe the gradual destruction of the human spirit, of basic human dignity. . . . People live their lives in a state of permanent humiliation. These are features of the totalitarian system which can neither be filmed by television cameras nor easily explained to visitors. In order to be seen they have to be experienced."

The infliction of the Soviet-type system on Eastern Europe gave rise to a new ruling class, one that owed everything to communism in general and to Soviet power in particular. Moreover, the less social support this class enjoyed, the more it tended to identify itself with the Soviet Union, its sponsor and protector. Moscow could count on the fealty, indeed servility, of those who so directly depended on the Kremlin for their own survival. Self-interest, as well as ideology, thus created a tight bond of loyalty and dependence, with Stalin deified at the apex of a disciplined pyramid of power.

But the apparent external cohesion of the Soviet bloc obscured the underlying internal fragility of the new regimes. That fragility surfaced shortly after Stalin died. By the early 1950s, the luster of the mirage of Marxism-Leninism's grand oversimplification was already beginning to dissolve in the face of harsh realities. The limited initial enthusiasm for communism had largely faded as the creeping awareness of Western Europe's much more rapid recovery bred disillusionment and resentments. Moreover, the abrupt disappearance of Stalin in 1953 deprived the Soviet leadership of a towering and intimidating personality.

As soon as political splits developed within the Kremlin leadership, and as soon as Soviet leaders began to tamper with the Stalinist legacy, crises mushroomed in Eastern Europe. The resulting upheaval in East Germany in 1953, followed by massive political instability in Poland and by large-scale violence in Hungary in 1956, would certainly have caused the collapse of communism in all of Eastern Europe, had it not been for the direct Soviet military intervention. Even in a country initially as well predisposed toward Moscow as Czechoslovakia, the experience with the Soviet-style system proved to be totally disillusioning. The Prague Spring of 1968, which was also crushed by Soviet arms, demonstrated the persisting unwillingness of the people to accept as permanent a political and socioeconomic system so explicitly derived from an alien tradition. The Soviet military occupation in turn further dramatized the condition of continued dependence and the status as puppets of the East European Communist regimes.

Not surprisingly, disaffection tended to be strongest in the cluster of states with the deepest cultural ties with Western Europe: East Germany, Czechoslovakia, Hungary, and Poland. For them, sovietization meant a profound break with both their political and cultural past. For a while, even history and tradition can be suppressed and driven from the surface of social life. A geopolitical doctrine based on domination through overwhelming power, such as the Brezhnev doctrine, can define the outer limits of dissent, creating the illusion of stability and even prompting the outward appearance of resignation. For a while, also, cultural life can assume external forms of doctrinal obeisance and even national aspirations can be muted. Underneath it all, however, resentment, frustration, and hope continue to ferment, waiting for an opportunity to assert themselves again.

The successful Soviet military interventions have taught the East Europeans that a direct challenge to Soviet preeminence and to their communist systems will not work. The West will not help them. Their frightened Communist elites will appeal for Soviet help. And the imperial Soviet rulers will use force to prevail. Hence, more indirect and more patient methods would have to be applied. The transformation would have to come from within, take essentially peaceful forms, and occur gradually. In a sense, a strategy of historical stealth would have to be persistently pursued. To be successful, it would have to involve the co-optation of at least a portion of the ruling class and entail some informal coordination with proponents of change in adjoining East European countries. It would also have to take advantage of propitious splits within the Soviet leadership.

Moscow's determination to use arms, if necessary, to keep communism in power in Eastern Europe has had a further, unexpected effect. It obviously reassured even the weakest Communist elites, such as the one in Poland, that the Kremlin will not permit their resentful peoples to rise successfully against them. That, quite naturally, served to enhance the sense of personal and political security of the native Communists. At the same time, the enhancement of the elite's security has had the paradoxical effect of narrowing the gap between such elites and their peoples. By fostering an enforced sense of shared destiny between the rulers and the ruled, these elites became more susceptible to the appeal of deeply felt national aspirations. By becoming more entrenched politically, and by feeling more confident historically, the Communist ruling class gradually became less servile nationally.

Furthermore, the Stalinist period was too short to replough totally the East European societies, to erase their sense of cultural and national identity, to destroy their specific political traditions. With time, but in varying degrees, a sense of distinctiveness increasingly surfaced—and to the detriment of Soviet control. In East Germany, it focused on the increased pursuit of closer human contacts with the rest of Germany. In Romania, it involved the emergence of a rabidly nationalist and highly personal dictatorship reminiscent in many ways of the prewar Romanian fascist Iron Guard. In Hungary, it focused on the energetic effort to promote a more decentralized economic system and on a quiet opening of social-cultural contacts with neighboring Austria. Even in super loyal Bulgaria, it assumed the form of an ambitious program to carve out a distinctive and highly specialized economic role. Only in dispirited Czechoslovakia, following the Soviet occupation of 1968, did quiet resignation seem to prevail throughout the Brezhnev years.

CHAPTER 9

Polish Society's
Self-Emancipation

The biggest change and the greatest challenge both to continued Soviet control and to the distinctive trademarks of the Soviet-type system took place, not surprisingly, in Poland. It is, after all, the largest and ethnically the most homogeneous of the Soviet-dominated East European states. Its modern history has been defined largely in terms of opposition to Russian domination. Its Roman Catholic religion, which sets Poland apart from its immediate neighbors and traditional enemies, serves to reinforce the sense of nationalism and imbues it with a doctrinal content directly at variance with communism. Almost everything in Polish society and in Polish history conspires against a communist system imposed on Warsaw from Moscow.

The word *conspires* is not a mere literary flourish. It describes accurately the contemporary Polish posture toward the prevailing communist system in Poland and toward the unequal relationship imposed by Russia. The 125-year-long subjugation of Poland by its neighbors has deeply ingrained the tradition of conspiratorial resistance into the national psyche. To resist repeated partitions, and to preserve their national identity, the Poles had to learn how to practice an internalized national life, quietly conspiring among themselves to evade the often brutal attempts to stamp out all signs of national consciousness. The fact that during the nineteenth century the Russians applied the most severe repressions thus conditioned the Poles for a more sustained resistance in the twentieth century—to a doctrine not only alien to their traditions and religion but forcibly grafted upon their society by these very same Russians.

Some anti-Russian sentiment permeated even the servile ruling

Polish Communist elite during the worst years of Stalinism. In the early 1980s, an enterprising Polish journalist, Teresa Toranska, undertook a series of in-depth interviews with the last surviving (and by then quite aged) members of the very top Polish Stalinist leadership. Published initially as an underground volume, entitled appropriately *Oni* (or *They*), the interviews reveal the extent to which even this group of dedicated Stalinists harbored deep-seated resentments against Moscow. They not only portrayed one another as having been Moscow's vassals but also accused one another of having served as direct agents of the NKVD (and later the KGB), while individually posing to Toranska as having been the key *saviors* of Poland from direct incorporation into the Soviet Union.

More important, the enduring strength of the national sentiment enabled Poland to preserve throughout the Stalinist era some important islands of national autonomy and authenticity. The Roman Catholic church was the most important. Some intellectual autonomy was also preserved, though to a much more limited extent. After 1956, the peasantry was freed from the oppressive efforts to impose Soviet-style collectivization on Polish agriculture. The scope of political and doctrinal control over the society by the state was thus significantly reduced.

The spontaneous social effort to inculcate the young with the history of the Polish underground resistance during World War II, to both the Nazi and the Soviet invaders, played an important role as well. The more the Communist regime maligned that resistance, the more attractive its traditions and sacrifices became to the younger postwar generation. This helped to sustain large pockets of passive and quiet conspiratorial resistance to spiritual communization. That passive resistance kept open the option of reaching out someday for more ambitious societal self-emancipation.

That day dawned in the 1970s. By then disenchantment with the existing system had become pervasive. Even the social strata originally sympathetic to some of the Communist-sponsored social reforms had come to view both the Soviet Union and the regime in Poland as brakes on social progress. The intellectuals were thoroughly disaffected and totally reoriented toward the West. The ambition of every aspiring scholar or creative artist was to spend some time in the West, with the Soviet Union viewed as a provincial backwater. American-sponsored cultural and academic exchanges, notably those developed over a number of years by the Ford Foundation, had a major impact, undoing two decades of regime-sponsored efforts to link Polish culture with that of its eastern neighbor. Polish youth had long forgotten its initial (and, in any case, quite partial and brief) infatuation with the notion of building a new society and was acutely aware of, and attracted by, the West's new life-style, technological progress, and cultural experimentation. The emancipated peasantry was almost totally Catholic and traditional in its outlook.

The biggest change in political attitude occurred in the industrial working class. Though numerically weak in prewar agrarian Poland, it had a rich syndicalist tradition and was generally of a socialist orientation. The Polish Socialist party (PPS) had been in the forefront of the struggle for Poland's national rebirth and had played a major role in the World War II underground. After the war, the Communists crushed the party, and its remnants were amalgamated into the new ruling party, totally dominated by Moscow's Communists. That ruling party then effected the postwar industrialization of the country, creating thereby a new post-peasant first-generation industrial class more susceptible to Communist ideological and organizational mobilization. It is noteworthy, for example, that the 1956 workers' rebellion in Poznan, which precipitated the emergence in Warsaw of a less servile Communist regime under Władysław Gomułka, was undertaken by the older, more traditional, and more politically aware workers, but with less resonance among the new first-generation industrial proletariat.

By the 1970s, two centrally important developments drastically altered the situation: First, the new industrial proletariat developed a political consciousness of its own, much more akin to the earlier Polish socialist tradition but also imbued (because of its recent peasant origins) with a strong religious spirit. Second, it had forged new links with the politically active anti-communist intelligentsia of a social democratic orientation. This was a powerful coalition, capable of articulating an alternative program (thanks largely to the intellectuals) and of generating political pressure (thanks largely to the newly politically motivated workers). Moreover, a protective and encouraging arm was extended by the mighty Catholic church, led until the 1980s by a universally respected primate, Cardinal Wyszyński, to whom even the Communist leaders reluctantly deferred.

These social currents gained a symbolically important spearhead through the appearance of a genuinely charismatic worker-leader, Lech Walesa. His personal history and political maturation was a microcosm of these broader trends. Born in a peasant family, brought up in a deeply religious environment, turned into a dockyard worker in Gdansk through Poland's postwar industrialization, disaffected by the continued poverty of the urban proletariat, converted to anti-communism by the privileges and abuse of power by the self-centered party officialdom, politicized by the bloody confrontation between the dockyard workers and the police in the early 1970s, and eventually assisted by a group of intellectual political activists, Walesa became the leader and the symbol of the movement that galvanized Poland and gained worldwide recognition.

The name of that movement, *Solidarność*, or Solidarity, also took on great symbolic importance. The essence of totalitarian rule is the elimination of any autonomous political life and the atomization of society. The objective is to make certain that every individual is left alone to face the system as a whole, feeling isolated and often adrift in his or her internal but never publicly expressed opposition. Solidarity conveyed the very opposite message. It signaled a new reality of shared consciousness, of collective confidence, and of an alliance between different social strata or classes. It confronted the Communist regime on a broad front: ideologically through its reliance on religion and through its emphasis on democracy and intense commitment to patriotism; organizationally through its nationwide structure and through its alliance with the intellectuals, the young, and especially with the church.

Solidarity also capitalized on the tangible failures of the communist system. The country's Communist leaders, having borrowed during the early 1970s some $30 billion from the West, simply squandered, through ineptitude and corruption, that massive injection of capital, which could have been used to revitalize the economy. The resulting economic crisis necessitated the austerity measures that not only sparked worker unrest but also destroyed any lingering social respect for the country's Communist rulers. Communism no longer represented social advancement for any major social class.

The peasants despised the regime because of the bitter encounter with collectivization and hence did not even credit it for the land reform of the mid-1940s. The urban masses suffered acutely under continuing housing shortages, poor services, endless queuing even for the simplest essentials of life, and escalating food costs. Even the educational system no longer served as a source of social promotion, long a point of special pride on the part of the Communists, who liked to contrast it with the situation in prewar Poland. A study presented to a conference of the Polish Sociological Association and reported in the underground publication *Wola* on June 1, 1987, documented this stagnation:

> A comparison of prewar and postwar workers, presented by Jerzy Krezlewski, a sociologist from Poznan, made a deep impression. . . . He presented precise numerical data proving that . . . despite the "actual existing socialism," the Polish People's Republic workers are on the same, or lower level as Polish workers of the inter-war period. What is worse, the situation of the Polish workers is the worst in Europe at the present, and is comparable to the situation of workers in the Third World countries. The information that while there has been some improvement in the access of workers' children to state universities (before the war, 25% of students, currently 31%), the greatest progress in this respect has been achieved by Catholic universities, where a majority of students come from workers' families, was greeted with surprise.

The shared consciousness of deprivation and politicization, and a sense of wider social solidarity, could not be destroyed even by the imposition of martial law in December 1981. By then a new national consciousness had been forged, one that integrated into the outlook of the masses the very traditions and even historical memories that the Soviet-sponsored regime had for thirty years strived to eradicate. The restoration of the authentic national personality became the enduring legacy of the more promising period of Solidarity's open existence, and it had the effect of transforming Poland's political landscape.

Solidarity thus precipitated the spiritual self-emancipation of the country, even though the preexisting political framework continued because of martial law. Nonetheless, that political framework, despite formal institutional continuity, was henceforth filled with a different substance. Martial law was able to destroy and suppress the surface organizational aspects of Solidarity, but it could not prevent the emergence of a de facto alternative political elite and the associated rebirth of genuine political life in Poland—even if that new life still operated partially below the official surface.

CHAPTER 10

From Social Solidarity to Political Pluralism

The rebirth of political life represented for communism in Poland a shattering defeat. It meant the undoing of several decades of emulation of the Soviet experience. It meant nothing less than the end of the totalitarian phase in the history of the Polish Communist regime.

The Communist regime still ruled, and even exercised a monopoly on power, but it no longer was able to monopolize the political life of the country. That life acquired an authenticity of its own and an existence independent of communist political control. It manifested itself in a variety of ways, ranging from truly conspiratorial activity to semi-open political debates, clubs, and demonstrations. The imposition of martial law in December 1981 was the critical catalyst: It precipitated the emergence of a flood of underground publications, which—according to a list from underground sources—produced between the end of 1981 and the end of 1987 some fifteen hundred underground newspapers and journals, and some twenty-four hundred books and pamphlets. It also prompted the formation of a large number of conspiratorial political groupings, ranging from the social democratic left to the more conservative Catholic and even ultra-nationalistic right wing.

The underground press was not merely anti-communist and anti-totalitarian. It increasingly articulated comprehensive and concrete programs of political, economic, and social reforms, prepared by well-organized study groups and commissions. Indeed, on many critical issues, such as the ecological devastation of the country or the backwardness of Polish agriculture or the organization and management of the industrial sector, the thinkers in Poland's autonomous political sector had more to offer than the regime. This was due in large measure to the fact that by the mid-1980s, with communism discredited and with the Polish regime widely perceived as an incompetent copy of the Soviet system, it became more respectable in the community of experts and intellectuals to collaborate with independent and even somewhat subterranean initiatives than with the government.

The revival of political life also meant the resurfacing of the traditional variants of the precommunist political scene. Initially, the most active and visible were social democratic offshoots of the regime itself. Disappointed ex-Communist activists, even some who were once active as fanatical Stalinists, increasingly turned to social democracy as a remedy to existing ills and injustices. They could draw on the rich traditions of the prewar Polish Socialist party and on its physical remnants in resuscitating a socialist alternative to the status quo. Their quasi-Marxist orientation tended to give them a certain limited legitimacy even in the eyes of the less dogmatic Communist bureaucracy.

The success of the democratic left in organizing the Workers' Defense Committee (KOR), despite periodic harassment by the police, was the point of departure for the intellectuals' alliance with the workers. That, in turn, produced the historically decisive appearance of *Solidarność*. It also paved the way to the reemergence of other political orientations, which had been brutally suppressed during the Stalinist phase. These included groupings based on the outlook of the prewar Polish leader, Marshal Józef Piłsudski, with their central emphasis on national independence and on collaboration against Moscow with such suppressed non-Russian nations as the Ukrainians, Lithuanians, and Byelorussians; on the teachings of the prewar conservative and intensely nationalist theorist, Roman Dmowski, who favored an ethnically homogeneous and Catholic Poland allied with Russia against Germany; and on the legacy of the founder of the Polish peasant movement, Wincenty Witos, who stressed the key role of an independent land-owning peasantry in the political life of the country.

These political groupings modified and updated their programs to fit the circumstances of the time, and it would be a gross oversimplification of the new political mosaic to define it in terms of a simple resurgence of the past. The conservatives, for example, cited the alleged economic successes of the Reagan administration and of the Thatcher government in their advocacy of free enterprise as the only solution for Poland's deepening economic crisis. Others pointed to

Sweden as a relevant model of allegedly successful social democracy. And all drew sustenance from the teachings of the Polish pope and internalized his Catholic social doctrine, especially his emphasis on the centrality of "personalism," in their programs.

Lively doctrinal debates were but one manifestation of the revival of a genuinely national political life. Debates on how to regain control over the national destiny were equally wide-ranging. Some favored pragmatic and progressive evolutionary change, including even some measure of collaboration with the existing regime, provided that the regime was willing to respect social autonomy and permit free trade unions. Lech Walesa symbolized that approach.

Others argued that nothing short of the regime's collapse would permit the needed reforms, and that a renewed confrontation was inevitable. To avoid a Soviet military intervention, some stressed the need to forge a common front of the suppressed East Europeans. To that end, they actively sought to forge a regional East European coalition of opposition movements. Still others argued that internal Soviet difficulties precluded direct Soviet action, that the Communist regime could not evolve, and that preparations therefore should be made to topple the regime. In Polish Silesia, that point of view had especially strong support, and it was propounded by a tightly disciplined, deeply conspiratorial organization appropriately called Fighting Solidarity.

But whatever the political leanings, nostalgia for true independence pervaded the emerging autonomous political dialogue. This was even conceded by the official Polish Communist press. Warsaw's *Rzeczywislość* on January 31, 1988, summarized this national yearning with remarkable frankness:

> Poland does not have its own politics, and it is impossible for Poland to have autonomous policies. This view seems very popular in our society. . . . There is a far-reaching conviction that we are dependent on our Eastern neighbor and that this neighbor determines Polish politics, which therefore ceases to be Polish and becomes a mere extension and function of Soviet politics. One may say that this view, held mainly by the opposition and a favorite view of theirs, has penetrated the national consciousness quite deeply. It is accompanied by nostalgic sighing and memories of the interwar period, when the Sec-

ond Republic allegedly had its own independent politics, not dictated
by anyone outside.

The revival of Polish political life had a further and equally important consequence: It meant the rebirth of an alternative political
elite, potentially capable of replacing someday the existing Communist rulers. That, too, was a far-reaching development, undoing
a central characteristic not only of Stalinism but also of Leninism.
By the mid-1980s, Poland was no longer a political wasteland, with
only the Communists representing a politically articulate social stra-
tum. The Communists, thanks to their Soviet backing, were still in
power. But they no longer monopolized political thought, political
life, or—in the minds of many—the country's political future.

Moreover, the Polish Communists were themselves undergoing a
transformation. The regime was headed by a professional military
man of a modestly aristocratic background who, though an apparently
committed Communist, by speech and manner conveyed some superficial impression of continuity with the country's past. In that respect,
Wojciech Jaruzelski differed significantly from Poland's initial postwar Communist leaders, who were manifestly of an alien doctrinal or
even ethnic formation and who flaunted their servility to Moscow. To
compete for political loyalty in the setting of an emerging de facto political competition, the general's regime had to relax considerably its
own censorship of the press and books. Otherwise, underground publications would have flourished even more. But the price was a more
open debate on national issues, on subjects previously taboo, prompting a further dilution of the official ideology itself.

Indeed, by the mid-1980s it was unclear how much of the ideology
remained intact. Stalinism was totally and even officially discredited.
Only lip service was still being paid to Leninism, especially in any joint
commemorative events with the Russians. But the substance of the doctrine of the ruling party was becoming not only vague but also in some respects increasingly reminiscent of more traditional Polish socialism.

Quite revealing and typical of this trend was an article published
in mid-1987 by the official ideological journal of the Polish Communist party, *Nowe Drogi* (no. 6, 1987). Although authored by an
obscure party theorist, it subjected the orthodox Leninist interpre-

tation of socialism to a withering critique, and the magazine gave it
considerable space. It began by noting that ongoing changes in
Poland were creating "an irrepressible impression that the basic
canon of the principles on which our present social and economic
conduct has been based is being put into question." *Nowe Drogi* then
stated that it was necessary to reexamine in that context the basic
assumptions on which the existing system was built, namely that
socialism would "produce higher forms of social life . . . abolish the
exploitation of man by man . . . eliminate exploitation by foreign capital . . . do away with social injustice . . . eliminate social plagues—
unemployment, limited education, absence of medical care, home-
lessness . . . ensure the victory of rationalism over all forms of irra-
tionalism." The party's journal then posed the question: "What can
be said about this program after 40 years of implementation?"

The response of the party's own ideological organ was brutally frank:
"Unfortunately, it is difficult to say 'yes' to these questions." More than
that, it went on to concede that the current policies of the Communist
government entail "in many ways . . . a return to the forms that were
previously condemned." Private ownership was being restored, foreign capital was being invited, market-mechanisms were being introduced, incomes were being differentiated, unemployment was to be
tolerated, religion was being favored. "Does this mean," it agonized,
"that we are departing from socialism when making changes like this?"

The answer was a prolonged case for reform of the system—
including all of the above steps—in the name of efficiency, greater
initiative, and genuine social justice. Even official atheism was to be
rejected because "the moral aspect of religion has a sufficient number
of points in common with socialism for holding a religious world
outlook to be considered favorable to socialism." Hence, "there is
no reason for socialism actively to combat the religious world outlook." The journal went on to repudiate the role of "the omnipotent
state" and to insist on initiative from below. Social conflicts were to
be resolved by negotiations and compromises, and to prevent domination by more powerful interests "it is necessary to create a system
of institutions and regulations" (i.e., pluralism).

According to the authoritative *Nowe Drogi*, those who oppose these
changes have "a very vulgar" understanding of socialism and equate
it with the preservation of "the current power structure in an unal-

tered form." Moreover, the journal stated that such party officials "think and behave in this way, as if the essence of socialism was the exercise of power and not the purpose for which power is exercised." *Nowe Drogi* concluded, "Attitudes of this kind deprive power of all its other significant aspects, and the means becomes the end." It would be difficult to ask for a more succinct denunciation of the essence of the Leninist legacy or for a more damning description of the true motivation of the current Communist rulers.

It should come as no surprise, therefore, that another Polish spokesman advocated in the leading Warsaw daily, *Zycie Warszawy*, on August 22 and 23, 1987, the cross-fertilization of Marxist and Catholic social thought and expressed gratification at the increasingly widespread use in Poland of the concept of "socialist personalism," thus adapting to the official doctrine a tenet of the current pope's teachings. Even if designed largely for tactical reasons in a country with an overwhelming allegiance to Catholicism, reinforced by special feelings of loyalty to a countryman pope, such statements unavoidably corroded the materialistic and atheistic orientation of the doctrine, while strengthening the appeal of the most important competing institution, the Roman Catholic church.

Public soul-searching by both the party's mass media and its ideologues reflected—but also stimulated—the accelerating dilution in Poland of the Marxist-Leninist doctrine. This dilution posed even the hitherto remote possibility of an evolutionary transformation of the party itself. Indeed, unlike the Soviet party, the Polish ruling Communist movement, increasingly swamped by a politically awakened and historically self-conscious society, appeared increasingly vulnerable to a slow but ultimately decisive process of political metamorphosis into forms more compatible with the traditional Polish political culture.

To be sure, such a process was being resisted. The ruling party officialdom remained determined to hang on to power. One way to do so was to crush periodically the reform movements that threatened its power, but then to adopt, as its own, major portions of the reform programs. That worked in the 1950s, the 1960s, and the 1970s—though each wave of reforms chipped away some portion of the original Stalinist edifice. As a result of such progressive attrition of the Leninist-Stalinist system, in Poland of the mid-1980s the needed further reforms threatened both the remnants of Stalinism and even the very essence of Leninism itself: the combination of dogma with organizational regimentation.

The scope of the needed reforms, however, was now massive. The economy needed decentralization, political life needed formal pluralism, society needed maximum opportunity for individual creative self-expression. Jaruzelski and his leadership thus faced a dilemma far more acute than that confronted earlier by any of his predecessors. Gomułka and later Edward Gierek still could strive to save the communist structure by making some concessions, even major ones, while hanging on to the key levers of power: decollectivization, but still retention of overall political control over the economy; accommodation with the church, but still official censorship and monopoly over the mass media; even toleration for some political opposition, but still firm mastery over the means of coercion.

In contrast, Jaruzelski faced a much starker choice: either continued socioeconomic stagnation, with the risk of an eventual political explosion, or a wide-ranging political and economic pluralization, with its inevitably deleterious consequences for the Communist monopoly of power. After the enthusiasm generated by the era of Solidarity, and following the polarization generated by martial law, partial reforms could no longer suffice. At the same time, there was not much breathing room left in the communist system for implementing half measures. For a while after the imposition of martial law, social apathy and political fatigue gave the Polish Communist regime a respite, and superficially its power even seemed secure. But the basic socioeconomic problems of the country had deepened in the meantime, and the choices became more starkly defined.

To revive the economy, the introduction of the market-mechanism was necessary, and even Jaruzelski's professional economic advisers confessed as much. But that step could not be separated from increased political pluralism. The acceptance of an open political life based on the principle of dialogue and contestation was necessary for economic progress. That life already existed on its own, because of the society's self-emancipation, but it lacked institutionalization and formal acceptance by the regime. To render de jure what already existed de facto required a fateful leap into qualitative systemic change, a leap that the ruling officials naturally feared.

Communist fear of political pluralism was not merely a matter of ideological conditioning. It was motivated even more by the fear of loss of privilege. In a medium-sized European country of 39 million people—of whom, according to numerous polls, at most only 10 percent are sympathizers of the regime—the overwhelming proportion of the responsible social positions remained reserved almost exclusively for party members. According to the official weekly, *Polityka* of May 14, 1988, 900,000 of the country's 1.2 million managerial posts were held by party members, which—as the paper itself stated—"means that almost 50 percent of the members of the party, which totals just over 2 million members, are in charge of other people." In 1986, the weekly noted, 444 persons were appointed to the very top managerial positions, and of these, 94.3 percent were party members. Two-thirds of Poland's university rectors, four-fifths of its school directors, and three-fourths of its health service directors were also party members.

The mounting social demands for genuine political pluralism posed a threat to such entrenched privilege. The beleaguered regime's response to the society's increasing self-assertiveness was to promote the notion of "socialist pluralism." Aware of its political weakness and of its social isolation, but apparently no longer pressed by the Kremlin to engage merely in repression, and also anxious to obtain Western economic relief, Jaruzelski's team embarked, with evident reluctance and much hesitation, on a program of political concessions. He created a Consultative Council, composed in the main of nonparty figures with a reputation for intellectual independence, to serve as his advisory body. The council was able to vent (though not directly correct) a variety of social grievances. Censorship was lifted from a large number of previously taboo subjects. Political opposition was permitted to express its views, although not in the official channels. Independent clubs and discussion groups sprung up, contributing to the further revival of genuine political life. Periodic anti-government demonstrations were occasionally tolerated, perhaps as safety valves for the release of social frustration. The worsening economic situation also gave rise in mid-1988 to intense discussions between government spokesmen and representatives of the Catholic church, as well as leaders of the only partially submerged *Solidarność*, regarding the possible formation of an "anti-crisis" or a "pro-reform" national coalition.

These concessions reflected the regime's weakness, its economic failure, and its ideological disorientation. The ruling party, by taking refuge in the slogan "socialist pluralism," acknowledged that the days of the Leninist monopoly of power and of the Stalinist suppression of all political life were gone forever. But the "socialist pluralism" that the party now offered was still a far cry from the "democratic pluralism" that the self-emancipated society was now demanding: Society sought not merely the right to criticize and to offer suggestions to the ruling party, but the right to share in the political decisions and eventually even the right to make basic political choices.

The difference between "socialist pluralism" and "democratic pluralism" was thus fundamental. Power sharing was the central stake, and that was the abyss dividing Leninism from social democracy. At some point over the next several years, the turning point will come. In the meantime, barring either a dramatic collapse of the regime, which would almost certainly produce a Soviet intervention, or a sudden adoption by the regime of a policy of massive repression, which would probably lead to a popular rising and in turn a Soviet intervention, the most likely prospect for communism in Poland is the continued attrition of its foreign-imposed characteristics and its progressive political "polonization." With Stalinism already officially repudiated, with only lip service in the main being paid by the regime to Leninism, and with the continuing attrition of the Soviet features of the Polish system, the gap between Poland and its original Soviet model will likely become wider still. Indeed, it is increasingly a matter of time before the communist system in Poland will be truly communist on the top political level alone.

The Communists—once revolutionaries themselves but now their rulers—have thus been defeated in the first stage of the revolutionary process directed against their rule. That stage was once well defined by the Italian Marxist theorist Antonio Gramsci as involving the battle of ideas. The next phase according to him involves laying siege on the state itself. It is here that the Communist economic failure has become the secret "fifth column" of the forces of democratic pluralism. That failure has helped to demoralize the Communist officialdom, to alienate the masses, and increasingly even to isolate the top political leadership. It means that gradually, and no doubt grudgingly, the Polish Communist leadership will have to yield, piece by piece, its monopoly of political power, or be faced at some point by all-consuming revolutionary violence.

CHAPTER 11

The Emerging
Regional Unrest

A new development made the prospect either of the gradual attrition of Communist rule or of a revolutionary upheaval against it increasingly worrisome to the Kremlin: Many non-Communist activists in Poland were increasingly seeking to link the cause of Poland's emancipation with that of its East European neighbors. Gorbachev's attempts at reform made such efforts easier and even gave the activists the needed platform. They could point to the absence of reforms in some of the neighboring East European countries, not to speak of the Soviet republics of Lithuania and the Ukraine (where Polish political-cultural influence easily radiated), as evidence of anti-socialist rigidity and unwillingness on the part of the local Communist leaders to emulate the Soviet example.

Gorbachev's flirtation with revisionism, and his loose talk of the sovereign rights of all Communist states, was also dissipating some of the fear previously inspired by the Soviet suppression of the Prague Spring. There are some striking parallels in this regard between the impact on Stalinist Eastern Europe in the mid-1950s of Khrushchev's sudden legitimation of Tito's heresy with Gorbachev's flirtation with ideas previously associated with unorthodox East European reformers. There could be no doubt that *perestroika* not only inspired greater hope in Eastern Europe but provided the opposition with a convenient tactical legitimation.

In that context, the Poles took the lead in generating a wider coalition of East European democratic opponents to the existing Soviet-type systems. Given the self-emancipation of Polish society, they could more easily congregate, organize, and move about than their

129

more policed fellow dissidents in the neighboring states. For the other East Europeans, any such activity entailed higher risks and costs than for the Poles, whose earlier sacrifices had won them a measure of official toleration. Moreover, the Poles had a more developed tradition of conspiratorial activity and, given their history, a natural propensity toward thinking in regional terms as the strategic point of departure for resisting Soviet (and, earlier, Russian) domination.

In 1986, the Polish opposition even launched a special journal dedicated to the promotion of *regional* opposition to Communist rule: *Nowa Koalicja* (*The New Coalition*). Its cover symbolically referred not only to Warsaw, Prague, Bratislava, Budapest, Bucharest, and Sofia—all East European capitals—but also to Kiev, Minsk, Vilnius, Riga, and Tallinn—all capitals of adjoining Soviet republics with the potential for nationalist separatism. In 1987, a joint meeting of prominent oppositionists from Poland and Czechoslovakia was held in a secret border location in the Tatra mountains on the nineteenth anniversary of the Soviet invasion of Czechoslovakia. The participants issued a communique demanding basic human rights and sent a special message of solidarity to the Soviet academician Andrei Sakharov, long the symbol of Soviet dissidence. The group also hailed Gorbachev's reforms in the Soviet Union and cited them as a justification for more far-reaching changes in Eastern Europe.

The ritualistic bow to Gorbachev's *perestroika* was unlikely to reassure the Soviet leaders. To them, developments in Poland undoubtedly were threatening enough, without the further aggravation of a wider East European coalition against Soviet domination. While apparently the Kremlin has been reluctantly willing to accommodate itself to greater Polish autonomy, as the painful alternative to bloody (and internationally costly) repression, the Soviet leadership could hardly tolerate the spread of the Polish contagion to the adjoining East European states. That prospect would pose nothing less than a mortal danger to the cohesion of the Soviet empire itself.

Yet the contagion continued to spread. In early 1988, in even bolder undertakings, the first joint statements of the democratic opposition from Poland, Hungary, Czechoslovakia, and East Germany were issued, calling for the democratization of their countries. In the first instance, 300 signatures were attached; on the second occasion, 438 people signed, including some from Yugoslavia and even the Soviet

Union. These events were unprecedented and entailed a psychological and historical breakthrough. It was the first time since Stalin's imposition of regional hegemony that a joint East European opposition to Soviet rule was able to coalesce and express itself openly.

This was followed by the issuing of a joint Polish-Czechoslovak statement, signed openly by twenty-six representatives of Polish and Czechoslovak oppositionist groups, on the occasion of the twentieth anniversary of the Soviet invasion of Czechoslovakia. It demanded a revision of the Warsaw Pact so that the right to sovereignty of individual states would be fully respected. In that connection, it also asserted "that the documents relating to the Soviet interventions in Berlin in June 1953, in Hungary in 1956, in Czechoslovakia in 1968, and the threat of intervention in Poland in 1980 and 1981; to the mass arrests of Polish citizens in 1939 and 1941, and in 1944 and 1948, the Katyn massacre in 1940, the murder of Imre Nagy and several hundred of his supporters; to the Cominform's activities; and to the mass murders by the Czechoslovak courts in 1948 and 1956, must be published."

Moscow's dilemma in the pursuit of an internal Soviet *perestroika* was thus compounded by the challenge posed by the dramatic changes taking place mostly in Poland but also in much of Eastern Europe. Formulating a response was not an easy task. In addition to the potentially explosive national impulses, a mounting regional economic crisis helped propel these political changes. That crisis, rooted in many of the same causes as the Soviet Union's own difficulties, undercut the effectiveness of a response based on simple police suppression. Putting people in prison would not increase the GNP, and it could even spark a regional explosion. Thus, the Soviet leaders, and their East European counterparts, had to exercise caution.

In the meantime East European economic difficulties were likely to mount, thereby intensifying political unrest. With the exception of the heavily subsidized East German regime (the beneficiary of a multibillion dollar annual aid package from West Germany), none of the region's Soviet-imposed regimes could be described as a socio-economic success. All their economies performed more poorly than their approximate Western counterparts. Some, notably Romania and Poland, were even abysmal economic failures, with the situation in the Romanian case made doubly bad by the emergence of a highly corrupt personal dictator who fostered a cult of the personality comparable only to that of Enver Hoxha in Albania or Kim Il Sung in North Korea.

The grim condition and the even grimmer future of the communist economies of the region were summarized in stark terms in a *New York Times* survey on December 20, 1987, which concluded that "while the newly industrialized countries of the third world are building factories with the most advanced technology, Eastern Europe is increasingly a museum of the early industrial age. . . . Eastern Europe is rapidly becoming part of the third world—and many third world countries are surpassing it economically. . . . Singapore, an Asian city-state with only two million residents, exports 20 percent more machinery to the West than all of Eastern Europe."

Together, regional economic deterioration, the progressive self-emancipation of the Polish society, and the struggles over *perestroika* in the Soviet Union were unleashing contradictory but essentially unsettling forces in Eastern Europe. Out of continuing deference to Moscow, leaders in every capital paid lip service to Gorbachev's reforms. That, however, had the undesirable effects not only of legitimizing internal pressures for major reforms but indirectly also even of sanctioning the Polish example, particularly because of the close personal links between Gorbachev and Jaruzelski. As a result, every regime in the region was under increased pressure to strike out on its own, in order to find some indigenous solution to mounting economic problems, or to reach a new internal sociopolitical balance.

Although the overall trend of the reforms was away from the traditional Soviet model—indeed, reform became more and more synonymous with de-sovietization—the specific policy reactions of the ruling parties varied greatly. Bulgaria and East Germany were able to hew to Moscow's line most closely, given their relative economic stability and very effective social regimentation. Indeed, the GDR had itself become the model for the politically more cautious Soviet reformers, while in Bulgaria the Soviet *perestroika* unleashed a flurry of inconsequential innovations in the economic sector, nominally modeled on Gorbachev's ideas, but with the Bulgarian leader, Todor Zhivkov, pointedly stressing after the Soviet Special Party Conference in June 1988 that Gorbachev's proposed political changes had "exceptional importance for the Soviet Union."

A more difficult economic situation plagued Hungary, Czechoslovakia, and especially Romania. Hungarian economic reform, essentially a halfway compromise between statist doctrine and a limited free market, ran into serious difficulties coincidentally with the political issue of succession to János Kádár, the country's undisputed leader since 1956. With Hungary caught in the never-never land between the recognized need for continued economic decentralization and the ruling party's interest in continued centralized political control, the economic reforms sputtered and even started to turn sour. International debt mounted, and economic activity flagged. Inflation and unemployment appeared, giving rise to growing social unease, while corruption within the bureaucratic elite reached massive proportions.

These tensions between the political and the economic dimensions of Hungarian life inevitably complicated the search for acceptable economic remedies, unleashing an intense struggle between doctrinarians and technocrats. The overall trend, however, continued to point in the direction of additional decentralization, the further expansion of the market-mechanism, the adoption of personal taxes, and intensified efforts to develop joint ventures with foreign capital, all resulting in the further dilution of the Soviet version of socialism. Much as in Poland, the Soviet ideology was particularly discredited among the masses, with forty years of intense indoctrination having bred a peculiar type of political amnesia, well-illustrated by the revealing interviews conducted by Radio Hungary on the occasion of the May 1, 1985, celebrations.

The interviews were conducted at random on Budapest's main square, the Karl Marx square, with passersby asked who Marx was. The replies, as broadcast, were as follows:

First passerby: "Oh, don't ask me such things."
Radio Budapest: "Not even just a few words?"
First passerby: "I would rather not, all right?"
Radio Budapest: "Why not?"
First passerby: "The truth is, I have no time to study such things."
Radio Budapest: "But surely you must have heard something about him in school."
First passerby: "I was absent a lot."

Second passerby: "He was a Soviet philosopher; Engels was his friend. Well, what else can I say. He died at an old age."

Third passerby: "Of course, a politician. And he was, you know, what's his name's—Lenin's, Lenin, Lenin's works—well, he translated them into Hungarian."

Fourth passerby: "It was mandatory to study him so that we would know."

Radio Budapest: "Then how about a few words?"

Fourth passerby: "Come on now, don't make me take an exam of my eighth-grade study. That's where we had to know it. He was German. He was a politician and . . . I believe he was executed."

In Czechoslovakia, issues dormant since 1968, and seemingly settled once and for all by the Soviet invasion, were reopened in part by Gorbachev himself. During his visit to Prague in early 1987, Gennadi Gerasimov, his spokesman, gave a most revealing answer when asked in a public press conference to cite the principal difference between Gorbachev and Alexander Dubček, the leader of the Prague Spring of 1968. His answer was just two words: "Nineteen years." He thereby implied that Dubček had been merely premature historically but not really a seditious revisionist. The possibility that the Gorbachev regime might be reconsidering the propriety of the Soviet intervention in 1968, a notion openly voiced by Gorbachev's supporters during the Moscow celebration in November 1987 of the seventieth anniversary of the Bolshevik Revolution, doubtless had a chilling and disturbing impact on the Czechoslovak Communist leaders, who had been put in power by that intervention.

Worst off was Romania. Its deteriorated economy was almost on a war footing, with food shortages, absence of heat and electricity in wintertime, and practically no consumer goods. The regime took refuge in virulent nationalism, stressing the cultural uniqueness of the Romanian nation and of its leader's allegedly seminal doctrinal contributions to world socialism. The cult of personality of the country's dictator, Nicolae Ceauşescu, assumed truly stupifying dimensions. He was extolled regularly in the Romanian press. For example, the party's daily, *Scinteia*, in July 1988 typically acclaimed him as "the hero among the nation's heroes, eminent fighter, revolutionary patriot and thinker, prominent personality of the international communist and workers movement, hero of peace, and symbol of the struggle for the defense of independence and sovereignty of nations and for the establishment of a new world order" who has singlehandedly caused "Romania's name [to be] spoken with admiration and respect everywhere."

The Romanian regime also indulged in strong doses of repression against its ethnic minorities, notably the several million Hungarians living in Romanian Transylvania. In an extraordinarily brutal undertaking, Ceauşescu undertook the forcible amalgamation of thousands of villages inhabited by Transylvanian Hungarians into standardized agricultural towns, on the grounds that this would advance their entry into the stage of full communism. This forcible resettlement, which prompted many Transylvanians to flee to Hungary, provoked, not surprisingly, strong protests from Budapest. Both Communist regimes then sought to mobilize public support through the appeal to traditional nationalism, with the result that Hungarian–Romanian relations precipitously worsened.

Indeed, by the mid-1980s Marxist internationalism was dead in Eastern Europe. Traditional nationalism was dominant. The Bulgarians, for instance, openly pursued a chauvinistic persecution of their Turkish minority. The Poles and the East Germans engaged in an open dispute about maritime borders. The Hungarians and Romanians were hurling public charges at each other over the ancient issue of Transylvania. The Czechs and the Slovaks were arguing about the proper allocation of economic resources for internal development. Only on the subject of the Russians were the Poles, the Czechoslovaks, the Hungarians, and the Romanians inclined to share a similar perspective!

But open and normal political life was still absent from Eastern Europe. Outside of Poland, dissent was still confined to relatively small groups, to occasional underground journals, to periodic assertions of protest. But the potential for the sudden revival of such life was clearly increasing, drawing ideological legitimacy from Gorbachev's *glasnost* campaign, encouraged by what has been transpiring in Poland, and facilitated by new means of communications as well as by the growing access to the West, which the Communist regimes had to accept out of economic necessity. It is almost a certainty that at some point in the relatively near future, given some major economic or political upheaval, politics as the expression of authentic social aspirations for multi-party democracy will truly return to the life of Eastern Europe. The Soviet-type subordination of society to the state, with its deliberate political castration of society, is gradually coming to an end.

While not matching in scope or intensity the Polish society's self-emancipation, the revival of political life has gone the furthest in Hungary. Political life was beginning to stir on the Danube. By 1987, the Hungarian political opposition was becoming an established reality, sufficiently confident to stage semi-public gatherings and even some demonstrations in Budapest. Oppositionists have been able to hold informal discussions, and to voice demands for an open dialogue with the government. Underground publications have also begun to proliferate. Moreover, even within the upper levels of the Communist regime voices were being raised to the effect that the status of the political opposition should be formally regularized. Imre Pozsgay, the head of the regime's umbrella organization, the Patriotic People's Front—who was viewed by many as Hungary's most liberal-minded top leader—went so far as to suggest in late 1987 that the current one-party dictatorship had to be viewed as a "transitional" arrangement.

In one important respect, this development differed politically from Poland: Much of the impetus for this political renewal came from the more intelligent leaders of the ruling party itself. More sophisticated and politically more secure than their nationally more isolated Polish counterparts, and heavily engaged in maneuvering for succession, they were willing to concede publicly that the existing regime had to be altered, that some forms of pluralism were inevitable, and that "the leading role of the Party" had to be redefined. They recognized that Kádár's days were numbered and maneuvered intensely to determine his successor. Open competition among them not only interacted with social pressures from below but also contributed to the reemergence of a political dialogue no longer confined just to the party's top leadership.

Thus, political change in Hungary, unlike in Poland, was driven to a significant degree by revisionist impulses from the top down. The country's Communist political leadership, determined to preempt the growing social pressures for more basic reforms, moved decisively in May 1988 to renovate itself, and thereby to regain firm control over the pace and direction of further changes. The party leaders succeeded in replacing János Kádár with Karoly Grosz, an energetic and much younger leader, whose previous ideological conservatism was an assurance to the party officials that reforms would not get out of hand, just as his relative youth provided an augury of greater dynamism and innovation.

A simultaneous shake-up of the Politburo, which gave the reformist orientation a clear majority, was even more important. It was significant that Pozsgay, viewed by many as the eventual leader of a more genuinely democratizing Hungary, was given a seat in the top party body. But the real moment of truth for the new leadership will come only when the internal economic difficulties inherent in the shift from a state-run to a market-based economy begin to interact with the rising demands for political pluralism. At that point, the demands for a genuine multiparty system—which were increasingly voiced openly in Budapest—will collide head-on with the desire of party officials, perhaps even including the reformers, to retain their hold on power. Thus, the Hungarian people, though in a more subtle and less turbulent manner than Polish society's self-emancipation, might provide one of the earliest tests of the still very uncertain capacity of Leninism to die peacefully.

There were rumblings in Czechoslovakia and Romania as well, despite much tighter police controls. In Romania, large-scale workers' riots erupted in early 1988. In Czechoslovakia, Dubček, who since 1968 had been consigned to political death, broke his silence in January 1988 through a remarkably outspoken interview with the organ of the Italian Communist party, *L'Unita*. Drawing explicit parallels between his own policies of 1968 and those currently pursued by Gorbachev, Dubček condemned both the Soviet intervention and the rigidly doctrinaire policies subsequently pursued by his Soviet-installed successors. Though official Prague denounced his views, orthodox Czechoslovak party leaders could not have been much reassured by the comments almost simultaneously made in the organ of the Japanese Communist party, *Akahata*, by a Soviet academician supportive of Gorbachev's *perestroika*, that the Soviet intervention into Czechoslovakia had been an error. Moreover, the simple fact that Dubček felt bold enough to express publicly his continued fidelity to the goals of the Prague Spring signified that Czechoslovakia would also, before too long, be experiencing a political rebirth.

The likely cast of any renewed political life in Eastern Europe was foreshadowed by the public opinion polls taken among East European travelers to the West by Radio Free Europe. Even though such polls tended to focus on those who had official permission to travel, and who planned to return, they almost uniformly indicated that communism had the committed support of at most only about 15 percent of the population, with the figure somewhat lower in Poland and somewhat higher in Bulgaria. The vast majority of the respondents identified themselves with essentially West European–type political parties of a social democratic, Christian democratic, or liberal orientation. In the late 1970s, social democracy still tended to exert considerable attraction. But by the mid-1980s a sharp increase in the attraction of an explicitly free-market economy, which was viewed by growing numbers as more successful than socialism, prompted a rise in interest in some form of conservative liberalism.

These polls also confirmed the enormous impact on political attitudes of the revolution in mass communications. In addition to Radio Free Europe, the Communist mass media now had to contend with the massive diffusion throughout the region of video cassette recorders, and the dissemination through them of uncensored films, political discussions, and dissident platforms. With the number of VCRs available to East Europeans rapidly increasing, and despite official efforts to impose some controls, the traditional Communist control over domestic mass communications was disintegrating. By 1988, it was estimated by *Radio Free Europe–Radio Liberty Report* on January 20, 1988, that there were approximately 1 million VCRs in Poland, 300,000 in Hungary, 150,000 in Czechoslovakia, and 50,000 in still tightly controlled Bulgaria.

This progressive, though uneven, resurfacing of politics was closely related to a reviving sense of a historically and especially culturally distinctive *Central*—not East—European identity. In Czechoslovakia, where authentic political life was more severely repressed than in Poland or even in Hungary, the emphasis on a distinctive regional cultural identity also represented a substitute for more direct political self-assertion. It is noteworthy that in his interview, Dubček pointedly stated that in speaking of Europe "it is no coincidence that I do not use the terms 'West' and 'East'. . . . Because of its geographical location, its traditions, and its experiences, Czechoslovakia belongs to Central Europe." Moreover, the historical self-identification, particularly of the Czechoslovaks, the Hungarians, and the Poles, with a *Central European* regional identity involved a repudiation of the Soviet-sponsored notion of a shared "socialist" culture. The significance of this should not be underestimated, given the several decades of effort by the Kremlin to inculcate the notion of a shared cultural community, with Moscow as its epicenter.

Beyond the rejection of Moscow as a radiating cultural center, a positive content also animated the notion of a Central European identity, a reality pregnant with regional import. It portended the emergence of a wider cultural community, somewhat reminiscent of the old Austro-Hungarian empire and of the nineteenth century cultural concept of a "Mitteleuropa." It implied the notion that "Europe" was not an entity neatly divided into two entities—a Western Europe and an Eastern Europe, with each subject to an extra-European power—but a cultural-historical community with overlapping but also distinctive layers of shared experience, values, and culture. Inherent in this perspective is a vision of a future Europe in which Western Europe could then interact naturally or "organically," so to speak, with an autonomous, perhaps even neutral Central Europe. Such a more distinctive Central Europe could, in turn, have more links and connections of its own with the *real* Eastern Europe—the Baltic states, Ukraine, and European Russia itself—than Western Europe could ever develop.

The historical import of this cultural trend is thus revolutionary. Linked to the progressive revival of genuine internal politics within individual East (or Central) European states, it foreshadows nothing less than the prospective attrition of the existing division of Europe into two separate blocs. Such attrition would permit the reemergence of more authentic East European systems, based on homegrown traditions and not on externally imposed doctrines. Accordingly, the organic rejection of an alien doctrine by a region that again was feeling itself to be a Central and not an Eastern Europe is the point of departure for the eventual dissolution of the globe's last remaining multinational empire.

CHAPTER 12

Imperial Retrenchment

"The situation in a number of countries of socialist persuasion remains unstable and is susceptible to regression," noted Aleksandr Bovin, a close Gorbachev supporter, in *Izvestia* on July 11, 1987. This rather unique admission, by a leading Soviet commentator, of basic weakness on the part of regimes that Moscow had installed more than forty years ago signaled the Kremlin's growing recognition that the Soviet-imposed institutional and ideological homogeneity could no longer be maintained. As a result, Soviet regional strategy had to shift from the assertion of the ideology to the defense of the empire as such.

Three principal dimensions of the requisite strategy of imperial defense became clearly discernible by the late 1980s. All involved continuity—none were a sharp break with the past—but together they were designed to reinforce the formalistic doctrinal ties with bonds of genuine and tangible interest. The first element involved enhanced emphasis on military coordination and common geopolitical interests; the second stressed intensified economic cooperation and integration; and the third placed special emphasis on the joint stake of the party elites in the retention of their power and privileges, but in a setting of greater tolerance for domestic diversity. Together, Moscow hoped, these three strands would produce a formula capable of nullifying the emancipating pull of the increasingly more authentic politics and culture of Eastern Europe.

The geopolitical dimension was especially important in preserving an imperial relationship with Poland and, to a lesser extent, with Czechoslovakia. Both countries remained concerned about their future relations with Germany, and some form of positive political association with a powerful Russia (of whatever ideological formation) was to them a necessary source of needed reassurance against any potential German territorial aspirations. In turn, for Moscow these basic national concerns

140

provided a useful substitute for the waning ideological bonds, and they also served to justify the continued existence and even reinforcement of the Warsaw Pact—which otherwise even the rulers of these countries might view as an imperial infringement on their sovereignty.

Accordingly, in the late 1970s and early 1980s, Soviet efforts to reinforce the military integration of the bloc were greatly intensified. Despite strong Romanian opposition, and also some evident reservations among the Polish military, Moscow succeeded in imposing a new command arrangement for the Pact. It enabled the Soviet High Command to assume direct control of the Pact's various national armies upon the initiation of an attack on NATO even without the prior knowledge of the East European political authorities. Startling details of this Moscow-imposed arrangement became known to the West in the early 1980s as a result of the defection to the West of Polish Colonel Ryszard Kuklinski. The tightened command system, as well as other measures designed to enhance military integration, was part of the Kremlin's very deliberate policy to strengthen the Warsaw Pact as the principal instrument of the political and military subordination of the region to Soviet control.

This increased emphasis on reinforced political-military bonds, designed to compensate for the fading vitality of ideological ties, was matched by greatly intensified efforts to expand the scope of economic integration of the East European Communist states with the Soviet Union. In addition to existing state-to-state cooperation, the Soviet leaders in the mid-1980s launched a number of initiatives to develop direct cooperation between branches of industry and even between individual firms. Such direct cooperation, undertaken outside of local national control, has stimulated fears in Eastern Europe that the initiative represents yet another Soviet design for gaining greater direct control over the region's economy. These concerns could hardly be assuaged by Gorbachev's openly stated interest in stimulating East European investments in the Soviet economy or by the emphasis placed by Moscow on using East European connections with the West to gain access for the Soviet Union to the latest Western technology.

To many East Europeans the Soviet stress on closer and more integrated economic links represents yet another phase of the prolonged process of sovietization of their societies. Having been compelled not only to imitate the Soviet model of industrialization, but also to adopt the Soviet-type industrial organization, the new emphasis on lateral links and on joint investment poses the real danger of the further isolation of Eastern Europe from the rest of the continent and thus of impeding the process of its evolutionary self-emancipation. The prospect of having to share Moscow's technological retardation, which such a closer union with the Soviet economy clearly implies, is just as ominous.

In this respect, an interview by the Soviet ambassador, Vladimir Brovikov, with Polish radio on October 31, 1987, was quite revealing. After hailing the "new impetus to cooperation" generated by lateral agreements on the industrial branch level between Soviet and Polish enterprises, and observing that several hundred enterprises were already involved, the Soviet ambassador went on to deplore the "many problems," "difficulties," and "timidity" that have impeded the expansion of such ties. He went on to assert that his embassy has "acted energetically to overcome the barriers in this sphere," thereby confirming reports of Polish reluctance.

Last but not least, from the Soviet point of view, an important potential benefit of these efforts to enhance "interdependence" was to make the East European party elites more directly dependent on the economic well-being of the Soviet Union. It is probably not an accident that the Soviet efforts to develop more binding economic relationships went the furthest with Poland, the country that indeed signaled the greatest determination to achieve self-emancipation. In April 1987, Gorbachev and Jaruzelski signed a joint declaration of cooperation in ideology, science, and culture between the two ruling parties, the first of its kind in the Soviet sphere. One may surmise that here the interests of Gorbachev and Jaruzelski overlapped, for the latter must have recognized an eventual threat to his and his elite's power in the progressive reemergence in Poland of a political life based on an increasingly self-emancipated society. This would help to explain the apparent eagerness with which the Jaruzelski regime responded to Gorbachev's efforts to intensify the region's economic and even ideological links with the Soviet Union.

Closer economic ties that generate bonds of special interest and tighter military links that rest on shared geopolitical concerns were thus to serve as compensation for the inevitable appearance in the region of increased ideological and systemic diversity. That diversity,

Moscow finally came to realize, could not be crushed, and efforts to impose a doctrinal homogeneity, based on a mindless imitation of the Soviet experience, were proving to be counterproductive, stimulating a more intense organic rejection of the Soviet model. That was why at the seventieth anniversary of the Bolshevik Revolution the Soviet leader formally renounced any desire to dictate how socialism was to be built within specific national settings. But that renunciation, in turn, made it all the more important that Moscow forge alternative bonds of unity, lest the result be the accelerated dissolution of the Soviet empire.

The undeniable fact was that Gorbachev's *perestroika* was permitting trends to surface that were inevitably loosening the bonds of control and dependence. His talk of "a common European home"—designed to draw West Europeans away from America—had the unintended effect also of legitimating Eastern Europe's drift toward the unifying Western Europe, thereby further eroding the Soviet imperial edifice. All of that sharpened the conflict between the region's subjective desire for emancipation and its continued objective subordination. The result could be a prolonged process of decay, of hopelessness punctuated by periodic bursts of unrest, and of growing instability. The region clearly needs, and greatly desires, an orderly transition from Soviet-type state socialism to some form of a multiparty democratic welfare state. It aspires even more to be part of a larger, truly democratic and pluralistic Europe, of which it feels itself to be culturally an integral part.

However, its political-economic elites cannot guide an evolution in that direction because they know that success would render them socially obsolescent and historically dispensable. This explains the reticence of even the Hungarian leadership, whose regime today is probably the most reform-minded in Eastern Europe. Therein lies the cause of the continued attraction of frightened Communist rulers to closer integration with the Soviet Union and of the consequent lingering tragedy—and explosive danger—of the East European condition.

Ultimately, the inability to promote peaceful evolution and to provide for genuine social participation in key political decisions, including eventual power sharing, could prove to be the undoing of communism in Eastern Europe. Simply put, the peoples of the region now predominantly view their communist systems as the central obstacle to their own well-being and to social progress in general. Indeed, the mood within large portions of their publics is today dominated by the potentially revolutionary consensus that a fatal flaw exists in the Soviet-imposed systems of Eastern Europe.

That fatal flaw is the communist party's monopoly of power, and its root cause is Soviet domination. Forty years after the imposition of communism on Eastern Europe, the elimination of both is now widely seen as the necessary precondition to social rebirth.

PART IV

Commercial Communism

The reform of Chinese communism is probably fated to be successful. That success will benefit China, but it will also be costly both to communism's ideological orthodoxy and to Chinese communism's political homogeneity. In brief, unlike its organic rejection by Eastern Europe, communism in China faces the prospect of organic absorption by the country's enduring traditions and values.

In the course of the next several decades, a more modern and more powerful China will likely become a major political and economic player on the world scene. In the process of guiding that historical rebirth of China, the country's Communist rulers are themselves experiencing a significant redefinition of their guiding ethos. Their dominant outlook, and even their political vocabulary, are becoming less characteristic of a revolutionary party claiming to be the representative of the dictatorship of the proletariat and more that of a modernizing party of the dictatorship of China's emerging state-sponsored commercial class.

To be sure, the Chinese Communists were never truly a proletarian party. Rather, most of its political leadership was composed of initially disaffected student radicals who became Marxist revolutionaries. These visionary activists then successfully translated the mutually reinforcing nationalist, agrarian, and urban resentments of an awakening but denigrated China into a triumphant ideological revolution. They carried out this revolution under the banner of a proletarian Communist party dedicated to the task of remaking China through a crash program of industrialization initially—notably in the early 1950s—modeled heavily on the Soviet experience. Two decades later, in response to repeated domestic setbacks, the party's next generation of leaders—though still led by a dominant survivor of the original revolutionary generation, Deng Xiaoping—directed the party

147

toward a different approach. A wide opening to the outside world—
which foresaw China's eventual active involvement in that world as
a significant commercial participant—became the means for achieving social modernization.

The historical trajectory of Chinese communism thus differs significantly from communism in Eastern Europe or in the Soviet Union.
Unlike that of Eastern Europe, Chinese communism is largely homegrown. It was neither imported from abroad nor imposed by an outside force. Chinese Communist leaders, in most cases, were not even
Moscow trained. The principal figures in the revolution rose through
the ranks. Some, like Mao Zedong and General Chu Teh, were student radicals who rose into command positions of an agrarian-based
revolutionary army. Others, like Zhou Enlai and Deng Xiaoping, obtained their first serious exposure to Marxist doctrine as students in
Western Europe, notably France, prior to becoming more directly involved in revolutionary activities at home. All shared in the unifying
experience of the Chinese Red Army's legendary Long March.

The example of the 1917 Bolshevik Revolution was of inspirational
importance to the young Chinese leaders—but they did not view it as
a binding model. China's conditions and its history differed so profoundly from Russia's that the Chinese leaders felt justified in redefining the Marxist-Leninist doctrine to their special circumstances.
More important, as the legatees of China's ancient civilization, they
had the intellectual and cultural self-confidence to carve out their own
revolutionary experience and to design their own strategy. Even after
the Soviet victory in World War II, when Stalin's personal prestige
reached its apex, the Chinese leaders were quite prepared to disregard
his strategic advice—which was to seek a revolutionary victory not all
at once but only by stages—and proceeded with an all-out revolutionary assault. Their final triumph in 1949 further intensified their sense
of separate indentity and their political confidence, in stark contrast to
the experience of their Soviet-subservient East European comrades.

Unlike their comrades in the Soviet bloc, Chinese Communists could
relate their ideology more effectively and quite directly to China's own
history. Ideological appeal was derived not only from social conflicts,
such as the agrarian hunger for land and the urban resentments
against industrial exploitation, but also from the deep feelings of in-
jured patriotism produced by a century-long national humiliation in-

flicted on China by Western imperialists that were subsequently set aflame by the Japanese invasion. China's extraordinary history sunk to its nadir in the nineteenth century, and it stimulated among many culturally proud Chinese the most intense feelings of resentment against both the hated outsiders and their own impotent and decadent rulers.

The rise of modern nationalism and the appeal of a doctrine of radical social renewal thus coincided historically in China. Chinese communism was able to blend them into a formula in which historically conscious patriotism and communism were not mutually exclusive propositions. Indeed, for many Chinese the Communist victory simultaneously represented a nationalist emancipation from hated foreign domination. In Soviet-dominated Eastern Europe, where for many communism meant submission to a foreign power, that was not at all the case. Even in the Soviet Union, the partial blending of communism and nationalism took place only in the trying days of the war against the Germans.

As a result of this fusion of nationalism and communism, Chinese revolutionary leaders, who set about to build a communist society, were quite naturally inclined to draw on their own cultural and social traditions, without looking over their shoulder at the Soviet experience or seeking to anticipate the Soviet reaction. China's phase of imitating the Soviet Union was thus quite short-lived. For the first few years after the revolutionary victory, and in the setting of intense animus toward the hostile United States, ideological kinship with the Soviet Union expressed itself through spontaneous—and not enforced—admiration for things Soviet and by imitation of the Soviet Union's initial state-directed industrialization.

In retrospect, the brevity of this phase and the alacrity with which the Chinese Communists turned to drawing on their own traditions and values in seeking to renovate China was remarkable. Once that turn took place the immersion of Chinese Communist leaders in their genuine national identity had to produce a significant redefinition of Chinese communism itself. China's developed culture—with its distinctive Confucian philosophy, with its unique tradition of the state-serving mandarin class, and with its advanced commercial skills—simply represented too strong a force not to exercise a powerful formative influence.

CHAPTER 13

China's Double
Three Tries

Communism in power is China's third major effort in the twentieth century to overcome its backwardness and to undo its national humiliation. Once in power, communism also dramatically altered its course three times in trying to create a new and more modern China. In each successive phase, Chinese Communist policy became less and less dominated by the precepts of an ideology shared in common with the other communist states, notably the Soviet Union, and more and more influenced by adaptations of that doctrine to China's specific conditions, established traditions, and more pragmatically defined national needs.

Few Westerners can fully appreciate the gap that developed in the course of the nineteenth century between the Chinese sense of their own unique, self-contained, and (to them) culturally superior civilization and the Chinese consciousness of their weakness in the face of the humiliations often deliberately inflicted upon them by the intruding European powers. A panoply of treaties, conventions, and extra-territorial arrangements imposed on China during the nineteenth century made tangible not only the inferior status of China as a state but also the inferior status of the Chinese as a people. That degradation collided with the Chinese sense that their past—even their relatively recent past—had been both culturally richer and even politically mightier than those of their arrogant intruders.

In fact, China's accentuated economic and political decline was of relatively recent vintage. Even as late as the eighteenth century, the per capita national income of the average Chinese was roughly comparable to that of the average Briton. Moreover, as recently as 1860

150

China ranked second in the world in terms of manufacturing output. According to Paul Kennedy's *The Rise and Fall of the Great Powers*, Chinese industries produced 19.7 percent of the world's manufactured goods—a share only barely surpassed by Britain's 19.9 percent and considerably ahead of all other competitors. Indeed, at the beginning of the twentieth century, China was the world's undisputed leading manufacturer, accounting for roughly one-third of the globe's output and outdistancing by far any other state. These facts refute the widespread Western perception of China as a stagnant and decadent empire, a ready victim for the more energetic and enterprising Europeans. They also help to illuminate the intensity of Chinese resentment against the West and the impatience with which the Chinese sought to erase the gap and thus to *restore* China to its historical preeminence.

As a result, this century has witnessed three major bursts of intense Chinese effort to reawaken, reorder, and reenergize their country. None of these can be seen as an isolated and compartmentalized historical phenomenon. Each was both preceded and followed by events that were part of a larger chain of historical causality, which was driven by the mounting Chinese resentment of their degraded condition. But these events can be conveniently personalized in terms of the leadership exercised by the three outstanding Chinese revolutionary figures of this century: Sun Yatsen, Chiang Kai-shek, and Mao Zedong.

Each drew political strength from rising nationalism, especially that of China's students, as well as from the intensifying resentments of China's poor. Each borrowed political ideas from the outside world to forge both a movement and a doctrine designed to restore China to greatness. Sun Yatsen's republican revolution of 1911 represented an early attempt to adapt to Chinese conditions essentially Western notions of constitutionalism, republicanism, and nationalism, influenced in part also by the seemingly successful Japanese imitation of the West's industrial and organizational accomplishments. Sun's efforts coincided with the convulsive agonies of China's old imperial system, and that gave them their historical timeliness, although the cultural and political remnants of the past eventually proved too resilient for his effort to succeed.

After a period of unrest, one of his disciples, who came to dominate the subsequent two decades of China's turmoil, raised the standard of renewal. Chiang's revolution was also an attempt to adapt Western notions of modernity to the more turbulent Chinese conditions, though in this second attempt the mixture differed greatly. Nationalism was juxtaposed to Marxism as the unifying sentiment, although Chiang himself had been exposed to Soviet training and had at one time collaborated with the emerging Chinese Communist activists in the struggle for a new China. That collaboration ended in 1927, with the collapse of the so-called United Front, which initiated twenty-two years of almost uninterrupted struggle with the Communists. Chiang placed central emphasis on military organization as the means of overcoming China's debilitating political fragmentation. He created a single monopolistic party, the Kuomintang, which resembled the Communist party in the Soviet Union and the fascist parties of Europe, to express a new sense of national unity. Chiang's own conversion to Christianity, combined with his stress on China's traditions and his seeming cultivation of the mandarin style, further underlined the complex interaction of old domestic roots and novel external impulses in the struggle for China's renewal.

Like Sun, Chiang also failed to translate the resentments against the past into a successful formula for shaping the future. The war with the Japanese initially elevated him into the symbol of national resistance but later sapped both his strength and his appeal. He was unable to overcome the twin blights of warlordism and corruption within his own movement, while his own patriotic star gradually dimmed. Chiang's faltering permitted the emergence of an alternative formula for change, one that mobilized more dramatically both the national and the social frustrations of contemporary China, that defined them in more explicit doctrinal terms, and that based them on a more disciplined and effective political organization. The Communist movement and the Communist Red Army, which had been led since the Long March of the mid-1930s by the homegrown Marxist leader Mao Zedong, proved ideologically and organizationally superior in the conclusive contest for control over the historical shape and philosophical content of China's post–World War II great awakening.

The new leader, a convinced Marxist but also an innovator in the realm of revolutionary theory, creatively adapted the notions of a proletarian revolution to the agrarian setting of China. Active since the early 1920s in the incipient Chinese Marxist movement, Mao had gained sufficient stature by the 1940s to formulate an independent Chinese revolutionary doctrine. Indeed, when the seventh congress of the Chinese Communist party convened in the Chinese Red Army headquarters in Yenan during the late spring of 1945—some four years before the final victory of communism in China—his ideological contributions were hailed as "Mao Zedong thought" and were elevated to the status of the party's guiding principle as the extension of Marxism-Leninism-Stalinism. This act testified not only to Mao's considerable intellectual arrogance but also to the political self-confidence of the Chinese Communists.

Yet, like his two predecessors in this century's quest for China's renewal, Mao was a patriotic Chinese steeped in his country's history. As historians of modern China have noted, one of his heroes was the first Qin emperor, who unified China in 221 B.C. Mao's admiration for him was doubtless related to the realization that contemporary China's lack of unity contributed directly to its decline. Historians have also noted that certain striking affinities existed between the Chinese Communist notions of a dominant and reformist government and the Qin dynasty's emphasis on discipline and permanent governance by a morally and spiritually superior mandarin class imbued with an explicit philosophy.

At first, however, the new order not only prevailed over the old, but it also dominated the thinking and the programs of China's new national leadership. Communist doctrine and the earlier communist experience in the Soviet Union provided the point of departure for the initial efforts to remake China. With time and with the progressive realization of the failure of the orthodox communist model, a formula that blended the new doctrine with the wisdom of China's own experience began to emerge and to define a less dogmatic program for achieving the country's full rebirth. In the context of both the social and national awakening of China, Mao's victory over Chiang led to three massive Communist attempts—two of which were extremely costly—to erase the historical gap that had opened so widely to China's disadvantage during the previous century.

The first effort—which culminated in the so-called Great Leap Forward—was derived largely from the combination of doctrine and the availability of Soviet help. Once the Communists had consolidated their power throughout the country after their final victory in 1949, the country embarked—in keeping with the grand oversimplification's faith in the socially miraculous benefits of heavy industry—on an ambitious program of industrialization. To that end, Soviet aid and techniques were to be assimilated as rapidly as possible, in a push in many ways reminiscent of Stalin's first five-year plans. Soviet advisers flooded into the country, Chinese students flocked to Soviet universities, and Soviet accomplishments were extolled in the Chinese press. But the Chinese leaders were impatient and unwilling to accept the notion that their development had to go through several historical stages on the long road to socialism. Their doctrinal impatience, and the inclination not to rely merely on the Soviet experience, culminated in the crash program enunciated at an unusual second session of the Eighth Party Congress in May 1958 both to collectivize Chinese agriculture and to industrialize the economy.

Admittedly, to justify this dramatic leap into the industrial age of a country that, according both to the official doctrine and objective statistics, was still a predominantly backward agrarian society, Mao needed a new ideological formulation. Never shy in tinkering with their doctrine, in September 1956 the Chinese Communist leadership arbitrarily proclaimed at the initial session of the Eighth Party Congress, the first held since the victory of 1949, that China had already entered "the advanced stage" in the construction of socialism. With the achievement of the grandiose goals of the Great Leap Forward, China would thus soon be ready to enter the stage of actual communism. Symbolic of the role of bitter national memory of foreign imperial domination, China's goals were defined not only in terms of the Marxist dogma, but also in terms of equaling and then surpassing the industrial capacity of Great Britain, the country which had been China's only peer in industrial production a bare century earlier—and which also had inflicted the worst humiliations on China.

The fanatic and quite brutal effort to restructure the Chinese peasantry into the so-called People's Communes produced a calamity of enormous proportions. Literally millions of peasants—by some estimates 27 million—died in the ensuing dislocations, violence, and famines. China fared little better in the industrial sector, and the economic situation worsened with the emerging rupture in Sino-Soviet relations, which by the late 1950s produced a veritable termination of all Soviet assistance. This prompted major disruptions in the ongoing industrial projects, especially as Soviet technicians abruptly departed, Soviet spare parts became unavailable, and the Chinese industrial sector was left suddenly entirely on its own. Overall economic performance was simply dismal, with the Great Leap Forward degenerating into a historically retrogressive calamity. According to G. C. Chow's *The Chinese Economy*, between 1958 and 1962 agricultural output actually dropped by 28 percent, light industry by 21 percent, and heavy industry by 23 percent.

Fantasy about the future soon gave way to paranoia about the present. The painfully felt failure of the Great Leap Forward contributed to the even more dramatic second phase in Chinese communism's triple attempt at remaking China. From the mid-1960s on, Mao pursued a deliberately inspired program of quasi-anarchistic upheaval, euphemistically called the Cultural Revolution. A paroxysm of violence seized China, with the now elderly and increasingly disabled Mao egging on his subordinates to destroy one another in a process of purported revolutionary renewal. The Soviet experience was now explicitly denounced and viewed as contributing to counter-revolutionary revisionism. Revolutionary purity was to be revived through internal struggles against both the ruling officialdom and past traditions.

As a result, China from 1966 to the mid-1970s experienced a series of brutal purges, mass killings of literally hundreds of thousands of party officials and military leaders (among them some of the most respected figures of the Long March and of the Chinese Revolution), and the imprisonment or exile to forced labor camps of several millions. While the precise numbers will never be known, this period was in many ways comparable to the worst years of the Stalinist terror and purges. The violence, though largely stimulated by Mao and several of his key associates, was fed also by the intensifying struggles for political succession, in the course of which at least two of Mao's would-be heirs were physically liquidated.

It took several years of patient maneuvering by Mao's subtle associate, Zhou Enlai, and the gradual rehabilitation of some of the surviving former top leaders, such as Deng Xiaoping, for the destructive dynamics of the Cultural Revolution to be brought under control. With Mao's death in September 1976, the process of normalization finally gained momentum. But even then five more years had to pass before power became firmly consolidated in Deng's hands. Only by the Twelfth Party Congress in September 1982 were his principal rivals formally removed from power, thereby firmly committing China to a new approach in seeking the elusive goal of national recovery and international prestige. Announced in the late 1970s and described as "the four modernizations"—in agriculture, industry, science and technology, and defense—the new program that was fleshed out gradually over the next several years postulated an altogether pragmatic opening to the Western world and an increasingly evident willingness to tamper with ideological orthodoxy at home.

That new course also corresponded to the fundamental change in China's international position: Not only had full relations with the United States been restored in late 1978, but a wide-ranging economic and political relationship, stimulated by shared fears of Soviet expansionism, had also begun to emerge, paralleling the rapid growth in Sino-Japanese trade. The shift in China's external relations contributed to the abandonment of the dogmatic vision of a world inevitably destined to undergo a nuclear war and to the adoption of new and more flexible principles guiding China's increased involvement in international commerce and diplomacy. The emerging reform program was to become, in effect, China's equivalent to Japan's Meiji Restoration, which had so dramatically plunged Japan into the modern world.

CHAPTER 14

Political Conflict
and the Birth of Reform

The new program was born in the context of a bitter power struggle and bitter power struggles defined its substance. It took approximately ten years of continuing political strife for China's emerging dominant figure, Deng Xiaoping, to forge and impose a comprehensive blueprint for a dramatically altered course of China's development. As had happened earlier in the Soviet Union, in the course of the titanic struggles between Stalin and Trotsky, ideology came to be reshaped in large measure by the vagaries of personal as well as political conflict. In the course of the 1930s, Mao had redefined Marxism-Leninism to put primary emphasis on peasant radicalism as the source of revolutionary energy; Deng was now to redefine socialism in order to enhance individual economic and commercial productivity.

The initial political arrangement after Mao's death in 1976 involved a sort of dual power. Continuity with Mao was seemingly assured by the assumption of governmental direction by his younger protégé, Hua Guofeng, while the restoration of normality and the abandonment of the Cultural Revolution was signaled by the assumption of de facto direction of the party by one of the most prominent victims of that revolution, Deng Xiaoping. Formally, Deng appeared to be proclaiming his fidelity to the teachings of Mao. In 1979, he stated that every Chinese citizen had to be bound by "the four principles": the socialist way, the dictatorship of the proletariat, leadership of the party, and Marxism-Leninism and Mao Zedong thought. In fact, however, under the guise of proclaimed continuity, Deng embarked on a deliberate revision of the established party line, in the course of which he had to overcome a series of truly major political obstacles.

These obstacles ranged from generational stagnation through political and ideological orthodoxy to actual open opposition within and outside the party—each of which complicated the process of shaping and imposing an alternative approach for China's entry into the modern world. The generational factor was rooted in the geriatric nature of the post-Mao top Chinese leadership. Though Hua, the nominal top leader, was relatively young by the prevailing Chinese standards, the top leadership was composed in the main of Mao's contemporaries, most of whom were not prepared to defer to Deng either personally or doctrinally. Moreover, and quite naturally, the majority of these veterans viewed with the greatest suspicion not only Deng's efforts to formulate a new approach but also his strident calls for a rejuvenation of the top cadres themselves.

These considerations interacted with political and ideological factors. Although Deng's reform program emerged only gradually, his initial call for the "four modernizations" was ideologically ambiguous because it neither postulated major alterations in the role of the party nor questioned explicitly the continued need for the dictatorship of the proletariat. But the more traditionally minded Chinese Communist leaders had to feel uneasy about the stress placed on rapid modernization based to a large extent on an opening to the West. In their content, even these early proposals clearly entailed the progressive enhancement of managerial considerations and the attrition of the party's special role and were quite evidently not driven by doctrinally orthodox assumptions regarding socialist construction.

To complicate matters further, open opposition to the established Communist dictatorship suddenly surfaced—an opposition encouraged and emboldened by Deng's even initially modest reform moves. Student activism, in dramatic contrast to the days of the Cultural Revolution, now took on a decidedly anti-establishmentarian and a doctrinally subversive Western democratic slant. Even as early as 1978, it manifested itself dramatically through mass demonstrations and through posters on the famous "Democracy Wall," not far from Beijing's Forbidden City. A slogan posted by one of the student leaders, Wei Jingsheng, captured the central message of the protesters: "Without democracy, no modernization!" But Deng was no closet liberal. That became amply evident when Wei's call for this "fifth modernization" earned him fifteen years in prison.

Political caution and ideological conviction both dictated Deng's response. Caution demanded the clearest repudiation of any sympathy for the would-be student democratizers because anything less would galvanize the party leadership and officialdom against the desired reforms. Such reforms, after all, were designed to restore normalcy for the ruling party in the wake of the massive disorders of the preceding decade as well as to advance the country's modernization. That conviction was reflected in the determination to maintain control *from above* over the reform process, lest it become a spontaneous upsurge that could eventually again threaten the party's primacy. To Deng, reform did not mean the abdication of power either by himself or by his party.

On the contrary, unlike Mao's impulsive revolutionary romanticism, Deng sought to pursue reform in a setting of stability and continuity, thereby making possible a long-term program for China's socioeconomic renewal. That required not only the rejuvenation of the leadership, but also an orderly succession to Deng himself. Otherwise, the party could again be plunged into the kind of disorders that in the preceding two decades had so badly damaged the country and devastated its leadership. But to assure an orderly transition, the top leader first had to consolidate his power, weed out any existing or potential rivals, set the course firmly, as well as designate and then entrench his successors. That has been Deng's central agenda since the early 1980s.

He pursued this agenda through several difficult stages, with remarkable perseverance, in spite of some serious setbacks. By 1982, he succeeded in formally removing Hua Guofeng from power, in routing the most radical remnants of Mao's immediate entourage— the so-called Gang of Four, among whom was Mao's widow and all of whom were sentenced to long prison terms for their criminal culpability in the brutalities of the Cultural Revolution—and in advancing his own chosen team of younger successors. In an important formal action, the Twelfth Party Congress in September 1982 confirmed his choice of Hu Yaobang as the next party leader and of Zhao Ziyang as governmental head. On the level of power, Deng had achieved a significant breakthrough.

But the issue of doctrine and program remained. For the next several years intense internal debates continued, and eventually caused a new political crisis. In these debates, Hu evolved from a relatively cautious endorser of limited reforms—with his keynote address to the Twelfth Party Congress in 1982 not breaking much new ground—to the leader spearheading not only of comprehensive economic reform but also of the much more controversial argument that basic *political* reforms had to accompany economic changes. In his view, economic reform, confined just to economics, would falter. He developed this argument—which gets to the heart of the prospects of reform in all Communist states—both publicly and, in a significantly sharper fashion, privately.

In the summer of 1986, Hu held a long private session and then entertained privately at dinner a former top-level U.S. official. (Incidentally, that dinner, held in the Great Hall of the People, was itself symbolic of the new spirit: Instead of the traditional Chinese menu, the official, who happened to be this author, was treated to the best of the French "nouvelle cuisine" and French wines!) In a five-hour discourse, Hu unfolded his views on the needed economic and political reforms in China. He spoke with extraordinary frankness, without reliance on a single piece of paper, and employed concepts not normally flowing from the lips of top Communist leaders. He stated quite directly that the existing political system had to be restructured, though it would take some time for the top leadership to draft the basic documents defining the required changes. Nonetheless, he asserted that in China too much was controlled from the top, that the existing system of central control was too rigid and too stereotyped, and that therefore substantial decentralization was needed. He added that the widespread overstaffing of the central party and government departments—with several hundreds of thousands of senior officials huddled in 107 such separate departments —compounded the problem. In brief, the state machinery badly needed a drastic overhaul.

Hu recognized that political change required the introduction of the rule of law. He referred specifically to the importance of objective and fixed rules that apply to everyone. Without such rules, arbitrary and capricious decision making could reappear, with negative consequences for social development. He related this need to the desirability of separating more sharply the roles of the party and the state, criticizing the excessive engagement of the party in direct administration. Moreover, he went on to argue that it would be desirable to stimulate greater political participation in public debates on policy by enhancing the scope of participation in the political process of China's non-Communist "parties"—the Chinese equivalents to Eastern Europe's Communist-controlled parties that allegedly represented the special "nonantagonistic" interests of the peasants and the intelligentsia. These groups, according to Hu, currently were subject to excessive Communist direction.

Hu also displayed striking flexibility in his discussion of the nature and role of the official ideology. He defined as the core of Marxism its method for analyzing the world and for understanding its problems, as well as for providing direction for building a new society. Elaborating on this rather vague definition of a doctrine that traditionally had always stressed the centrality of several dogmatic propositions, he said that Marxism was itself in the process of development and had to be validated through tangible achievements. His doctrinal pragmatism was indicated by his observation that in recruiting new members in the countryside, the party henceforth would seek those who through their initiative could lead others into prosperity even though inevitably some people will become rich before others.

Underlying all of his comments was a curious ambiguity. The thrust of his argument, which he made quite explicitly and with considerable animation, was that basic political changes were needed, and that they had to parallel the economic changes that the party leadership was preparing to adopt in the pursuit of "the four modernizations." Since the broad thrust of the emerging economic program pointed in the direction of extensive decentralization, it followed that political change would have to involve an equally substantial dispersal of concentrated political power. He was neither hesitant nor ambivalent on these points. Moreover, he showed particular open-mindedness on the sensitive issue of ideology, defining Marxism in broad terms and without the usual list of Leninist imperatives.

Yet, when the discussion came to the question of the role of the party, the combined effects of vested political interest, of ideological conditioning, and of the special propensity of all Communist leaders to perceive themselves ultimately as the only correct interpreters of the complex reality around them resurfaced in the flat assertion that the ruling role of the party had to continue, as would "democratic centralism," Lenin's deliberate misnomer for mindless obedience. That, in turn, meant that the ultimate dilemma of change—namely, where to draw the proper boundary between economic and political reforms—remained unresolved.

Other top Chinese leaders, most of whom took less innovative positions than Hu, were even more perplexed and uneasy regarding this centrally important and truly complex issue. Personal rivalries doubtless also played a continuing role in the internal debates over the emerging program of reform. Deng's choice of Hu as his principal successor was presumably not universally acclaimed in the top party ranks, as evident in the reaction of the leadership to the large-scale student riots that again broke out in December 1986. Several hundreds of thousands demonstrated in China's major cities, calling for greater freedom, pushing for democratic reforms, and generally challenging the party's claim to a monopoly over the reform program. In a reflexive response, the party leadership suppressed forcefully these outbreaks, which were led in many cases by the children of the party's officialdom. At the same time, the party elders personally petitioned Deng for Hu's dismissal, blaming him at least partly for the recent turmoil and for an excessive inclination toward political and ideological revisionism.

Hu's removal reopened the issue of succession, and kept open the question of the overall strategy of reform. Deng again confronted the need to set the course and to assure political continuity after he passes from the scene. It took much of 1987 for Deng to strike the new balance, to designate a new succession team, to codify more comprehensively the reform program, and to complete the process of weeding out remaining elderly opponents or skeptics. In January, Deng yielded to pressure—and perhaps he himself had become somewhat uneasy over his successor's penchant for spearheading political innovation—and Hu's dismissal was announced. During the spring and summer, protracted negotiations took place among the top leaders. By the fall of 1987, a new team was ready to be formally installed: Zhao had been shifted to take charge of the party, while Li Peng, a younger party leader who was a protégé of the late Zhou

Enlai and whom Zhou treated as an adopted son, was designated to become the new head of the government.

The two men clearly represented the reformist wing, though the party's officialdom could view neither as a threat to its vital interests. Both identified themselves with Deng's view that internal modernization had to be matched by an external opening to the world and both conceded that some carefully calibrated political changes had to match the more ambitious economic reforms. Both, however, also shared Deng's view that domestic political dissent could not be permitted to outpace economic reform—and that the former had to be suppressed so that the latter could continue under firm direction from above.

Zhao delivered the comprehensive statement of the overall Chinese approach to reform before the Thirteenth Party Congress in Beijing in late October 1987. After summarizing the various reforms undertaken since the late 1970s, he integrated them into a broader vision of the future and sought to give a coherent ideological significance to previous initiatives and future plans. The congress also installed formally a new party leadership composed at the top predominantly of Deng's choices, thereby producing the long-desired drastic rejuvenation of the party's top cadres. The leadership's commitment to reform was illustrated by the fact that Hu, far from passing into politicjal obscurity, remained in the Politburo and was prominently visible as part of the leadership during the congress' proceedings.

Thus, the congress marked an important milestone in China's post-Mao history. Henceforth, the internal conflict no longer centered on Deng's primacy or the desirability of comprehensive reforms, but rather on how best to pursue the reform strategy. To be sure, that question could—and at some point probably would—escalate into a wider disagreement over policy, particularly in the event of a new succession struggle. Future rounds, however, will likely be fought out by Deng's successors and in the setting of an ongoing and truly ambitious reform program.

CHAPTER 15

Reform Strategy
and Ideological Flexibility

Prolonged and intense struggles for power served as the catalysts for ideological change. In the setting of firmly and clearly established leadership, the communist system tends to rigidify its doctrinal orientation. Bureaucratic conservatism and dogmatic orthodoxy tend to reinforce each other, with dogma legitimizing established power and power protecting the established dogma. But since China experienced neither the twenty-five years of entrenched Stalinism under Stalin nor the twenty years of stagnant Stalinism under Brezhnev, China's ideology did not congeal like that of the Soviet Union. Mao's own policies involved several drastic reversals, while his later physical decline precipitated the almost two decades of political instability, punctuated by a murderous struggle for succession.

In the setting of an acute conflict for power—which ultimately means nothing short of a desperate struggle for personal survival, given the lethal character of politics within the communist system—ideology tends to become subordinated to the laws of the jungle, to become a tool of conflict, and hence to be periodically reinterpreted in keeping with the expediencies of power. All of that, in turn, serves to open gradually the door to other, more pragmatic criteria. Doctrinal concessions can increasingly be driven also by such mundane economic considerations as productivity and efficiency. In the process, doctrine becomes diluted.

As noted, a reform process with various zigs and zags had been gathering momentum since the late 1970s and culminated in the Thirteenth Party Congress in 1987. An event of historical importance, the congress provided the setting for three critical developments.

First, it was the forum for a comprehensive restatement of China's commitment to a decreasingly doctrinaire development and for an evaluation of the accomplishments of the reforms implemented in the course of Deng's efforts to consolidate his power. Second, it produced a detailed blueprint of China's further economic *and political* reforms. Third, in that context it articulated an important new ideological formulation designed to justify the long-term character of China's doctrinally flexible renewal.

By late 1987, the initial Chinese reforms already had a significant track record. The most impressive accomplishment, and initially the most doctrinally daring innovation, had occurred in agriculture. It had to give the Chinese leaders cause for satisfaction and faith in their course of action. Initiated at the Central Committee plenum in December 1978, the progressive decollectivization or decommunization of Chinese agriculture had prompted a dramatic surge in productivity. Indeed, over several years, China was transformed from a net importer of food to an actual exporter—in stark contrast to its Communist neighbor to the north, which even under Gorbachev remained frozen in its commitment to its wasteful collectivist system.

But this reform carried profound ideological consequences. It meant that the overwhelming majority of the Chinese people had ceased to live within a communist framework shaped by ideological impulses. On the contrary, empowered to control their land through long-term leasing and to sell their products freely on an open market with prices determined by the laws of demand and supply, rural society was now living economically and culturally within an environment fundamentally different from conventional communist notions. This break with the past entailed an inevitable de facto lessening of direct party control over much of China's population—though to the great advantage of China's economy. Centralized political control thus contracted as China's overall economic power expanded.

An ideological fig leaf for the decommunization of China's agriculture was contrived through the arrangement to "lease" the land to the peasants, rather than to cede ownership. In the formal sense, the peasants were still not landowners but lessees of the publicly owned soil. In reality, however, they were given total control over production. Moreover, by 1987 Chinese officials were broadly hinting that further steps would be taken to legalize the right to purchase and sell such "leases," thereby in effect restoring the right of private ownership. Their inclination to make such reforms both permanent and wide-ranging was doubtless prompted by the reforms' self-evident economic success. According to J. L. Scherer's *China Facts and Figures Annual, 1986*, gross agricultural output grew by 9 percent in 1978, by 11 percent in 1982, and by 14.5 percent in 1984, even as Soviet agriculture stagnated. In addition, this agricultural rebirth stimulated growth in the output of Chinese rural industry, which increased by a staggering 400 percent between 1981 and 1986 and which grew by a further 36 percent in 1987 alone.

Changes in other domains likewise had been under way since the late 1970s. On the whole, they, too, gave cause for satisfaction, though with some potentially serious warning signals on the horizon. When embarking on the agricultural reforms, the party leadership had also charted an ambitious new industrial program in order to achieve Deng's "second modernization." According to the party's daily, *Renmin Ribao* on March 9, 1978, its proclaimed goal was "to approach, equal, or outstrip" the industrial output of "the most developed capitalist countries." But Deng and his supporters quickly realized that this objective was overly ambitious. With the elimination in 1982 from the leadership of Hua Guofeng, Deng scaled down the grandiose industrialization programs, especially in heavy industry. In yet another ideologically significant deviation from the doctrinal imperatives of the past, he assigned a higher priority to light industry, as well as the already prospering rural industry.

The encouraging results of these broad shifts in priorities prompted in turn the "Decision of the Central Committee of the Communist Party of China on Reform of the Economic Structure" of October 20, 1984. It represented both the formalization of the steps already taken and yet another push forward in the progressive deideologization of the Chinese system. Defined as providing "the only road to prosperity for the whole society," the decision was short on doctrine and long on specifically needed changes. It flatly stated that since "no state institution can know the whole situation fully and cope with everything in good time," it was now timely and appropriate for "the enterprise . . . [to] be truly made a relatively independent economic entity." That independence was to be expressed in the hiring and firing of staff, in the procurement of needed supplies, in the setting of wages and of prices, and—within the framework of the overall national plan and subject to state taxation—in the reinvestment of profits and in the setting of specific targets.

This reform was paralleled by an opening for privately owned small-scale enterprises, especially in the consumer sector. Private initiative was declared as economically and socially functional in filling the many gaps inevitably left by state-owned enterprises still subject to the overall state economic plan and less oriented to a responsive satisfaction of consumer needs. Once that opening was created, Chinese society's cultural penchant for entrepreneurial initiative quickly manifested itself. According to a CIA report submitted to the U.S. Congress in April 1988, 300,000 such enterprises, as well as *20 million* additional one-person or one-family undertakings, had sprung up by 1987.

As Deng stated in 1978, the reforms in the rural sector and the unfolding changes in the industrial sector—which represented his two key "modernizations"—would be pursued in the context of a wide-ranging opening to the world, notably to the advanced Western world. Deng and his supporters viewed that opening as necessary both for strategic as well as economic reasons. Political and strategic relations with the United States were deliberately expanded, notwithstanding the continued disagreement over Taiwan. Economic relations with the United States grew with even greater momentum, and even more so with neighboring Japan. To further that expansion, in yet another example of ideological flexibility, the Chinese leaders established in the early 1980s several so-called special economic zones in the coastal regions of China, specifically Shenzhen, Shantou, Zhuhai, and Xiamen. Foreign presence and economic activity in these regions was to be attracted through an ideologically revolutionary set of special enticements and entitlements, creating in effect a series of capitalist islands within the Chinese economy.

Deng's objective was to foster China's world trade. Chinese leaders came to recognize, with much sharper acuity than their Soviet counterparts, that international trade could be the locomotive of internal development and that this has been a major source of impetus for the remarkable growth rates attained in recent decades by several of China's Pacific rim neighbors. But to foster that trade China had to be made economically attractive, and Deng sought to do so through the special zones, plus the domestic reforms. Again, those who mourned doctrinal purity could be cheered at least by the tangible results. By the mid-1980s, China's coastal region was experiencing an extraordinary burst in economic growth and productivity, with its cities undergoing a visible and impressive renewal. Since 1978, China's GNP has doubled. Its foreign trade has grown by almost 15 percent per annum since 1982. In 1987, China's exports soared by 25 percent, and China's foreign trade reached the respectable level of $80 billion, quadrupling the 1978 level.

At the same time, China's willingness to permit relatively large numbers of its more able—and, in many cases, politically better connected—students to study abroad was not only symbolic of the opening to the world, but also significant both in its doctrinal as well as practical consequences. The result was an inevitable loss in direct ideological control, conceded—though with some official reluctance and occasional tensions—in order to gain the benefits of the West's more advanced technology and science. Most striking in this respect was the fact that the largest number of such students were sent to the United States, the erstwhile ideological enemy. It has been estimated that by 1987 some twenty-seven thousand Chinese students were studying in American universities, compared to merely a few score from the Soviet Union. Harvard University reported in 1988 that Beijing University had become one of the top ten feeder schools in the world for Harvard's graduate programs.

The pace of these changes, their ideological flexibility, and the dilemma of accommodating simultaneously a state and a private sector within an increasingly complex economy inevitably produced tensions and difficulties. The Thirteenth Party Congress thus required Chinese leaders not only to take stock of what had been achieved but also to face up to the problems created by the reforms. These difficulties confronted the Chinese leaders with the need to decide whether to retrench or whether to plunge forward with even more ambitious reforms, lest the program of change slacken, stall, and then stagnate. They chose the latter. The congress thus provided the platform not only for the definition of the needed further changes but also for the articulation of an important ideological justification for China's comprehensive reforms.

Several warning signals testified to the fact that such reforms were not painless. In agriculture, decommunization produced a massive proliferation of small household farms, numbering 180 million. After an initial burst in productivity, their excessively small acreage made capitalizing on economies of scale impossible. As a result, further significant increases in agricultural yields became unlikely. Clearly, some form of amalgamation would have to be encouraged. Moreover, the loosening of central controls over production quotas and marketing had prompted many peasants to turn to the more lucrative cash crops instead of cultivating grain. The resulting price spiral compelled the Chinese authorities to increase substantially the subsidies provided to urban consumers in order to compensate for the rising inflation.

Corruption was also becoming a growing problem. Prompted by the sudden opening to free enterprise and the intrusion of foreign capital, especially in the new special economic zones, the temptation to get rich quick proved irresistible to a number of Chinese officials. Chinese press reports have cited incidents in which officials have cost the state millions of dollars—and in one case over a billion dollars—through smuggling, fraud, and open profiteering. Bribery to receive access to scarce goods or materials, at the levels of both producers and consumers, became a pervasive problem. Abuse of political power and favoritism in allocating economic resources, such as fuel, also became more widespread. All of this prompted party leaders to launch a campaign in January 1986 seeking the "rectification of party style." But as long as resources are distributed not just by the market but also by the state and party apparatus, these types of corruption will likely continue.

Last but not least, the coexistence of an economy based on centrally and arbitrarily set prices with an economy driven by the market created massive confusion for the Chinese planners, for the increasingly independent managers of state-owned industries, for the emerging new private entrepreneurs, and for foreign businessmen. The confusion in the pricing system was the source of major bottlenecks in the economy, and it also contributed to potentially dangerous inflationary pressures. How to extricate China from this conundrum is likely to remain the principal economic, as well as a major doctrinal, dilemma facing, and probably also dividing, the Chinese leaders.

Political problems also surfaced. First, unavoidable dilemmas arose as a result of economic decentralization in a centralized political setting. As the former gathered momentum, it was bound to collide with the latter. Chinese leaders had to choose between compromising on the decentralization or yielding on political control. Concessions on the political front inevitably meant a further contraction in the administrative role of the party. Second, and related to the first problem, a more restrictive role for the party opened the doors to more overt political dissent. The saliency of this problem was heightened by the emergence of such dissent among students and intellectuals. To party leaders, the intolerable demands for further political liberalization—which intensified in the latter 1980s—were the painful concomitants of the tolerated economic changes.

To the credit of the Chinese leadership, they did not respond by viewing these dilemmas as confirmation of their worst—and ideologically inspired—fears of the capitalist contagion. Instead, as a result of their determination and confidence, they recognized these difficulties as the unavoidable consequences of a successfully unfolding process of reform. Accordingly, the Thirteenth Party Congress—dominated by Deng's chosen successors and the new generation of top leaders—did not retrench. Symbolically, the Chinese leadership appeared in a variety of elegantly cut Western-style suits (unlike their counterparts in the Soviet Politburo who seem to be collectively tailored) and comported themselves with the foreign press like successful Pacific rim entrepreneurs. Substantively, the congress went beyond the reaffirmation of the leadership's commitment to renewal and focused in concrete terms on needed future economic and political changes.

In the economic realm, General Secretary Zhao Ziyang boldly stated that by the early 1990s only about 30 percent of the Chinese economy would be subject to central planning. Foreign investment would be further stimulated by the deliberate adoption of what might be called the coastal strategy. This would involve a program for selectively accelerated development of China's maritime provinces, which are inhabited by approximately 200 million people. This part of China would join, ahead of the rest of the country, the Pacific rim's new co-prosperity sphere, and would do so on the basis of creating greater scope both for domestic free enterprise and for foreign capital. To encourage the latter, even land would be made available for foreign purchase.

Zhao's speech and the more detailed subsequent proposals clearly indicated that the domestic industrial sector would be subjected not only to further decentralization, but also to the expansion of its private component. The official party paper, *Renmin Ribao*, on June 28, 1988, flatly rejected any notion that the growth of private enterprise had been excessive, arguing, "It is untrue that private enterprises are developing too fast in our country or that they are too many in number." It also projected that eventually private enterprise should account for about 10 percent of China's total industrial output. Factory managers would be given the power to retain profits and to use them for investment as well as incentive bonuses. A bankruptcy law would be introduced, while the personnel of the state bureaucracy would be drastically pared by 20 percent. In agriculture the focus would be on the encouragement of larger-scale but still private farming. But in one area—price reform—the Chinese leaders hesitated. This reflected both practical economic difficulties and special ideological sensitivity. Out of a concern over potential runaway inflation, the leadership remained wary of a comprehensive defreeze. That, in turn, meant the issue of price reform would continue to perplex and perhaps even to divide Chinese decision makers.

Perhaps even more important than the economic reforms was the evident inclination of the new Chinese leaders to address the issue of political change. In his programmatic report, whose title "Advance Along the Road of Socialism with Chinese Characteristics" placed special emphasis on the uniqueness of China's condition, Zhao acknowledged that "the deepening of the ongoing reform of the economic structure makes reform of the political structure increasingly urgent." Having recognized the connection between the economic and the political dimensions of renewal, he went on to assert that "the key to reforming the political structure is the separation of party and government," an important conclusion which Gorbachev and the Soviet reformers drew publicly only a year later. In his speech, Zhao outlined the steps needed to move matters in that direction, placing special stress on the need to develop an impartial, professional, and highly trained public service to be chosen on the basis of competitive examinations and whose career patterns would be determined entirely by their professional performance rather than by political or ideological criteria. With this civil service, reminiscent perhaps of a mandarin class, the party officialdom would be detached from direct involvement in administration but would remain in charge of energizing the system and of providing the needed links between policy and public opinion.

To be sure, though these steps indicated a serious recognition of the reciprocal causal link between effective economic reforms and greater political flexibility, they were still a far cry from anything even remotely approximating a Western-style pluralist democracy. At the very best, they were a modest step away from the traditional concentration of power at all levels in the hands of the ruling party and a step toward a political system based on established rules of procedure and administered by a public service guided by objective standards of conduct. In that sense, the more arbitrary and coercive attributes of the political system could be viewed as receding, though Zhao quite explicitly stated that "we shall never . . . introduce a Western system of separation of the three powers and of different parties ruling the country in turn."

To legitimate China's commitment to a long-term program of development based on an increasingly mixed economy, and pursued in a setting in which the party commands but does not directly administer, the Chinese leaders formulated a special ideological concept: "the primary stage of socialism." The departures from orthodox Marxism-Leninism were justified by reference to the undeveloped character of the forces of production and to the uniqueness of China's historical condition. Zhao defined the expected length of this "primary stage" with some specificity:

> We are not in the situation envisaged by the founders of Marxism. . . .
> So we cannot blindly follow what the books say, nor can we mechanically imitate the example of other countries. Rather, proceeding from China's actual conditions and integrating the basic principles of Marxism with those conditions, we must find a way to build socialism with Chinese characteristics, through practice. . . . It will be at least 100 years from the 1950s, when the socialist transformation of private ownership of the means of production was basically completed, to the time when socialist modernization will have been in the main accomplished, and all these years belong to the primary stage of socialism.

Although foreshadowed in some earlier statements by Hu Yaobang, the formal adoption of the concept of "the primary stage" provided a dramatic contrast to the ideologically ambitious claims of the 1950s. At that time, the party line claimed that China was already well advanced along the road to socialism and building socialism on the basis of universally valid Marxist-Leninist principles that were further enriched by the thought of Mao Zedong. Zhao's new formulation was obviously designed to justify both the pragmatic changes being implemented and the need for a prolonged period of nonsocialist economic growth.

In effect, China's modernization was to be based on the long-term assimilation into its economy of such capitalist elements as the market-mechanism, private ownership, foreign investment, venture capital, unemployment and bankruptcy, as well as private farming. Moreover, a major part of China was to develop ahead of the rest of the country through an intensifying commercial assimilation into the outside world. All of this was to be coordinated by a neutral civil service and supervised by the ruling party, with the latter somehow assuring that the process would eventually take China into the stage of advanced socialism and, later still, communism.

Indeed, in propagating the concept of "the primary stage of socialism," Zhao created an ideological formula largely devoid of ideological content. That was presumably intentional. Absence of doctrinal substance maximized tactical flexibility, though the formula clearly foresaw a long-term process, to last over several generations, of quasi-capitalist development. However, this lack of ideological mooring carried important potential consequences. Such a prolonged phase of development inevitably would breed its own economic and political dynamics. These might reshape the objective context within which the party wielded power, even if on the subjective level the party might feel that it was not deliberately doing so. As a result, questions would inevitably arise as to how the party could hold on to power and justify its control, especially if Chinese society and the Chinese economy were increasingly reshaped by the dynamics of that quasi-capitalist development.

Thus, ideological difficulties are bound to mount. The traditional concept of the dictatorship of the proletariat—with a self-appointed ruling party representing the proletariat—is over time simply incompatible with the economically pliable formulas put forth by the Chinese leaders and with their notions of a state administered by an undogmatic, professional, functionally oriented state bureaucracy. Presumably anticipating this doctrinal dilemma, the Chinese leaders casually supplanted at the Thirteenth Party Congress the phrase "dictatorship of the proletariat" with the oxymoronic term "the people's democratic dictatorship"—words altogether devoid of the specific class content of the once-sacred Marxist-Leninist formula. Finally, their paramount emphasis on national uniqueness as the determinant of doctrine—not just at the margins but at the core of the dogma—made a mockery of any universally valid precepts regarding the processes and substance of socialist construction.

Yet, China's reforms require this kind of doctrinal elasticity in the definition of socialism. Shortly after the congress, Hu Qili, one of the younger leaders elevated to a top position by that congress, demonstrated just how far the words could be stretched. Addressing the party's propagandists and seeking to give them guidance on the party's new general line, he authoritatively reasoned that "whatever benefits the development of the productive forces is required or permitted by socialism, and whatever does not benefit it is contrary to scientific socialism." Not surprisingly, these ideological gymnastics opened the doors to a much wider infusion into China of new Western ideas. Especially within Beijing's think tanks, this intrusion generated a special fascination with theorists of the postindustrial society such as Daniel Bell, of the social consequences of the new information technologies such as Ilya Prigogine, and of the shape of the future such as Alvin Toffler. To a growing number of Chinese thinkers, these Western perspectives had more to offer regarding the real substance and direction of the "primary stage" than "the books" of Marxism-Leninism which Zhao's own words were helping to delegitimize.

All this inevitably posed a key question: When does ideological flexibility turn into doctrinal dilution? That the answer might be "not before too long" was conveyed symbolically by the announcement in Beijing on—of all days—May 1, 1988, of the termination of the publication of the party's theoretical journal, *Red Flag* or *Hong-qi*. Once the principal source of doctrinal guidance, the magazine had in recent years become the platform for conservative, dogmatically anti-reformist views. A new publication—to be titled with Deng Xiaoping's phrase, *Shishi qiushi* or *Seek Truth from Facts*—was to take its place. This particular fact spoke for itself.

CHAPTER 16

The Real
Cultural Revolution

The tone and tenor of the Thirteenth Party Congress indicated that the majority of the Chinese leadership, and especially its younger members, did not worry much about doctrinal niceties. Their principal concern was that China develop efficiently, steadily, and on the basis of the widest possible exposure to, and assimilation of, the latest Western technology and science. That was to be the primary purpose, and the central justification, for their own exercise of power.

A few days after Zhao had addressed the Beijing congress, Gorbachev also delivered a major programmatic statement to the assembled Soviet party elite, who had gathered for a festive commemoration of the seventieth anniversary of the Bolshevik Revolution. His speech, which culminated many months of debate and preparation, sought both to summarize what had already been accomplished and what had yet to be done in the quest for *perestroika*. Together, Zhao's and Gorbachev's speeches provided some suggestive comparisons regarding the pace, the nature, and the scope of the reforms pursued by each as they grappled with the practical consequences of the failure of the communist doctrine.

On the level of both dogma and practice, the Chinese were ahead of the Soviets in seeking social renewal and modernization. Compared to Zhao's bold commitment to a pragmatic and long-term "primary stage of socialism," Gorbachev offered an ideologically tepid case. He provided neither a clear-cut ideological definition of the significance of his efforts nor an understandable time frame for *perestroika*'s life span. In doctrinally vague terms, he defined restructuring as "a

175

specific historical stage in our society's onward advance. And to answer the Leninist question from what to what are we passing, it has to be said quite definitely: We are imparting new qualities to socialism—a second wind, as they say." It was doubtful that much long-term guidance could be derived from such elusive formulations.

Gorbachev also initially demonstrated less willingness to innovate in the area of the party's own role. Though he called for democratization, especially at the level of the soviets (or councils) in order to enhance self-government and for more objective legal standards, he coupled these admonitions with a flat reaffirmation of the party's central role: "Time demands that in the new conditions, too, the party should proceed at the head of the revolutionary renewal. . . . The growing role of the party is a logical process." Unlike the Chinese, the Soviet leadership in 1987 was still unwilling to consider yanking the party out of the business of administration. Nor was it ready in 1987 to match the politically critical Chinese decision to limit the top party leader (and also the prime minister) to a maximum of two five-year terms of office.

It took approximately one year—as well as perhaps the power of the Chinese example—for the Soviets to follow suit. The Soviet mass media during 1987 and 1988 gave the Chinese reforms detailed and increasingly sympathetic coverage. One can only assume that the Soviet leaders were not indifferent to the possibility that China might prove both more innovative and successful. In any case, in the summer of 1988 the Soviet party, prodded by Gorbachev, finally adopted similar limits on the tenure of office by high officials, and it also approved proposals for pulling the party out of the management of local government.

The slower Soviet pace—despite Gorbachev's revisionist inclinations—undoubtedly constituted an expression more of the collective orientation of the top Soviet leadership than of Gorbachev's own inclinations. But that time lag was what politically mattered. It defined the contrasts between the Soviet and the Chinese approaches. A Soviet journalist who supported Gorbachev, Fedor Burlatskiy, captured the essence of that difference, especially in terms of the approach toward ideology, when he summarized in *Literaturnaia Gazeta* on April 20, 1988, the reactions of a Soviet audience to his impressions from a trip to China:

Not long ago, after my return from China, I had an opportunity to speak about the reforms there. Specifically, about the way family contracts were successfully used there to solve the food problem, to increase grain production by more than one-third in 5–6 years, and to raise peasants' living standards threefold. Suddenly a venerable professor took the floor. This is what he said, literally: "All this is okay. But what was the price that had to be paid for it? The price that had to be paid was a retreat from socialism and the borrowing of capitalist methods. Is this not too high a price to pay for economic growth?"

That kind of argument undoubtedly was heard also at the top of the Soviet leadership. It represented the major obstacle to more doctrinally ambitious reforms. As a result, the Chinese were bolder not only ideologically but also practically. Their reforms went further than those of the Soviet Union. That was especially true in agriculture. But it was also the case in urban and rural industry, in foreign trade, in foreign investment, in consumer goods, and in private enterprise. In China, peasants, in effect, could own their land. Thousands of wholly foreign-owned ventures were permitted to operate in the special economic zones. The service sector witnessed a proliferation of private enterprises. A major shift toward the production of consumer items has been encouraged, in part through rural workshops and small factories. Last but not least, unlike the Soviet Union, China made significant cuts in the size of the army and in defense expenditures. In all these sectors, changes in China were more tangible than those in the Soviet Union.

Moreover, social receptivity to these changes was also more evident in China. In fact, this social receptivity is the major reason why China will probably succeed, while the Soviet Union will probably falter. Unlike the Soviet peasantry, China's peasants had not been wiped out. Therefore they could respond to the new opportunities by higher production. Unlike the Russians, the Chinese people have a talent for entrepreneurship. Unlike Russia, China before communism never had a state that dominated or stifled independent economic life. With a commercial tradition more deeply rooted and socially widespread than in Russia, China enjoys better prospects not only for a commercial revival within China but also for a significant growth in China's role in world commerce. Finally, China is predominantly inhabited by one people, the Han, whereas the Soviet Union is a coerced amalgam of many nations. A decentralized China will still be one China; a decentralized Soviet Union most probably would become a dismantled Soviet Union.

As a result of its more clearly and more confidently defined sense of direction, China's leadership adopted a course of action in which *perestroika* preceded *glasnost*, while in the Soviet Union not only did *glasnost* come before *perestroika*, but also more debate about reform took place than actual implementation of reform. Accordingly, seasoned observers of the Chinese scene were inclined to assess the prospects for further changes in relatively optimistic terms. Their consensus was that China stood a reasonable chance of sustaining high rates of growth for about the next decade, barring some inherently unforeseeable natural calamity or political disaster. Consequently, by the year 2010 China's overall economy (though certainly not its per capita output) might even surpass that of the Soviet Union, a development pregnant with ideological as well as political import.

Still, any projection into the future must be sensitive to possible discontinuities and dangers. Both political as well as economic setbacks could adversely affect these otherwise promising prospects. Several specters must be haunting the farsighted Deng. Struggles for succession could again split the leadership. Disagreements over the social and economic effects of the coastal strategy could intensify conflicts over policy. Commercial communism could degenerate into corrupt communism, with corruption first contaminating and demoralizing the party officialdom and then eventually prompting a repressive and politically centralizing reaction. In the meantime, inflation could turn the urban masses against the regime, while increasing economic pluralism could breed escalating civil unrest and rising demands for more democracy.

Power rivalries have in the past precipitated major policy changes. That could happen again. It is far from certain that Deng has succeeded in fully entrenching his two chosen successors. Once he is gone from the scene, their power could be challenged or events could push them, or one of them, in other directions. Given the ambitious and very complex scope of the reform program, difficult choices and policy differences will inevitably surface as the reforms encounter practical difficulties. These, in turn, are likely to interact with personal rivalries and accentuate the resulting political conflicts.

A possible major issue of contention pertains to the so-called coastal strategy of China's modernization. Apparently favored by Zhao, it envisages an inevitably uneven process of development, with the coastal regions acting as the locomotive of growth and in the process developing much more rapidly than the rest of the country. In effect, the 200 million Chinese inhabiting the coastal regions get a head start in joining the modern and prosperous non-Communist countries of the Pacific rim. The proponents of the strategy calculated, and hoped, that the rest of China would eventually benefit from this strategy's technological and economic spin-offs.

Other Chinese leaders were less sanguine—and even saw dangers in this strategy. Its very success would accentuate socioeconomic differences within the country, push ideological flexibility beyond tolerable limits by encouraging predominantly capitalist values, and repudiate altogether the egalitarian tradition so deeply embedded in the concept of socialism. *The Beijing Review* (April 25–May 1, 1988) reported that some party officials were "afraid that the strategy will slow down the development of inland areas" and stressed the danger that inland China "will slip even further behind as coastal areas develop." In addition, the economic emancipation of the coast could also precipitate an inflationary spiral even more severe than the one already stimulated by the ongoing reforms, thereby imposing new hardships on the urban population and perhaps even causing public unrest. China's new prime minister, Li Peng, has on record advocated greater caution in the pursuit of reforms, with special emphasis on the continued need for price controls, and has endorsed the coastal strategy in more restrained terms than his colleagues.

Inflation is probably the greatest menace to the ongoing reforms. Every Communist effort at experimentation with the partial adoption of the market-mechanism—be it earlier in Yugoslavia, more recently in Hungary, or lately in China—has tended to trigger inflationary spirals. These were due to the fact that removing controls, in addition to unleashing economic dynamism, tends also to reveal major gaps in the functioning of the communist economy, precipitating an excess of demand over supply but without the elasticity of response inherent in a true market economy. Fear of worker unrest because of inflation has inspired some second thoughts even among reform-minded Communist leaders in every communist country that has toyed with reforms.

Future policy conflicts, according to such prominent scholars of contemporary China as Michel Oksenberg and Harry Harding, are thus likely to occur not between reformers and anti-reformers, but rather between ambitious reformers who are driven largely by pragmatic economic imperatives and cautious reformers who fear that economic dynamics could prompt political and ideological complications. If the economy prospers, as seems likely, the process of subordinating the ideology to economic pragmatism will continue. If it does not, as could happen, some retrenchment, in the context of renewed power struggles, becomes likely. But even then, the broad commitment to change is likely to continue, with the prospects high that China will sustain in the years ahead growth rates above those of the Soviet Union.

An even more complicated problem is likely to arise in the political-institutional domain. China has moved forward with its restructuring largely on the basis of an initiative from above. Unlike the Soviet leadership under Gorbachev, Chinese leaders have made little effort to generate from below a public campaign of "democratization" as a means of bolstering the efforts from the top down. Instead, they have preempted that by explicitly acknowledging that political changes will have to parallel economic changes, and by suggesting how this might come about, especially through the disengagement of the party from the state administration. This has enabled the Chinese leadership, with power more firmly held in Deng's hands, to control the process and to push forward. In many respects, what Deng succeeded in doing is more suggestive of Ligachev's notion of *perestroika* imposed from above than of Gorbachev's use of *glasnost* as the catalyst for *perestroika*.

The question does arise, however, whether Deng's actions in the political realm will prove sufficient. China's economic program is truly ambitious. China's opening to the world, especially of its coastal regions, is wide and the interaction with the outside world is expanding rapidly. Under these circumstances, the pressures for genuine political liberalization, and then for true democratization, are bound to increase. Symptoms of this process are already proliferating and will likely become more visible. The role of the party, its control over mass communications, and its monopoly on policy making, are all likely to come under challenge. At the same time, political dissent will be more difficult to suppress in the setting of economic changes congenial to greater social and economic, and hence also inevitably political, pluralism.

Major political-institutional problems will therefore surface in the future. They may become more acute if the economic program falters. That would provide additional grist for mutual political and ideological recriminations among the top leaders. But if the economic renewal remains relatively successful, as now seems likely, that will breed pressures from below for greater democracy because these impulses are inherent in the substance of the ongoing economic reforms. At some point, almost certainly within one or two decades, the Chinese Communist leaders will have to face the fact that productively creative socioeconomic pluralism is incompatible with a system of one-party rule that rejects political pluralism.

That incompatibility could pose a problem of serious dimensions. A brief comparison of the political reforms publicly recommended by Fang Lizhi, a physicist hailed as China's Sakharov, and those officially advocated by Zhao illustrates the dramatic gap between the Communist idea of "democratization" and the Western ideas of genuine pluralism and popular sovereignty. In his speech before the Thirteenth Party Congress, Zhao clearly endorsed Deng's notion of putting economic reform before political reform. Fang, on the other hand, reversed this order of priority. "Without democracy," he said, "there can be no development."

In terms of substance, Zhao's democratization involved the separation of party and state, the decentralization of power, the streamlining of bureaucracy, and the enhancement of legal standards, but did not include a genuine role for the people in selecting their leaders or forming overall policy. He called for "a channel for the demands and voice of the masses to constantly reach the higher levels" and for a policy of regular "social consultation and conversation." He also endorsed the concept of allowing multiple candidates to compete for elected positions on the local level, though the nominating procedures apparently would remain in the party's domain and the scope of such elections constricted. At the same time, he denounced those who advocated "bourgeois democracy"—Marxism-Leninism's code word for free elections through a secret ballot.

Meanwhile, Fang and his followers called for genuine democratization in the Western sense of the term. In a speech at a Shanghai university, published in *China Spring Digest*'s March–April 1987 issue, he declared that "complete Westernization is the only way to modernize" and emphasized the political dimension of such reforms. "Clearing our minds of all Marxist dogma is the first step," he said. Then he argued that any valid concept of democracy had to be based on human rights:

> Not long ago we asked for [a] democracy not quite different from relaxation of restrictions. However, it is important to note that democracy is quite different from relaxation of restrictions. The critical component to the democratic agenda is human rights, a touchy issue in our country. Human rights are fundamental privileges that people have from birth, such as the right to think and be educated, the right to marry, and so on. But we Chinese consider these rights dangerous. Human rights are universal and concrete, but at present we lump freedom, equality and brotherhood together with capitalism and criticize them all in the same terms. If we are the democratic country we say we are, these rights should be stronger here than elsewhere, but at present they are nothing more than an abstract idea.

After denouncing any concept of democratization that implied "something performed by superiors upon inferiors" and that did not involve accountability of political leaders to the people, he took aim at Beijing's political reforms: "Our government does not give us democracy by loosening our bonds a little. It gives us only enough freedom to writhe." The question of political freedom is thus yet to be faced by the Chinese leaders, and it is bound to be an unsettling issue.

In the meantime, the reconstruction and modernization of communist China will continue to transform both the country and its brand of communism. Unlike the drastic phases of the earlier Communist programs, today's reforms are generally more in keeping with the cultural traditions of the country. Unlike Gorbachev's *perestroika*, they do not go against the grain of historical conditioning. They are also an expression of cultural self-confidence—a distinct Chinese quality—and this permits China to send thirty thousand of their best young people for study abroad without paranoiac fears of ideological contamination. Unlike the Russians, the Chinese, who view themselves not only as a nation but also as a civilization, are not driven by thinly suppressed inferiority complexes toward the West. That enables them to see their own technological backwardness as merely a temporary condition in the five-thousand-year-old and culturally superior civilization. Foreign know-how can thus be assimilated without precipitating deep cultural or ideological anxieties, and without the compulsion to posture in order to hide China's temporary shortcomings.

Two additional and also peculiarly Chinese factors will help the reform program. First, the shift within China toward a less centralized, less collectivistic, and less bureaucratic communism that seeks to revitalize commerce, external trade, and entrepreneurship is likely to exploit a major external asset: the forty million Chinese living overseas. Many are wealthy and are engaged in the kinds of pursuits that the internal reforms seek to nourish. Most retain a special attachment to China and are already responding constructively to opportunities to help in the building of a more modern China. Indeed, in the coastal regions designated for a special foreign presence, overseas Chinese capital is already making its presence felt. That capital investment includes, according to knowledgeable Hong Kong financiers, as much as $15 billion, and perhaps even more, quietly invested in China's export industries by Chinese capitalists from Taiwan. One has to assume that the Communist government in Beijing simply chose to be ideologically open-minded regarding this matter!

Second, the return of Hong Kong to China in 1997 will further reinforce the thrust of change. While Hong Kong will experience many complications in the process of reintegration into a larger and still-communist China, Hong Kong's impact on China will inevitably serve to strengthen the forces of change. It will increase China's global commercial presence, and introduce into China extraordinarily skilled, world-class financial and commercial personnel. It cannot help but strengthen the nonideological impulses in economic policy-making.

Hong Kong's return to China will thus have major economic significance. Within a decade, China will be absorbing a small but vital and extremely wealthy capitalist city-state, with a current GNP of about $40 billion, a world trade of more than $60 billion (or about two-thirds of China's foreign trade), a valuable commercial, industrial, and tourist infrastructure, and a large Chinese-speaking as well as foreign business community. Even allowing for the chance that residual ideological impulses will lead Beijing to try to contain Hong Kong's impact, sheer self-interest will dictate policies that by and large preserve Hong Kong's special role as a commercial and financial center, with its influence and values then inevitably radiating not only into China's maritime region but also into the country at large.

China's government will have one additional reason to be tolerant in its treatment of Hong Kong: its preoccupation with the future of Taiwan. The Chinese passion for reunification stems from the residual resentments over past foreign domination and is inherent in the Chinese sense of nationhood. It remains strong and sincere and is driven more by nationalism than by communism. Chinese Communist leaders must recognize that an ideologically motivated interference with Hong Kong's prosperity—beyond hurting China— would create a further obstacle to any eventual assimilation of Taiwan into some larger, cooperative arrangement with the mainland. To bring about a reunion through accommodation, Deng has openly advocated the possibility of a solution based on the formula of "one state, two systems," which would mean that Taiwan could preserve its highly successful free enterprise socioeconomic system even in the context of a loose reunification. How China handles Hong Kong will thus serve as an object lesson for Taiwan. That makes it doubly important that Hong Kong prosper and flourish after the reunion with China. Inevitably, that also means that Hong Kong's impact on China cannot be arbitrarily contained.

In brief, the existence of a rich overseas Chinese capitalist class that feels kinship with China and the prospective absorption of Hong Kong by China provide truly powerful reinforcement and further stimulus for the changes that China is undergoing. There is nothing analogous in the current Soviet situation. Reformist Chinese leaders are bound to draw political sustenance from these favorable circumstances, specific to China's situation.

Growing compatibility of the increasingly diluted communism with the country's cultural and national traditions is also important in the less easily defined area of values. These are especially important in a country in which a public philosophy of considerable sophistication and depth had for many centuries played an important integrative role. It is impossible to peruse a comprehensive history of China—such as a recently published volume, *The Cambridge History of China*, edited by J. K. Fairbank and Denis Twitchett—without being impressed by the degree to which Chinese society has been permeated and regulated by principles deeply rooted in the Confucian system of both thought and rules. It is the remarkably internalized consciousness of these principles, and the extent of the people's immersion in them, that makes Chinese society so very different from most others, where traditions, habits, and values tend to be less explicit, less defined, and less intellectually systematized.

If Chinese Communist leaders succeed in their present course, they may produce the real cultural revolution in China: a fusion of the traditional values of their people with the cultural dictates of modernity. The former has long stressed the Confucian notions of natural laws, of high-minded motivation and education in the official mandarinate, of social cooperation, harmony, and hierarchy in economic activity, and of respect for age and ancestry. The latter places a premium on innovation, creativity, communication, efficiency, and risk taking. Both also put a high value on individual motivation as the locomotive of change, thereby removing the taint of vice from commercial profit. A future Chinese leader, even one who calls himself a Communist, could well endorse the Confucian classic which Harvard University's China scholar, Roderick MacFarquhar, is fond of quoting: "Possessing virtue will give the ruler the people. Possessing the people will give him the territory. Possessing the territory will give him its wealth. Possessing the wealth, he will have the resources for expenditure. Virtue is the root, wealth is the result."

Under Mao, a head-on collision took place between communism and these more traditional values. With the state acting not as the traditional paternalistic protector of society but as its destroyer, the earlier Great Leap Forward and the Cultural Revolution became unmitigated disasters. In contrast, with the growing complementarity between Deng's pragmatic programs for the future and the more deeply engrained values from the past, today's reforms augur a better tomorrow for China. The result will have profound implications for both China and communism. China will join the front ranks of the world's powers and thus will reclaim for itself its previous status. In the process, however, it will redefine the substance of its communism, with the symbolic ideal no longer represented by an industrial worker toiling in a state-owned steel foundry but a high-tech commercial entrepreneur competing actively on the Pacific rim's international market.

Ideological dilution will be the price of such success. Modern China may enter the twenty-first century still ruled by communism, but it will not be a communized China.

PART V

Discredited Praxis

Fermenting in the Soviet Union, repudiated in Eastern Europe, and more and more commercialized in China, communism has become a globally discredited ideology. Marxist-Leninist "praxis"—the unity of theory and action—no longer commands respect even among party members as a universally valid guide to social reconstruction. As a result, the prospects for the international advance of communism have plummeted.

Around the world, people now equate Soviet-style communism with arrested development. This perception is dominant in both halves of Europe, in the Far East, in Southeast Asia, and in North America. It is also beginning to permeate the perspectives of the opinion leaders in Latin America and Africa. In the more developed parts of the world, including the so-called newly industrializing countries, few see in communism a relevant program for the future. In the developing world, the shortcomings of the Soviet model of development are graphically demonstrated by the fate of the several countries that chose to emulate it. Even China's improving performance cannot compensate for this perception of communist failure because the more recent Chinese economic successes have been accomplished largely by very evident diversions from past communist "praxis."

The new global consensus represents an epochal change and carries devastating political consequences for world communism. Communism today is attractive primarily to those who, frustrated by their underprivileged condition or ethnic suppression, see in it a shortcut to political power. Poverty, backwardness, and ethnic hostility provide the most fertile settings for its appeal. But the notion that communism, once in power, means stagnation and waste is a dramatic reversal of the views preponderant as recently as a mere two decades

189

ago. It involves a massive alteration in political attitudes regarding the critical question of the proper relationship of the individual to society and of society to the state. Ultimately, therefore, the shift in the global perception is one of fundamental philosophy and of basic outlook—and not just of political style or allegiance. It is historic in nature.

The decline in the ideological significance and in the political zest of contemporary communism was poignantly illustrated by an obscure gathering in Prague in mid-April 1988. It brought together representatives from ninety-three Communist or pro-Communist parties worldwide to observe the thirtieth anniversary of the last remaining Soviet-sponsored international Communist organ, the *World Marxist Review*, and to consult together on the state of the Marxist doctrine. The meeting's very obscurity was symbolic. Some years earlier such a meeting would have commanded major attention from the world's mass media. Yet it went unnoted in the Western media and received only some brief and perfunctory notices in the Communist press.

The *World Marxist Review* was all that was left from the more heady days of the Comintern, the central organization of the Communist International, located for about two and a half decades in Moscow, or even from its more limited postwar successor, the Cominform, set up by Stalin to supervise the work of the newly ruling East European Communist parties. But that lingering legacy made the work of the *Review* all the more important to Moscow, for it represented that last formal device for coordinating doctrinal positions and also for updating the common doctrine in changing times. Accordingly, Anatoly Dobrynin, who was then a secretary of the Soviet Central Committee and an important foreign policy adviser to Gorbachev, headed the Soviet delegation. Delegations from the Soviet-dominated East European states were on an equally high level.

The meeting itself, however, was basically a fiasco. The doctrinal debates were tepid, listless, and largely formalistic. Dobrynin spent much of his time propagating Gorbachev's new foreign policy, while on doctrinal issues his major contribution was to foreshadow the approaching demise of the proletariat as the basis for Communist power. As quoted by Prague Television on April 15, 1988, Dobrynin said that "a new technical revolution is starting and it requires the mastering of computer technology and robots. Thus, whether we like it or not, whether we want to or not, we have to restructure the working class too." He was less clear on what the implications of this were for the alleged party of the proletariat, but he did postulate that a further implication of the scientific revolution was that "all human interests have priority" over class interests. From this assertion, he drew the implication that global peace was a higher value than even a socialist revolution, a notion that might not be all that appealing to the more frustrated and radical parties aspiring to power. Since Dobrynin clearly defined peace largely in terms of U.S.-Soviet relations, the somewhat familiar burden of his message—despite the references to the new scientific revolution—was that the revolutionary process had to be subordinated to the interests of the Soviet Union.

Perhaps the most revealing aspect of the conference was conveyed by those who did not attend. The Chinese Communist party, as had been the case for a number of years, totally ignored the entire enterprise, while the world's most influential nonruling Communist party, the Italian Communist party, in the words of the official report, "has sent a letter to the editor of the *World Marxist Review* notifying him of its decision to cut off relations with the journal." Secretary Dobrynin was left to revel with his East European counterparts and with the representatives of such sundry organizations as the Communist party of Saudi Arabia, the Left party–Communists of Sweden, the Communist party of Luxembourg, the Senegal party of Independence and Labour, the Communist party of Nepal, and so forth.

Even the Soviet delegates must have sensed that the event signaled a further stage in the serious deterioration of the global condition of the Communist unity of theory and practice. Communist theory was fragmenting while Communist practice was now widely viewed as a failure. Unintentionally, the meeting thus symbolized the worldwide breakdown of disciplined subordination of the Communist parties to Moscow's control. It also made clear the disappearance of doctrinal uniformity, the broader fading of communism's popular appeal, and the consequent evident decline in the movement's political vitality. All this augured the approaching end of communism as a significant world phenomenon.

CHAPTER 17

From Revolutionary Comintern
to Annual Convention

By the 1980s, the revolutionary Comintern was but a distant memory, but a memory that stood in heroic contrast with the yearly convention of the elderly or at best middle-aged Communist functionaries and sympathizers who now annually assemble in Moscow on the occasion of the November anniversary of the Bolshevik Revolution. When the first session of the Comintern convened in Moscow in March 1919, about a year after the Bolshevik seizure of power, the air was pregnant with revolutionary expectations, despite the civil war still raging in Russia. Those in attendance were genuine revolutionaries, steeled by combat and by prisons. Their mood was optimistic. Ferment was growing in Central Europe, particularly in defeated and demoralized Germany, an advanced industrial society, which seemed historically ripe for the plucking, much in keeping with communism's diagnosis of history. Revolutionary expectations seemed about to be fulfilled, and the new organization—the Communist International—was set up to unite and guide the world revolutionary process.

Expectations rose even higher by the time of the Comintern's second meeting, in the summer of 1920. The new Red Army, which had largely won the civil war, now stood at the gates of Warsaw, and the road to the heart of Europe seemed about to open. Almost at the same time, a congress of oriental peoples was convened in Soviet Baku to raise high the standard of revolutionary war against colonialism, thereby launching a two-pronged offensive against the apparently disintegrating capitalist and colonial world. Flaming oratory of the most flamboyant Bolshevik leaders, such as Trotsky and Zinoviev, dominated the atmosphere at the meetings, and their eloquence reinforced the feeling that communism's international victory was not only inevitable but historically imminent.

Bolshevik revolutionary optimism was palpable. In the first issue of the Comintern periodical, Zinoviev had prophesied, "In a year, Europe will have forgotten about the fight for communism, because all of Europe will be Communist." By the opening of the second congress, he had hedged his optimism only slightly: "Perhaps we have been carried away; probably, in reality, it will need not one year but two or three years before all Europe is one Soviet republic." In presenting the manifesto of the Comintern at the congress, Trotsky proclaimed, "In different countries the struggle is passing through different stages. But it is the final struggle. . . . It is all-embracing and irresistible. It spreads, strengthens and purifies itself; and it is eliminating all the old rubbish. It will not halt before it brings about the rule of the world proletariat." Even Lenin joined in the euphoria, telling some French visitors, "Yes, the Soviets are in Warsaw. Soon Germany will be ours, Hungary reconquered; the Balkans will revolt against capitalism; Italy will shake. Bourgeois Europe is cracking at every seam in the hurricane."

Their confident rhetoric, however, barely screened the more mundane and politically serious efforts by the newly installed Soviet Bolshevik leaders, led by Lenin, to seize effective control over the world Marxist movement. In fact, the Russian Politburo from the start controlled the Executive Committee of the Comintern and insisted that admission into the Comintern required left-wing parties to adopt twenty-one stringent conditions. As a result, Moscow excluded a variety of social democratic and pacifist groups who were sympathetic to the Bolsheviks but less amenable to Bolshevik concepts of discipline and transformed the Comintern into a regimented and sectarian organization.

When Poland defeated the advancing Red Army in the battle of Warsaw in August 1920 and when revolutionary ferment in Germany and elsewhere faded, the Kremlin was forced to reassess communism's more immediate prospects. Lenin and the other Bolshevik leaders necessarily became more preoccupied with the consolidation of their domestic power, first through the New Economic Plan and later through Stalin's decision to build socialism in Russia independent of any direct connection with the world revolutionary process.

These decisions inevitably contributed to the further sovietization of the Comintern. It became increasingly an organ of the Soviet ruling party, closely connected to the Soviet secret police and intelligence apparatus, and dominated at the top by Lenin's and later Stalin's chosen lieutenants.

Stalin made no bones about it. As early as 1927, in a catechist statement, he set the absolutely correct standard for every true Communist. Stalin asserted that "he is a revolutionary, who without reservations, unconditionally, openly and knowingly . . . is ready to protect and defend the USSR, for the USSR is the first revolutionary proletarian state in the world, which is building socialism. He is an internationalist, who without reservations, without wavering, without making conditions, is ready to protect the USSR, because the USSR is the base of the revolutionary movement in the whole world."

Despite the heavy-handed assertion of Soviet control and despite the waning in the immediacy of revolutionary expectations, the Comintern still remained during the 1930s and into World War II for many non-Russian Communists a repository of their communist hopes and the focus of their political loyalty. Directed during the Stalinist era by the colorful Bulgarian revolutionary Georgi Dimitrov and by his Soviet counterpart Dimitry Manuilsky, the organization became a school for the development of a new cadre of leaders, totally disciplined and thoroughly Stalinist in outlook. As these Stalinist disciples replaced many of the more independent-minded foreign Communists whom Stalin had executed during the great purges of the 1930s, the Comintern became both the general staff and the training academy for the Communist leadership that Stalin put in power in East-Central Europe after 1945. Some were parachuted into Eastern Europe with Soviet instructions during the war, and others arrived on the coattails of the victorious Soviet army.

Paradoxically, such effective Soviet control over the Communist movement, as well as the desire to placate the Anglo-Saxon allies, made the Comintern dispensable. In 1943, Stalin ostensibly abolished it. The world was told—and the gullible believed—that the Soviet Union no longer controlled the international Communist movement. However, the centralized Moscow operation continued to be run by Dimitrov and Manuilsky throughout the war, after which Dimitrov himself became the new ruler of Bulgaria. His various Moscow subordinates, such as the NKVD agent Boleslaw Bierut and Comintern officials Klement Gottwald, Matyas Rakosi, and Walter Ulbricht became the heads of Communist-ruled Poland, Czechoslovakia, Hungary, and East Germany, respectively.

As the Cold War heated up, Stalin moved to re-create, on a narrower basis, a more formal instrument of Soviet international control. In 1947, he created the Communist Information Bureau, or the Cominform. Its special focus was the consolidation and integration into the Soviet sphere of the new ruling Communist parties, as well as the shaping of a joint strategy for the more important West European Communist parties, such as the French and the Italian. Some Soviet leaders apparently hoped that these parties might not only be able to accelerate America's disengagement from the continent but even come to power themselves. China's victorious revolution also contributed to a brief reawakening of revolutionary expectations, with the red flag now fluttering over more than one billion people.

Several factors contributed to the Cominform's relatively short life span. It was abolished in 1956, three years after Stalin's death, partly because none of his successors could match the personal prestige of the Communist dictators who had succeeded in winning power on their own, such as Mao in China or Tito in Yugoslavia. Tito had asserted his independence even of Stalin already in the late 1940s, while Mao's own differences with the Kremlin were in the process both of sharpening and of surfacing. In 1956, the Chinese pointedly signaled their support for the aspirations for autonomy of both the Polish and the Hungarian Communist leaders and pressed the post-Stalin Soviet leaders to dilute—if not yet abandon—their claim to the formal leadership of the world movement. They were echoed by the leader of the electorally most successful West European Communist party, Italy's Palmiro Togliatti, who coined the appealing term of "polycentrism" as the alternative to Stalinist centralism.

The Soviet desire to heal the breach with Yugoslavia, to avoid a rupture with China, to retain the Italian party within the fold, and to reduce tensions with such leaders as Władysław Gomułka in Poland, led to a series of gradual but still reluctant concessions. In addition to abolishing the Cominform, Moscow acknowledged in 1956 the right of the ruling parties to adapt the Soviet experience in building socialism to their own specific national conditions, though the Kremlin still inserted the caveat that the Soviet experience had universal validity. In any case, these concessions were made grudgingly, under pressure.

Reflecting the Soviet reluctance to abandon fully its centralist leadership, Khrushchev decided to convene in Moscow in 1957 a grand conference of all Communist parties. He sought to rekindle a greater sense of unity within the world movement and also to revitalize the Soviet control over it. In the course of a speech delivered on July 11, 1957, to the very supine Czech Communist leaders, the Soviet leader explained his goals quite openly: "What do we want? We want unity, closed ranks, and rallied forces. We acknowledge different paths, comrades. But among the different paths, there is one general path, and others are, as you know, like a big river with tributaries. In the same way there are specific peculiarities, but there is only one path, the Marxist-Leninist path."

From the Soviet perspective, the conference was, at best, a mixed success. It was the last major event that brought together not only the Soviet-controlled or pro-Soviet leaders of almost all ruling and nonruling Communist parties but also the Chinese. The Chinese at the time were embarking on their dogmatically motivated Great Leap Forward, and with their help the Soviets succeeded in obtaining the conference's approval (though with the Yugoslavs abstaining) for a condemnation of revisionism. The meeting did not, however, accept the Soviet proposal for an outright condemnation "of those who stress the national peculiarities of each country marching toward socialism" as "profoundly alien to Marxism-Leninism." Instead, it adopted a compromise formula that emphasized "the correctness of the tenet of Marxist-Leninist theory that the processes of the socialist revolution and the building of socialism are governed by a number of basic laws applicable in all countries embarking on the socialist path," while also promptly adding that "these laws are manifested everywhere alongside a great variety of historically formed national features and traditions which should be taken into account without fail."

Several dramatic events that followed the 1957 gathering—which was, in effect, the last gasp both of the Soviet supremacy and of Leninist-Stalinist preponderance in international communism—highlighted and accelerated the historical disintegration of Soviet-dominated Communist unity. In the 1960s, the Sino-Soviet split, which was motivated first by ideological differences and then fueled by the surfacing of deeply rooted nationalist antagonisms, broke into the open. The Soviet military intervention in Czechoslovakia in 1968 provoked widespread condemnation even from Communist parties, while the pronouncement of the Brezhnev doctrine further discredited any Soviet efforts at the promotion of international Communist unity. Not surprisingly, the rise of the Solidarity movement in Poland in the late 1970s was met with open displays of support from the Italian Communist party and some others.

Subsequent Soviet efforts to convene a similar gathering of the world Communist movement and to use it to set a Moscow-defined general line were thus unproductive. The last effort to do so, in 1981, was notable for its political and ideological emptiness. Gradually, the Soviet leaders themselves came to realize that nothing even remotely reminiscent of the Comintern and the Cominform could be resuscitated in the existing setting of ideological diversity, with that diversity intensified by the strong antagonisms among the various national parties. There was simply no predisposition among the world's Communist parties to accept Soviet initiatives designed to restore political and ideological unity, much less a desire for any Soviet-sponsored organization to institutionalize it.

The best that the Kremlin could now do was to use its annual celebration of the Bolshevik Revolution to hold, in effect, a convention of ruling Communist bureaucrats, of international Communist functionaries, and of various left-wing sympathizers, who would gather together in a largely ritualistic salute to their fading revolutionary dreams. The meetings were largely a mixture of ideological sloganeering, of behind-the-scenes haggling with the Kremlin hosts over levels of Soviet financial subsidies, and of gala parades, official receptions, evenings at the ballet, and personalized entertainment provided by the hospitality specialists of the KGB. These conventionlike gatherings contrasted dramatically with the revolutionary puritanism, the doctrinal fervor, and the sense of comradeship in the early, more pristine days of the Communist International, when the Comintern was actively plotting a real worldwide revolutionary strategy even while imposing the Kremlin's "general line" on its disciplined international agents.

The breakdown of discipline and the fading of morale were related directly to the attrition of the Soviet Union's own appeal as a model of socialism to the world's radical Marxists. The uninhibited Soviet admissions of socioeconomic failure, which under Gorbachev's *glasnost* became a veritable flood of self-accusatory condemnations, reinforced the already existing and widely shared view that much of what had transpired in the Soviet Union during the Communist era had been a wasteful and cruel disaster. Denunciation of the Soviet experiment could no longer be equated with hostile anti-communist propaganda. Soviet journals and spokesmen were competing among themselves in exposing a multitude of present shortcomings and in surfacing past crimes.

Soviet spokesmen frankly conceded the resulting drop in the Soviet Union's appeal even to the world's Communists. Writing in the mass-circulation *Izvestia* on July 11, 1987, commentator Aleksandr Bovin flatly stated that the internal Soviet "reversals, contradictions, crises, and stagnation" have discredited the Soviet model, which was once projected by Moscow and viewed by many abroad as deserving of emulation. A mere twenty years earlier, the Soviet system was still considered to be a serious alternative to the American "coca-colonization" of the world, with leading Western left-wing intellectuals, like Jean-Paul Sartre, contrasting Soviet puritanism and idealism to the alleged crass materialism of the transatlantic rival. Soviet leaders themselves at that time were brimming with optimism, with Khrushchev freely dispensing advice in the course of his Third World travels on how best to imitate the Soviet drive for rapid industrialization and modernization.

Twenty years later, the Soviet urban landscape was pockmarked with such features of delayed Americanization as the Pepsi logo or the McDonald's arch. They provided mute testimony to the tacit Soviet acceptance of the status of an inferior and pale imitation of the much more advanced—but once so derided—American consumerist system. Despite ringing ideological pronouncements to the effect that *perestroika* would build a healthier and more creative socialist system, its most tangible social impact involved the visible adoption of techniques and even some cultural modes of the previously denounced rival. This could not help but have a demoralizing impact on the remnants of the faithful who still assemble once a year in Moscow for the ritual of recommitment.

The failure of the Soviet Union as a relevant social model was a most serious blow to the world Communist movement. This explains the desperate search for an alternative focus of admiration. For a while, China seemed the leading candidate, with its apparent idealistic purity and total dedication. But that image faded with the depravities of the Cultural Revolution, with the exposure of Mao Zedong as a mass murderer on a scale at least as large as Stalin, and especially with the expanding scope of Sino-American cultural, economic, and political cooperation. Under those circumstances, China's evolving and occasionally corrupt commercial communism could hardly be viewed as the model for a social revolution.

The remnants of the true believers flirted also for a while with either Vietnam or Cuba, but neither proved capable of generating global appeal. Its postvictory brutalities and economic failure discredited Hanoi, while Fidel Castro's personal dictatorship smacked too much of fascism and depended so heavily on the Soviet dole that it could not offer an independently appealing example. After the Sandinistas took power, Nicaragua became the most recent refuge of the yearning Marxist faithful. But a movement aspiring to global relevance could hardly cite as its viable and generally applicable social model a relatively primitive and rather chaotic rural society of three million people. In the quest for a relevant model, no substitute existed for the Soviet system—a fact that magnified the significance of its failure as the beacon of world communism.

Thus, the sectarian annual convention in the Kremlin provided the sad epitaph for a movement that once proudly called itself the Communist International. Its ritualized proceedings were the tattered remains of its once-claimed universally valid revolutionary "praxis."

CHAPTER 18

Political Irrelevance
in the Developed World

In theory, communism should have been most successful in the developed world. According to classical Marxist doctrine, the socialist revolution should have taken place in developed countries as the historically inevitable consequence of the crisis of capitalism within industrialized society. As late as 1961, the Soviet party was proclaiming, in its newly adopted program, that "the inevitable process of decomposition has engulfed capitalism from top to bottom" and that "the general crisis of capitalism" was underway.

The Soviet proclamation was both explicit and detailed. It stated that

> The general crisis of capitalism finds expression in the following: the continuous defection of new countries from capitalism; the weakening of the position of imperialism in economic competition with socialism; the disintegration of the imperialist colonial system; the aggravation of the contradictions of imperialism with the development of state-monopolistic capitalism and the growth of militarism; the intensification of internal instability and decay of the capitalist economy manifest in the growing inability of capitalism to fully use the productive forces—low rates of production growth, periodic crises, constant failure to utilize production capacities, and chronic unemployment—the mounting struggle between labor and capital; the sharp intensification of the contradictions of the world capitalist economy; the unprecedented intensification of political reaction on all fronts; the rejection of bourgeois freedoms and establishment in a number of countries of tyrannical fascist regimes; and the profound crisis in bourgeois policy and ideology.

200

Not only was this diagnosis wrong, but by the late twentieth century an even more stark proposition stood out: the more advanced the society, the less politically relevant its communist party. This is the central surprise of communism's confrontation with history. While it has failed where it was expected to succeed, it has succeeded—but only in terms of seizing political power—where, according to the doctrine, conditions were said to be historically premature for its success. This paradox ultimately served to deprive communism of its central asset: the sense that it was riding the crest of history, that it represented the future, and that its inevitable triumph was tantamount to human progress. Instead, communism's systemic failure within the socially retarded Soviet Union and its increasing irrelevance to the socioeconomic dilemmas of the much more advanced world signaled its doctrinal obsolescence.

The twentieth century thus did not become the century of communism. Its grand oversimplification could not encompass all the complexities of the advanced society's social structure. This structure did not correspond to Marx's antiquated view of the centrality of the industrial proletariat. Nor could the doctrine provide any meaningful guide for social policies that had to assimilate the creative innovations of ultra-science and high-tech. Moreover, the perversion of Marxism by the contributions of Lenin and Stalin reduced the doctrine to a sterile justification for arbitrary and dictatorial power, thereby further inhibiting its capacity to adapt to changing circumstances. In the democratic setting of the West, where choices were made on the basis of open debate, communism could not withstand the exposure of its manifest irrelevance to modernity.

Belatedly, even Soviet spokesmen came to realize that eclipse of communism in the twentieth century. Writing in the authoritative Soviet philosophical journal *Voprosy Filosofii* in mid-1987, E. Plimak, a scholar in the Moscow Institute of the International Workers' Movement, put it quite correctly: "Even relatively recently, Communists believed that the twentieth century would be the century of the world-wide triumph of socialism . . . this goal is receding into the distant future. The truth is that we underestimated the ability of capitalism to adapt to new conditions . . . we overestimated the speed with which socialism might spread." He was echoed even more pointedly by the previously cited Soviet commentator, Bovin, who abandoned any pretense at historical optimism by flatly declaring, "The prospect of socialist transformations in developed capitalist countries has receded indefinitely."

And so it has. In North America, communism is not even a political movement but a miniscule and aberrant sect, unnoticed in the political processes of either the United States or Canada. Little reason exists to expect this condition to change. Indeed, even during the days of the Great Depression, when the capitalist system sank into crisis and the public sense of its inadequacy was peaked, the Communist movement did not succeed in generating much public support. Not only did the creative response of the existing system, through the New Deal in the United States and through its equivalent in Canada, preempt and disarm the social appeal of communism, but public opinion instinctively sensed that Marxist-Leninist prescriptions were not relevant to the societies in the forefront of social-technological innovation.

Equally instructive, and for communism historically dismaying, is the disappointing condition of communism in Japan. As the country after America that is the furthest along in leaving behind the industrial era and entering the new technetronic age, communism should have made its mark by now. In fact, communism should have had a major chance of success in Japan. The country was devastated in the course of a war waged during the industrial stage of its development. Its postwar recovery revived a large urban working class. Its conflict with America should have left a residue of national antagonism susceptible to ideological exploitation. Last but not least, the tactically expedient—and historically understandable—Japanese allergy to nuclear weaponry provided a superb opportunity for the mobilization of national sentiment by the Japanese Communist party.

Despite these objective and subjective advantages, the Japanese Communist party's electoral strength has not exceeded in the entire postwar period the level of approximately 10 percent. It first attained that plateau in the 1949 election to the lower house. Despite some success in the formal recruitment of dues-paying members—whose rolls rose from about 87,000 in 1961 to about 465,000 in 1985—its relatively limited electoral support has remained stationary ever since. Its high point was reached in 1972, with 10.9 percent of the vote, while in the most recent 1986 contests for the House of Representatives its share dropped to 8.8 percent.

Moreover, this negligible total has been reached through intense efforts to identify Japanese communism with nationalism, not only by appealing to anti-Americanism but also by placing enormous stress on the independence of the Japanese party from either the Soviet or the Chinese Communists. Both of the latter have been explicitly accused by the Japanese Communists of pursuing "hegemonism," and at one point the Japanese party even broke formal relations with each. To cultivate domestic support, the Japanese Communists have loudly denounced the dictatorial traditions of the ruling Soviet and Chinese parties and have sought instead to identify themselves with Western-style social democracy and pacifism. In effect, they purchased their 10 percent share of popular support at the cost of Communist doctrinal unity, while the denunciations of the Soviet Union and China have reinforced the popular image of communism as a systemic failure.

To the great irritation of the Soviets, the Japanese Communists have even embraced the nationalist demand for the restoration to Japan of the northern islands held since World War II by the Soviet Union. The Japanese Communists, moreover, have gone even further than the conservative Japanese government by demanding the restoration not only of the four islands immediately proximate to Hokkaido but also of the entire Kurile Islands chain, which was formally ceded to the Soviet Union in the San Francisco Peace Treaty. In blunt and deliberately nationalistic words, the party's official organ, *Akahata*, on May 26, 1986, stated that these islands "were historically Japanese territories," that the Soviet seizure of them went "against the principles of scientific socialism," and that their "immediate return" was required "in conformity with international justice."

A deeper and perhaps even more troubling message was inherent in the failure of communism in Japan than the lost opportunity to capitalize on the wartime devastation and on the inevitable complications in the American–Japanese relationship. Japan, much like America, was by the 1970s in the forefront of global modernization, pioneering not only in scientific and technological innovation but also, as an inevitable extension of that dynamic, in social development.

It was doing so on the basis of principles regarding private property, free enterprise, political pluralism, and corporate management that epitomized in many ways Marxism's most severe condemnations of capitalism. Japan's system was not only succeeding economically and sustaining a very high degree of popular support, but also clearly setting an example of innovation that even Soviet or Chinese Communist leaders were now citing as in many ways worthy of emulation. This had to be doctrinally disturbing, for it carried the subliminal message that communism had become anachronistic.

If the failure of communism in the United States and in Japan can be assumed to have been historically troubling to the ideologically committed, its failure in Western Europe must have been doctrinally even more galling. According to Marxist tenets, communism should have been a political success in the region where its theories were originated and nurtured and where the theory foresaw conditions historically ripe for the triumph of the Marxist revolution. True believers could perhaps rationalize the failure in the United States and Japan as the result of the allegedly unique, hence doctrinally inapplicable, circumstances of these two countries. They could attribute the premature revolution in Russia to the Bolshevik strategy of snapping the weakest link in the chain of imperialism—a success which was then historically consolidated by Stalin's determination to build "socialism in one country." Still the construction of socialist society should have first occurred in Western Europe, the classical example of capitalist industrialization and the showcase of capitalism's inevitable and fatal contradictions.

Instead, by the end of the twentieth century communism in Western Europe is becoming, quite literally, not only obsolescent as a social program but also irrelevant politically. This is even true of the countries where in the wake of World War II, communism should have had a second chance, a spurt of vitality, and a renewed opportunity to come to power. In Italy, in France, and on the Iberian peninsula, the doctrinal polarization generated by the struggles against the fascist right should have benefited the most militant party of the left. In each of these countries, the unfinished process of capitalist industrialization favored the emergence of an increasingly class-conscious proletariat, politically attracted by the example of the Soviet Union. In each of these countries, the intellectual class was

disaffected from the status quo, tempted by cultural anti-Americanism, inclined at least to flirt with Marxism and in many cases even
to embrace it with intellectual enthusiasm. The setting, the conditions, and the timing were doctrinally perfect.

Yet the political record has again been one of failure. In Italy, the
Communist party (PCI) emerged from the war with enormously high
prestige and became the second largest party, commanding at its high
point more than one-third of the popular vote. By the mid-1970s, it
seemed ready, if not to assume power directly, then to share it through
a coalition with some of the non-Communist parties. The PCI personified the new phenomenon of Eurocommunism—a more refined
and moderate version of communism which was ideologically and
politically sophisticated enough to assume power in more mature
social and economic conditions.

But this did not happen. Instead, the progressive transformation
of Italian society, generated by the steady growth of the Italian economy, and the related rise in Italy's international prestige and self-
confidence contributed to the decline of the extreme left. The party's
fortunes hit a plateau and then gradually started to wane. From a
peak of 34.4 percent of the vote obtained in the general elections of
1976, the party's support gradually declined to 26.6 percent in the
general elections of 1987 and to 21.9 percent in the municipal elections of 1988. Even more suggestive of its dim prospects was the fact
that by the mid-1980s it could not attract large numbers of young
people. Among youth, the proportion who joined the PCI was only
half that of the population as a whole. In fact, no less than 21 percent
of its members were pensioners. Moreover, 40 percent of the membership originated from the traditional industrial sector at a time
when Italy's service sector was undergoing a major expansion. The
party thus represented Italy's past.

Compounding the problem was the fact that the party has been
able to obtain this respectable, though declining, popular support
largely thanks to its undisguised repudiation of much of what Soviet-
style communism has come to represent and to advocate. The party's
political decline would undoubtedly have been much more rapid if
it had not engaged in its highly publicized condemnations of Stalinism, of the Soviet invasion of Czechoslovakia, and even of Moscow's
Leninist tenets, while at the same time extending public support to

the Polish Solidarity movement and to other dissident activities in the Soviet sphere.

In effect, Italian communism averted its political demise, though it failed to prevent its political decline, by increasingly adopting the stance and the doctrines of once-condemned social democracy. It purchased political survival at the cost of doctrinal heresy. It not only abandoned Stalinism by its advocacy of "polycentrism" and its condemnations of the Soviet intrusions into Czechoslovakia and Afghanistan, but also increasingly deviated from the Leninist notions of strict internal discipline and doctrinal homogeneity. The Italian Communist party thus survived at the cost of wider Communist unity—publicly condemning the Soviet experiment as a historical failure while politically and ideologically embracing revisionism.

Unlike the Italian party, the misfortunes of the French Communist party (PCF) are rooted in large degree in its tactical and doctrinal inflexibility. It has remained both Stalinist and Leninist and has paid a high political price. The French party, like the Italian, was poised on the brink of political success immediately after World War II. Since wartime dislocations had intensified the socioeconomic tensions of France's somewhat delayed industrialization, the Communist appeal was certainly enhanced. Indeed, in 1948, the party stood as the single largest unified political force in France, seemingly ready to take power either through a confrontation or by electoral victory.

Instead, recent years have seen the PCF's precipitous decline to a condition of political marginality and doctrinal irrelevance. Outmaneuvered politically on the left by the resurgent French socialists, and with the French center-right benefiting from the country's economic and technological growth, the French Communists have found themselves increasingly viewed by the electorate as not relevant to their social concerns. In the 1973 and 1978 parliamentary elections, the PCF obtained 21.1 percent and 20.5 percent of the vote, respectively. In the 1981 presidential vote, it drew 16.1 percent of the electorate. In the 1986 parliamentary elections, its share fell to 9.8 percent. And in the 1988 presidential contest, it attracted a mere 6.8 percent of the total votes cast.

There is little reason to expect the French Communist party to regain its former preeminence. Its formal membership has drastically declined, as have the rolls of the Communist-dominated trade unions.

The restructuring of the French economy away from heavy industries has undercut the areas of traditional PCF strength. In economically dynamic areas, the party's losses have been the greatest, while France's economically ossified regions remain its last redoubt. Moreover, by focusing on the traditional industrial working class as the central historical actor, the PCF has undermined its own appeal to the rest of the French society, which during the last decade and a half has been undergoing an exceptionally rapid modernization. The most troubling prospect is the low regard in which young French voters hold the PCF, with only 3 percent preferring it over all the alternatives.

The collapse of the Communist mystique among the French intellectuals has contributed to the general decline in the appeal of Marxism in France. Once the dominant school of thought in the academy, in the French salons, and on the intellectually vibrant Parisian Left Bank, Marxism by the late 1970s had come to be viewed by those who shape the currents of French thought as largely passé and banal. Its place has been taken by a fascination with the implications for society of new techniques of communications and the processes not only of pluralistic democracy but even of free enterprise. French socialists scored their electoral gains by skillfully adapting to this mood. In contrast, the French Communists seemed still wedded to antiquated Stalinism and Leninism. In a country in which the intellect has a special political standing, the discrediting of communism as history's intellectually innovative tool was especially costly. In France of the mid-1980s, it was no longer socially fashionable or intellectually respectable to be a Communist.

The third area of Western Europe where a communist party also once stood a serious chance of coming to power was the Iberian peninsula. In both Spain and Portugal, the combination of social retardation and the internal decay of their quasi-fascist regimes appeared to offer the most fertile setting for the emergence of Communist power. Indeed, the conditions seemed almost designed to fit the classical Marxist formula: early industrialization, primitive capitalist ruling classes, reactionary right-wing political elites, intense social inequality and deprivation—as well as emerging and increasingly politically self-conscious industrial proletariats led by experienced and disciplined Communist parties, steeled by their

underground struggles. Political success in France and in Italy should
have been accompanied by political triumphs in Spain and in Portugal. Yet communism fared no better there.

The bitter struggle against the neo-fascist regime of Franco had
not only gained for the Spanish Communist party (PCE) widespread
international and domestic support but also permitted the party to
acquire an efficient underground organization. When the Franco
regime faded from the scene and the transition to democracy was
underway, the Spanish Communist party was well positioned to become the chief beneficiary of the political change. Instead, once it
had surfaced into the open daylight of renewed electoral politics, the
PCE promptly split into contending factions, reflecting the wider
doctrinal rifts in the international Communist movement. Its dominant faction tried to compete with the Spanish social democrats by
dropping Leninism from its platform and by seeking to combine its
continued adherence to Marxism with an explicit commitment to
democracy.

The Spanish people, however, remained skeptical, especially since
the memories of Communist terror during the Spanish civil war
remained relatively fresh. Moreover, the efforts of the PCE to identify
itself as the party of the democratic left worked to the advantage of
the Spanish Socialists, who could not be outbid in their adherence
to democracy. As a result, between the mid-1970s and the mid-
1980s, the Socialist vote climbed from about 30 percent to about 45
percent, while the Communist vote declined from about 10 percent
to less than 5 percent. As happened to their comrades in Italy and
France, the Spanish Communists also became increasingly marginal
as a political force.

A similar fate has befallen the Portuguese Communists. As in
Spain, it initially appeared that the Portuguese Communists were
destined to succeed. The end of the Salazar dictatorship had ushered
in a period of political instability in Portugal, which led some Western
observers in the mid-1970s to go so far as to write off Portugal as a
lost cause. The socialist successor to Salazar, Mário Soares, was
widely described as Portugal's "Kerensky," certain to be swallowed
up by the intensifying social chaos of which the Communists were
destined to be the political beneficiaries. Instead, the Portuguese
Socialists, benefiting from the active support of their West European

comrades, were able gradually to preempt the Communist appeal, to isolate the Portuguese Communists as doctrinal fanatics, to undercut their support in the rural areas by timely land reforms, and by the end of the 1970s to contain the Communist appeal at a high-water mark of just under 20 percent of the vote and then to push it down to about 12 percent by the mid-1980s.

In both Spain and Portugal, entry as full-fledged democracies into the European community also ignited a genuine sense of historical optimism among not only the intellectual and business elites but even among the masses. It created the feeling that a new era of opportunity and of rapid modernization was at hand, and that new spirit also worked to deprive the communist doctrine of much of its popular appeal. Increasingly, in these countries communism was seen neither as relevant to existing social dilemmas nor as a source of guidance for coping with the emerging problems of the future.

Elsewhere in advanced Europe, communism has become even less politically and doctrinally relevant. In Britain, it has largely disappeared, with the party rolls listing only ten thousand members. Its magazine, *Marxism Today*, has been able to gain a certain degree of intellectual respectability by regularly denouncing "ossified socialism" and by engaging in serious discussions of such once heretical notions as "market socialism" and "international competitiveness." In Scandinavia and West Germany, communism is no longer a political factor even worthy of notice. As in America, it is only a small and aberrant sect. In all of non-Communist Europe, of the twenty-two legal Communist parties, only nine received more than 5 percent of the vote in the most recent elections and only five more than 10 percent.

On the continent where Marxism originated, the Communist movement is today just a relic of that continent's first encounter with industrialization and a victim of the pervasive appeal of pluralist democracy.

CHAPTER 19

Socioeconomic Failure
in the Developing Countries

Though communism has been more successful in gaining political power in several underdeveloped countries, it has proven to be a systemic failure in all of them. Socioeconomic policies modeled on the Soviet Union have not produced the desired development and modernization. Over the last decade, such repeated failures have fostered a wider disillusionment in the Third World, not only with the Soviet example but with the communist doctrine itself.

Initially, it appeared that the post–World War II anti-colonial wave might be dominated by the Marxist praxis, creating an irresistible dynamic in the Third World in the direction of Soviet-led communism. That was certainly Khrushchev's expectation during the late 1950s and early 1960s. The Soviet Union seemed to be on the historical march, expecting soon to leapfrog the United States in the economic competition, while its experience in the "construction of socialism" was being hailed as universally applicable. Khrushchev proclaimed this message with great fervor to appreciative audiences in Indonesia, India, and in various African countries.

During this phase of communism's historical optimism, the Soviet leaders also revised their traditional notion of the world divided into two hostile camps, the encircled socialist camp—led by the Soviet Union—and the aggressive imperialist camp—led by the United States—with the latter effectively dominating directly and indirectly the less developed zones of the world. Accepting decolonization as an important and new historical development, and claiming that the major impetus for it came from the Leninist doctrine and from the support provided by the Soviet Union, Khrushchev propounded the

210

argument that the newly liberated countries now represented a "zone of peace" that itself could make a relatively rapid transition to socialism. The Soviet Union would aid the process by grants of military and economic assistance, by friendly ideological guidance based on the Soviet experience, and by deterring the imperialists from obstructing the inevitable progression toward full-blown socialism. The eventual result would be an encircled capitalist camp.

Although initially none of the leaders of the new states that Khrushchev was courting formally accepted the precepts of Marxism-Leninism, and although none proclaimed their regimes to be headed toward communism, socialism as the desired mode of socioeconomic organization gained considerable support during the first postcolonial phase of independent statehood. In different ways, the new governments of such major countries as India or Indonesia and of the new African states adopted some form of state socialism as the norm, though in every case insisting that they were blending it with their own specific national cultures. The leader of West Africa's new state of Guinea, Sékou Touré, responding to Khrushchev, expressed that mood when he stated, "The Marxism which served to mobilize the African populations, and in particular the working class, has been amputated of those of its characteristics which did not correspond to the African realities."

Nonetheless, the new leaders did find the Soviet support helpful and were inclined to flirt with Soviet-propagated doctrines, especially for political reasons. They were particularly attracted by Leninist techniques for the seizure and maintenance of power, and the concept of a disciplined and hierarchical ruling party was especially appealing to the new generation of rulers interested in perpetuating their personal authority. They quickly realized that Leninism's militarized approach to politics served their needs well, while some adaptation of the Soviet ideology would also buttress their power by providing a historical legitimation—namely, rapid development through socialism—for their nondemocratic rule.

Political expediency thus reinforced the intellectually fashionable preference for some form of socialism as the basis for nation building and as the shortcut to modernity. But the fashion did not last long, and the Soviet appeal proved to be quite transitory. In two major new countries, India and Indonesia, Soviet leaders invested much time and effort, but indigenous political circumstances effectively preempted the Communist appeal. In India, the Congress party, for all of its shortcomings and its flirtation with the socialist ideas of Harold Laski and the London School of Economics, maintained parliamentary institutions and remained committed to a mixed economic system. In Indonesia, the revolutionary impatience of the Indonesian Communist party precipitated in 1965 an armed collision with the army, resulting in the total physical liquidation of Indonesian communism.

For a while, Africa and Latin America looked more promising for the adoption of Communist programs. In Africa, radical tendencies were naturally intensified by the inherent racism of the colonial experience, and in southern Africa by the reality of institutionalized racism in South Africa itself. At the same time, the weaker and less homogeneous national identity of the newly liberated peoples enhanced the importance of a unifying doctrine to the new political leaderships. The appeal of the Marxist grand oversimplification was inevitably stronger in countries which badly wanted to leapfrog into modernity but which lacked strong intellectual and cultural traditions for formulating their own historical visions. Last but not least, since most of the African countries were smaller than India or Indonesia, the prospect of even limited Soviet economic assistance appeared more decisively important.

In the 1970s, several African countries thus embraced Marxism as their doctrine and proclaimed themselves to be engaged in the task of building socialism. Six—Angola, Mozambique, Madagascar, the Congo, Benin, and Ethiopia—even went so far as to adopt Marxism-Leninism as their guiding framework and stressed their fidelity to the broad outlines of the Soviet experience in building socialism. Nine others—Algeria, Libya, Cape Verde, Guinea-Bissau, Guinea, São Tomé and Principe, Zambia, Tanzania, and the Seychelles— became self-avowed socialist regimes, though stressing the centrality of their own national conditions in the actual implementation of socialist goals and avoiding any explicit identification with Leninism. All of them, however, did elevate the state into the central organ of socioeconomic change and organized political power around a single dominant and militarized party.

Reality proved unkind, however, both to the native, and somewhat naive, socialist hopes and to Soviet expectations. The levels of Soviet economic aid were inadequate to influence decisively internal economic development. Local mismanagement, corruption, and the dislocations caused by the abrupt rupture of economic relations with the former colonial powers produced in most of these countries large-scale economic failures. The richer ones, like Libya, or those with a more developed political tradition, like Algeria, moved rapidly toward the definition of more indigenous programs of social development. Algeria, for example, resumed a more cooperative economic relationship with the previously dominant colonial power, France. Others simply stagnated, while some, notably Angola and Mozambique, were further devastated by tribal and political conflicts, in which one side invited East bloc assistance and the other received South African aid.

In brief, the Communist record in Africa involved limited political success, marred by demonstrable systemic failures. The famine in Ethiopia was undeniably made worse by the incompetence and ruthlessness of the "socialist" regime, which even used starvation as a means for crushing internal opposition. In the neighboring east coast African state of Tanzania, economic stagnation contrasted negatively with the relative progress made by adjoining Kenya, which had adopted a much less doctrinally determined path of economic development. Kenyan agricultural production has grown at a rate four times greater than that of Tanzania, where communal agricultural programs have resulted in a massive failure. From 1980 to 1985, Kenya's GNP has grown at an average annual rate of 3.1 percent, while Tanzania's has increased by only .8 percent each year. During the same period, Kenya's industrial production rose 2.0 percent annually, while Tanzania's dropped 4.5 percent per annum. Kenya has also surged ahead in social indicators, such as infant mortality, health care, and education. On the west coast, one of the last acts of President Sékou Touré of Guinea before his death was to visit in 1980 the president of the United States in order to plead not only for economic assistance but also for guidance in economic development, while eloquently denouncing as misguided his own earlier reliance on the Soviets in seeking to build an African socialist state.

More generally, by the 1980s the very notion of socialist development, an idea with which the Soviet Union could identify and thereby benefit politically, was increasingly discredited in much of the Third World. Asia led the way in economic development, but in a demonstrably nonsocialist fashion. Those countries that took the Communist path—Vietnam, Laos, and Cambodia—represented spectacular examples of socioeconomic failure. Despite $2 billion of Soviet economic aid each year, Vietnam cannot produce enough food to feed its own people, with rice production actually falling for two successive years. Hanoi, in asking for foreign assistance, claimed 4 million people were now "near starvation." Its inflation rate stood at 700 percent. The government has defaulted on almost all of its foreign debt of $3 billion, while foreign exchange reserves dropped to a mere $20 million. Today, many of Vietnam's "boat people," who used to flee mainly for fear of political or ethnic persecution, set out to sea for purely economic reasons. Meanwhile, nearby non-Communist Thailand is enjoying an economic boom. With an average annual GNP growth rate in the 1980s of about 5 percent, and with a 9 percent increase projected for 1988, the Thais easily surpassed all other Southeast Asian nations and have positioned themselves to join the ranks of the newly industrializing countries in the 1990s.

In Africa, the remaining islands of socialist commitment were either stagnating or seeking to disengage from their socialist commitment. The drive toward privatization was gaining momentum in almost every one of the African countries that had once embarked on the Soviet-oriented road toward state socialism. After a quarter century of independence, many "socialist" countries in the developing world were poorer in terms of per capita gross national product than they had been at the outset.

The retreat in Africa from the Soviet-influenced notions of development has occurred on a wide front. In the tiny state of São Tomé and Principe, one of the first official acts upon reaching independence in 1975 was the nationalization of the country's vital economic resource, its cocoa plantations. A decade later, its East German–trained president was announcing the government's desire to sell the now unproductive plantations to private owners. Tanzania was following suit in the milling and tourist industries and was loosening its reins on agriculture. In Angola, money-losing state companies were to be sold to private bidders, and similar announcements were made during 1986–88 by the regimes of Benin, the Congo, and Ghana, as well as those of some of the otherwise less socialistically

inclined African states. Indeed, the growing danger was that some
of the African states, burned by their experimentation with Soviet-
style economics, were now overly inclined to find quick salvation in
the opposite method.

The failure of communism in Africa impacted inevitably on Soviet
policy. Moscow's policy gradually became more selective and geostrategic, less doctrinally motivated and less focused on economic
assistance. Already during the 1970s, the Soviet Union started to
reduce drastically its economic aid to the would-be African socialist
states, concentrating instead on key targets of strategic opportunity
—such as Angola or Ethiopia—which were related more to the geopolitical competition with the United States than to a wider expectation of a continental ideological triumph. Both of these states,
however, paid a high price for remaining the continued objects of
Soviet attention, with Ethiopia languishing as one of the world's
poorest countries (with a per capita GNP of only $110) and with
Angola torn apart by a civil war sustained by a Cuban military contingent of fifty thousand men financed and supplied by the Soviet
Union.

The Soviet trend toward geopolitical selectivity continued and accelerated during the 1980s. Soviet preoccupation with domestic reforms coincided with rising Soviet historical pessimism regarding the
short-term prospects for world communism. As a result, by the mid-
1980s, Soviet experts on Africa were encouraging their clients to
solve their economic problems by integrating themselves with world
markets and by attracting foreign investment, clearly signaling thereby
that the Kremlin was not about to foot their development bills. The
encounter of Africa with communism had thus bred mutual disillusionment.

The communist experience in Latin America also proved disappointing from the standpoint of the Marxist praxis. Neither in theory
nor in practice did the situation evolve the way Soviet or Latin American Communists might have expected. To be sure, from the strategic
point of view, the Communist victories in Cuba in the late 1950s and
in Nicaragua in the late 1970s represented important breakthroughs.
A Communist foothold was established, and sustained, in the Western
Hemisphere. That the region's preponderant imperialist power
proved impotent in the face of this challenge was undeniably a his-

torically significant development. It demonstrated that Soviet-backed regimes could be established under the very nose of the world's most powerful capitalist state, potentially serving as communism's Piedmont in the larger quest for a revolutionary transformation of the Latin American continent as a whole.

That revolutionary transformation seemed warranted both by the specific circumstances of the region, notably by its difficult relationship with the economically dominant neighbor to the north and by the apparent fit of the classical Marxist doctrine to the region's socioeconomic conditions. Although any sweeping generalizations regarding a large and highly varied continent require many qualifications, in broad terms contemporary Latin America approximates the conditions that first gave rise to the Marxist analysis. Its rural economy has been based on a largely feudal system, with the owners of enormous *latifundios* relying on the labor of landless peasantry, in some cases of badly treated, often semi-literate Indian stock. Its rapidly expanded urban centers contain heavy concentrations of unemployed or underemployed displaced peasants, emerging and increasingly politically assertive middle classes, and socially parasitic but often politically dominant bureaucratic-military elites. Its economic development has been most uneven, containing in some cases within individual states examples of rapid industrial and technological innovation and of the most primitive and socially benighted rural sectors. Compounding the difficulties of the continent's overall development has been the vulnerability of several of its national economies to the vagaries of the world's commodity markets as well as the crushing indebtedness produced by the inflow of petrodollars during the 1970s. Finally, the demographic explosion, with population growth rates among the highest in the world, has been placing the existing social structures under enormous and potentially catastrophic pressures.

A classical Marxist revolutionary situation should have, therefore, arisen in at least several Latin American countries. Moreover, the emotional and intellectual impetus for it should also have been provided by an additional radicalizing ingredient peculiar to Latin America: the region's intense and quite widespread anti-Americanism. Though that sentiment varied in intensity from country to country, and though only Mexico, Cuba, and the Central American states had

been most directly victimized by American expansionism and interventionism, by and large all Latin American societies were susceptible, particularly among their intellectuals and students, to an anti-
American perspective that blended nationalism with Marxism. The
United States was viewed not only as expansionist, exploitative, and
domineering, but also culturally crass, vulgar, and crudely materialistic. Among opinion makers, the fashionable anti-American formulas were quite reminiscent of the views that had some decades
ago dominated the left-wing salons of Paris.

In the most revolutionary sense, that feeling was best expressed
by the continent's most glamorous and charismatic figure, Che Guevara, who proclaimed the United States—in a simple but compelling
phrase—to be "the great enemy of mankind." More than Fidel Castro, Guevara became in the late 1960s and the 1970s the symbol of
a revolution that in his view, to succeed, had to be not only social
but also anti-American. Guevara, restless after the success of the
Cuban revolution and convinced that a wider regional revolution was
now possible, felt that the moment was ripe for militantly exploiting
these two motivations. In his view, all that was wrong with the status
quo was ultimately buttressed, and exploited, by America. Hence,
any genuine revolutionary struggle had to be focused on the central
enemy. That was the underlying theme of the romantic revolutionary
guerrilla activity that was pursued in those years in Bolivia, in Ven-
ezuela, and to a lesser extent in other countries.

This revolutionary fervor faded somewhat with Guevara's capture
and execution in Bolivia in 1967. Neither the Soviets nor Castro
actually shared Guevara's revolutionary romanticism. Both were determined, for good and expedient reasons, first to consolidate communism's new base in the Western Hemisphere before risking all in
a broad revolutionary quest. But the legacy of Guevara's indictment
of the United States, and his linkage of the social revolution to the
struggle against the United States, continued to have political impact
and formed the basis for any longer-range strategy of advancing the
cause of communism in Latin America.

Guevara's legacy—as well as Soviet hopes—received for a while
a massive and politically potent infusion of vitality through the appearance of "liberation theology," a doctrine that blended Marxist
analysis of capitalist evils with Christian compassion for the down-

trodden. American capitalism again personified the evil that had to
be expunged. It established, according to the theory, the condition
of "dependency" for Latin America, which in turn perpetuated the
social and personal degradation of the impoverished Latin American
masses. The doctrine took its name from the best-selling book by
the Catholic theologian Gustavo Gutiérrez, *A Theology of Liberation*,
published in 1971, which struck a most responsive chord on a
continent beset by social problems, imbued with a strong dose of
anti-American sentiment, and spiritually dominated by the Roman
Catholic church. As Gutiérrez put it, for Latin America, "oppressed
and dominated, the word *liberation* is appropriate, rather than development. . . . And for many in our continent, this liberation will
have to pass, sooner or later, through the paths of violence."

Liberation theology in this manner provided also the moral justification for revolutionary violence. A bridge was thereby created
between the Christian sense of outrage against moral evil and the
Leninist advocacy of disciplined revolutionary action. It made itself
felt in the course of the revolutionary upheavals in Nicaragua and El
Salvador, where devoted Communists and radicalized priests served
arm-in-arm, and more broadly in the widely shared view that revolutionary action was not only a moral impulse but, indeed, a moral
imperative. On the simplest popular level, it was illustrated by a story
recounted by another liberation theologian, José Miguez Bonino, of
a play staged in a Protestant church in an Uruguayan shantytown.
One actor asks, "Who, then, is Jesus Christ?" Another responds,
"For us, Jesus Christ is Che Guevara."

Given the fortuitous parallelism of the Marxist doctrine and of the
liberation theology, both of which were fueled by anti-Yankee sentiments, in a setting dominated by the material plight of the Latin
American masses and perpetuated not only by a discriminatory social
structure but also by an almost permanent economic crisis, it is
remarkable how unsuccessful Communist efforts have been to advance the revolutionary process. The establishment of Marxist-Leninist regimes in Cuba and in Nicaragua does not refute that
conclusion. The first is an isolated Caribbean island, which was
actually one of the more developed Latin American societies at the
time of the Communist seizure of power. The second is a small,
largely peasant Central American country. The revolutions in both

were motivated by highly bitter memories of direct U.S. interventionism. That national memory was more important as the source of political radicalism than was the appeal of Marxism, and the consolidation of communism in both was facilitated by American errors, hesitation, and lack of consistent policy.

Communism, however, should have made more political progress elsewhere, exploiting the rural and urban crisis inherent in the continent's nascent industrialization. According to Marxist doctrine, that stage of social development should produce the sharpest class contradictions, which should be susceptible to exploitation by the communist party. Yet neither legal nor illegal Communist activity has achieved a political breakthrough. Attempts at either urban or rural guerrilla warfare have failed, while the gradual democratization of Latin American politics has revealed the surprisingly limited Communist electoral appeal.

In fourteen recent national elections held in various Latin American countries during the 1980s, the best result obtained by the Communists (in some cases competing through parties not officially designated as Communist) was 26 percent of the vote in Peru and 17 percent in Guyana. Elsewhere, their total votes ranged from approximately 3 percent to 5 percent. In such key countries as Argentina and Brazil, their electoral strength was at the lower end of the spectrum, though in Brazil not one but two Communist parties competed, one pro-Soviet and one pro-Albanian! (The latter scored an electoral coup by obtaining the highest individual vote total for one of its candidates, twenty-nine-year-old Dr. Jandira Fegnalli, widely admired in her bikini as the sex symbol of Copacabana beach.) Communists did much better in the two elections that they themselves conducted: In Nicaragua they claimed to have obtained 63 percent of the vote and in Cuba 100 percent.

Several reasons lie behind this Communist failure. In recent years, the United States had adopted a somewhat more enlightened approach toward Latin America, particularly by identifying itself with the ideal of human rights. This not only helped to advance the cause of democracy in Latin America but also distanced the United States from the fading personal right-wing dictatorships. More important, however, was the rise of indigenous democratic forces, which were increasingly able to blend their quest for personal freedom with the advocacy of needed social reforms. The return of democracy to several leading Latin American countries helped to defang the revolutionary appeal. As a result, even some radical liberation theologians have come to identify social change with democratic values, seeing in the latter the fulfillment of their revolutionary aspirations while increasingly repudiating the Manichaean Communist vision.

Contributing to that fundamental change of mood has been the charismatic impact of the new pope, John Paul II, as well as the manifest decline in the attraction of Soviet-type "socialism." In the course of a visit to Latin America in January 1979, the pontiff remarked, "Ah, yes, liberation theology, but *which* liberation theology?" In this now famous comment, he was in effect setting out to recapture for the church the spiritual monopoly of the struggle against social evil, divesting liberation theology of its Marxist connection. In subsequent teachings and encyclicals, John Paul undeniably made strides in fashioning a de facto alliance between the moral impulse for a radical reconstruction of unjust societies with the promotion of pluralistic and democratic social change. On a continent with a rich Catholic tradition, this had a significant political impact. It reinforced the legitimacy of pluralist democracy and delegitimized the Marxist message.

At the same time, the direct political impact of the internal Soviet crisis should also not be underestimated. By the late 1970s, the Soviet model was rapidly losing its credibility. Subsequently, Gorbachev's own denunciations of Soviet failures provided additional confirmation for the most severe and critical foreign assessments of the Soviet experience. Moreover, since the conventional wisdom of Latin America's intelligentsia was very susceptible to views emanating from Paris, the emergence in recent years of a new consensus in France that the Soviet Union represented an example of arrested social development and that its state socialism was intellectually stifling further undercut the appeal of communism.

Contributing to the disenchantment with communism were the specific cases of Cuba and Nicaragua. Once the initial burst of enthusiasm for Fidel Castro's anti-American self-assertion had passed, Latin Americans became more aware of the actual social and economic failure of the Cuban revolution. Despite annual Soviet subsidies of about $5 billion, Cuba's economy has stagnated, with virtually all sectors of the economy failing to meet production goals. In 1986, Castro announced a cancellation of payments on Cuba's approximately $3.5 billion foreign debt and asked for a new twelve-year repayment plan with a six-year grace period. One of Cuba's main sources of hard currency has become reexports of Soviet oil, which Havana receives at a subsidized price and resells at the world price. At the same time, with sugar production lagging far below production targets, Cuba has been forced to buy hundreds of thousands of tons on the world market in order to meet its annual Comecon sugar quota.

This economic disaster has resulted from Castro's persistent adherence to Stalinist central planning. A bloated bureaucracy of 250,000 now manages an economy with a work force of only 3 million. In a major address at the Third Party Congress in 1986, Castro denounced a series of typical Communist economic irrationalities:

> . . . new industrial and agricultural facilities built in unpopulated areas, without housing facilities for the work force; very important agricultural programs—such as for citrus—where there are still sown areas without irrigation; irrigation projects which cannot be put into operation because they lack pumping facilities or electrical power; work shops and other facilities built without electrical hook-ups; housing developments built without urban amenities [i.e., roads and commercial and recreational facilities]. . . . We have the case of the central railroad, in which we have invested hundreds of millions of pesos without being able to exploit it efficiently since signals, loading and unloading areas, stations, etc., have not been completed.

Castro later told the Central Committee he had compiled a book of "economic irregularities" in which "every paragraph is a calamity."

Much the same was the case with Nicaragua. The economic incompetence of the Sandinista leaders and the militarization of the country created wartimelike deprivation. In early 1988, a can of imported pineapple slices cost a Nicaraguan earning an average salary about 20 percent of his monthly pay. A pair of trousers would cost almost an entire month's salary. Managua had no running water two days a week, and daily three-hour blackouts were the norm. Foreign debt rose from $1.6 billion to $7 billion. Inflation raged at an estimated 1800 percent in 1987, with real wages plummeting by 90 percent, and some economists predicted a possible hyperinflation of 10,000 percent in 1988.

Even more damning was the rapidly spreading awareness in the late 1970s and early 1980s of Cuba's miserable record on human rights. The fact that this island, with a population of only 10 million, contained more political prisoners than all of the other Latin American countries combined could not be indefinitely suppressed. The personal accounts of individual mistreatment in Cuban prisons—notably the much read story of his twenty-year-long imprisonment by Armando Valladares, *Against All Hope*—had a wide-ranging impact. They diminished Castro's personal stature and reinforced the image of communism as ultimately a repressive and dehumanizing system. The rising concern over Cuban violations of human rights had a special impact on the morally sensitive circles influenced by the liberation theology, contributing to the further intellectual and political isolation of Marxism.

The political future of Latin America is far from resolved, given the massive scale of its social and economic problems. The continent is undergoing revolutionary changes that are bound to produce sudden discontinuities and major upheavals. In the near future, communism may have better prospects in Central America and perhaps Mexico than elsewhere. Marxist-Leninists there can take advantage of the anti-American, nationalist, and radical impulses of significant portions both of the local intelligentsia and peasantry. Stepped up insurgency in El Salvador is likely to be replicated by intensified guerrilla activities in adjoining countries, Honduras and Guatemala. In both countries, favorable conditions for revolutionary action exist. The failure of the U.S. efforts either to accommodate or to unseat the Sandinista regime in Nicaragua, matched by the subsequent mishandling of the relationship with Panama, has generated in Central America a widespread sense that U.S. influence is receding and that the void can be filled by more radical regimes, enjoying Moscow's protection against U.S. intervention.

Accordingly, it is to be expected that the Soviet Union and Cuba will both encourage revolutionary trends in the region. They will do so cautiously, for they are aware of American sensitivities on this score, but they are not likely to ignore such tempting revolutionary opportunities. A widening revolution in Central America would provide historical validation for Castro's sense of his historical mission. From Moscow's point of view, it would serve as a valuable geopolitical distraction for its principal rival, the United States, while at the same time reviving Moscow's own rather flagging doctrinal optimism. In any case, Soviet strategists must view the region as the soft underbelly of the United States, and they are unlikely to resist any temptation to fan the region's revolutionary flames.

Ultimately, Mexico is likely to prove to be the major target. Much depends on whether the progressive weakening of the ruling Institutional Revolutionary Party (PRI) will lead to democratic pluralism or to ideological polarization. Over the years, with its symbolic links to the authentic Mexican revolution, the PRI has successfully preempted the Communist revolutionary appeal. With the PRI likely to be challenged in the years ahead by a stronger right and a stronger left opposition, one can expect that Mexican Communists will strive to polarize the country's politics, in the hope that they can eventually take over the Mexican left and steer it into more radical, and also anti-American, directions.

That this is a serious danger is attested by the results of the 1988 Mexican presidential elections. The left-wing splinter of the PRI, while losing to the party's official candidate, obtained at least 31 percent of the vote (and in all probability more), and it did so under an ideological banner that had distinct Marxist-Leninist overtones. The program of this movement, known as the National Democratic Front, included a formulation to the effect that "Dialectical Materialism, Historical Materialism, Marxist Political Economics, Scientific Socialism, and Communism are all parts of a fundamental, integrated Marxist-Leninist science whose creative application will allow us to understand accurately the role of the various social strata in the history of Mexico. . . . [A]ll members of the Cardenas Front of National Reconstruction . . . assign a high value to the study of Marxism-Leninism. . . ." These formulations aimed at fusing strong nationalist anti-American feelings with the more classical communist notions. The possibility of a Communist takeover of the radical left could portend a serious challenge in the event that the existing Mexican political system begins to fragment.

Communism in Central America, and perhaps in the future also in Mexico, may thus be able to tap potentially strong anti-American popular sentiments in a renewed effort at revolutionary violence. But farther south, it is more likely that during the coming years revolutionary activities will not reflect classical Marxism-Leninism ideologically or organizationally, but rather a variety of homegrown revolutionary doctrines. Some—like the Shining Path in Peru—may seek to adapt Marxism and Maoism to the messianic aspirations of the long-exploited Indian peasantry. Others may seek to re-create the radical urban guerrilla warfare that afflicted both Argentina and Uruguay during the 1970s. But it does appear increasingly likely that a historically significant and doctrinally orthodox triumph on the Latin American continent will elude communism.

CHAPTER 20

Global Ideological Disintegration

The cumulative consequence of communism's loss of revolutionary élan, of its manifest irrelevance to the politics of the advanced world, and of its failure to capitalize on the socioeconomic dilemmas of the Third World, as well as of its difficulties in creating functioning and united communist systems in conditions as diverse as those of Eastern Europe, the Soviet Union, and China, has been a deep ideological crisis. The essence of the crisis can be reduced to the necessity of choice between doctrinal purity and doctrinal unity.

Soviet leaders, who for many years considered themselves to be the masters of the movement and the interpreters of its dogma, gradually came to realize that purity could only be sought through sectarian squabbling among Communist parties. Insistence on purity would inevitably mean the end of unity. Unity, however, could only be preserved at the price of purity, with the common doctrine diluted to the lowest common denominator. With their own faith probably somewhat declining and with their effective control over the international movement in any case weakening, the leaders in the Kremlin eventually opted for unity over purity.

They did so reluctantly, over a number of years, and with much hesitation. At times, they tried to push the clock back and sought to reestablish a shared and strict orthodoxy of their own definition. Encountering resistance and fearing new splits, they would then grudgingly yield. In the process, the communist doctrine was not only diluted but also increasingly fragmented in both theory and practice. The communist praxis increasingly faded into the past, giving way to a pragmatism based on the centrality of diverse and specific national

225

conditions. What was once thought of as universal became increasingly dominated by the particular.

This might have been the historically inevitable fate of a doctrine that proclaimed itself to contain a globally valid prescription for social salvation, once that doctrine began to be applied to specific national settings. Particular political and social circumstances simply had to be recognized and accommodated, lest the doctrine be rejected as totally irrelevant. But any compromise with diverse reality inherently served to diversify the doctrine, and to elevate varying national priorities or conditions into doctrinal principles. Moreover, the sheer complexity of the emerging postindustrial society, and notably of those of its features most influenced by ultra-science and high-tech, called into question the once politically useful grand oversimplifications of Marxism-Leninism. Increasingly, these tenets came to be viewed as both dated and overly conditioned by parochial circumstances related to their specifically Russian origins.

However, the process of doctrinal disintegration was doubtless also accelerated by the bureaucratic heavy-handedness, ideological clumsiness, and political insensitivity of the doctrine's Soviet mentors. From the early Leninist years until some time after Stalin's death, the Soviet leaders insisted not only on their ideological supremacy but also on the practical political subordination of the Communist parties to the interests of the Soviet Union. This bred an intellectual and political resentment that was bound to erupt into the open at the slightest show of Soviet indecision. The Soviet failure to suppress the Titoist heresy in 1948 was the first signal that Moscow might not be able to fully assert its doctrinal domination, and the contagion of heresy spread more rapidly and openly after Stalin's death in 1953.

The subsequent thirty-five years saw a series of rearguard efforts by the Soviet leaders to preserve communism's orthodoxy and unity. The Kremlin's fight had to be waged on two fronts. The first involved a fight against other ruling parties, which resented Moscow's attempts to impose systemic uniformity on the processes of actually building communism. The second involved a struggle against parties aspiring to power, which were politically handicapped by the Stalinist legacy and were more inclined than Moscow to denounce it. On both fronts, setbacks for Moscow were the rule. The earlier split with Yugoslavia, barely patched up in the mid-1950s, was subsequently overshadowed by the massive and violent quarrel with China, while outside the Communist bloc the increasingly independent Italian Communist party led the march not only toward revisionism but to an open flirtation with social democracy.

The Soviet desire to repair the rift with China, and to avoid similar rifts with other ruling parties, eventually prompted the abdication by the Soviet party of any claim to formal ideological leadership. The Soviet quest for a wider, global Marxist unity also prompted the Soviets to tolerate the Italian party's embrace of essentially social democratic perspectives, including the de facto repudiation of Leninism. The Kremlin chose this course as the lesser evil, knowing full well that the Chinese self-assertion was bound to find tacit support in the other Communist capitals and realizing that the Italian example had already won endorsements from such far-flung Communist parties as the Japanese in 1976 and the Spanish in 1978.

Belated Soviet flexibility simply encouraged the further disintegration of the doctrine. The Italians in 1979 dropped from their party program the obligation for its members even to study Marxism-Leninism and in 1983 abandoned formally the once-hallowed Leninist principle of democratic centralism. In the meantime, the Chinese made headway in restoring their party relations with a variety of ruling and nonruling Communist parties, while at the same time repeatedly denouncing any Communist reliance on "rigidity of dogmas and harmful models" and rejecting categorically the existence of any "center of leadership" or the existence of any "leading party."

As a result, by the mid-1980s both democratic centralism as the key Leninist test of internal doctrinal orthodoxy and loyalty to the Soviet Union as the litmus test of proletarian internationalism were abandoned by the Kremlin, as they already had been by some other parties. At the Twenty-seventh Soviet Party Congress, Gorbachev humbly proclaimed that "the diversity of our movement is not a synonym for its disunity. In the same way, unity has nothing in common with uniformity, hierarchy with the intervention of one party in the affairs of another or with the pretension of one party to possess a monopoly of the truth." Indeed, he stated, henceforth even social democracy was to be welcomed as part of a broader and progressive coalition, engaged not so much in the promotion of a Marxist-Leninist revolution as in the deterrence of a nuclear conflict between the United States and the Soviet Union.

Implicit in this bow to diversity and in the attempt to forge a wider but inevitably looser coalition was the realization that Marxist historical expectations and Leninist political tactics have proven to be either anachronistic or erroneous. The impoverishment of the working class under capitalism did not occur, the anti-colonial wave did not turn into a Marxist-Leninist revolution, while the attempt to maintain Soviet political and doctrinal leadership in the Communist movement produced isolation and rebellion. Last but not least, the failure of the Soviet model discredited the notion of any universally valid doctrinal guidelines for socialist construction. Under these circumstances, the only sensible option was for the Soviet leaders to abandon their quest for the restoration of a coherent ideology and of cohesive political unity.

A historical watershed had thus been crossed. Having failed as a united movement in both the developed and the developing worlds, the era of a monolithic Communist movement built around a shared dogma was now irrevocably a thing of the past. The mid-1980s witnessed not only the end of the unity of communist theory and practice but also the end among Communist parties of unified doctrine and of united action.

PART VI

The Agony of Communism

The communist phenomenon represents a historical tragedy. Born out of an impatient idealism that rejected the injustice of the status quo, it sought a better and more humane society—but produced mass oppression. It optimistically reflected faith in the power of reason to construct a perfect community. It mobilized the most powerful emotions of love for humanity and of hatred for oppression on behalf of morally motivated social engineering. It thus captivated some of the brightest minds and some of the most idealistic hearts—yet it prompted some of the worst crimes of this or any century.

Moreover, communism represented a misguided effort to impose total rationality on social affairs. It posited the notion that a literate, politically conscious society could undertake to control social evolution, guiding socioeconomic change to purposeful ends. History would thus no longer be a merely spontaneous, largely accidental process, but a tool of humanity's collective intelligence and moral purpose. Communism thus aspired to blend, through organized action, political rationality with social morality.

Yet in practice, the excessive faith in human reason, the propensity of very acute conflicts for power to translate tentative historical judgments into dogmatic assertions, the inclination for moral outrage to degenerate into self-righteous political hatred, and especially the Leninist fusion of Marxism with the backward autocratic traditions of Russia transformed communism into an instrument of political oppression defiantly in conflict with its own moral impulses.

CHAPTER 21

The General Crisis

Communism today is in a state of general crisis, both ideologically and systemically. The scope of that crisis emerges with considerable force from five major developments:

1. For Communists around the world, the Soviet experience—an icon no more—henceforth must not be imitated but avoided. Communism thus no longer has a practical model for others to emulate.
2. In the Soviet Union, the communist system's insoluble dilemma is that economic success can only be purchased at the cost of political stability, while political stability can only be sustained at the cost of economic failure.
3. In Eastern Europe, communism's fatal flaw is the party's monopoly of power rooted in Soviet domination. Forty years after the imposition of communism, the elimination of both foreign and party domination is now widely seen as the necessary precondition to social rebirth.
4. In China, communism's ideological dilution will be the price of economic success. Modern China may enter the twenty-first century still ruled by communism, but it will not be a communized China.
5. The era of a monolithic Communist world movement built around a shared dogma has become a thing of the past. By the mid-1980s, the end has come to the notion of a movement of Communist parties unified in doctrine and action.

Cumulatively, this not only signals the general crisis of communism, but also foreshadows its fading as a major political and ideological force in the contemporary world. This crisis is currently reflected in the growing social unrest over the poor economic performance of the Communist states and in the loss of doctrinal con-

232

fidence among the ruling Communist elites. In the Communist countries, the notion that socialism represents a superior social system either is already discredited or is viewed with growing skepticism. Moreover, world communism no longer can point to any social model as its beacon for the future.

The classical Marxist-Leninist definition of "the general crisis of capitalism"—which the Kremlin in 1961 proclaimed was actually under way—fits well the current condition of communism. By merely substituting in that proclamation (see page 200) the word "communism" or a reference to the Soviet Union for "imperialism" or "capitalism" and the term "free enterprise democracy" for "socialism," a devastatingly accurate picture of contemporary communism emerges:

> Communism at its present stage of development is Soviet imperialism at the period of its decline and destruction. The inevitable process of decomposition has engulfed communism from top to bottom, including its economic and state structure, and its policy and ideology. . . .
>
> The general crisis of communism finds expression in the following: the continuous defection of new countries from the Soviet-influenced model; the weakening of the position of the Communist countries in economic competition with the advanced free enterprise democracies; the disintegration of the Soviet bloc; the aggravation of the contradictions of communism with the development of state-monopolistic socialism and the growth of militarism; the intensification of internal instability and decay of the communist economy manifest in the growing inability of communism to fully use the productive forces—low rates of production growth, periodic crises, constant failure to fully utilize production capacities, and chronic underemployment; the unprecedented intensification of political reaction on all fronts; the establishment in a number of Communist countries of personal tyrannies; and the profound crisis in communist policy and ideology.

While this definition, couched in Marxist terminology, encapsulates the general crisis of world communism, its extent and intensity, however, differs from country to country. The accompanying table is an approximate—and admittedly impressionistic—summary of the intensity of that crisis within individual Communist states. For communism, political success equals effective control, and the less coercion needed to assert and maintain total control, the greater the

Index of the Crisis Level in Communist States

	USSR	CHINA	EAST GERMANY	POLAND	CZECHOSLOVAKIA	HUNGARY	ROMANIA	BULGARIA	YUGOSLAVIA	VIETNAM	CUBA	NORTH KOREA	ANGOLA	MOZAMBIQUE	ETHIOPIA
Socialism has lost its attractiveness to masses	1	2	1	3	2	3	3	1	2	2	3	1	3	3	3
Social pessimism about future	2	0	1	3	2	3	3	1	2	2	3	2	3	3	3
Dropping standard of living	2	0	1	3	2	2	3	1	3	3	3	2	3	3	3
Communist party dispirited	2	0	0	3	2	2	3	1	2	1	1	0	1	3	1
Religious activity rising	1	0	0	3	1	1	0	0	1	0	1	0	0	0	1
Nationalism colliding with ideology	1	0	1	3	2	3	2	1	3	1	1	1	2	1	2
Economic privatization rising	1	2	1	2	1	3	0	0	2	1	0	0	1	1	0
Political opposition socially active	1	1	1	3	1	2	0	0	2	0	0	0	3	3	2
Political pluralization openly demanded from below	2	2	0	3	1	3	1	0	3	0	1	0	2	2	2
Regime on defensive on human rights	2	1	1	1	2	1	3	1	2	2	2	2	1	2	3
NATIONAL TOTALS	15	8	7	27	16	23	18	6	22	12	15	8	19	21	20

Numerical scale:

  3 = very true
  2 = true
  1 = partially true
  0 = not true

Crisis levels among Communist regimes:

Below 10 = not in crisis—4 countries
10 to 19 = crisis—6 countries
Above 19 = grave crisis—5 countries

success. Accordingly, even though all of the categories are not necessarily of equal importance, a cumulative high score would indicate a failure to achieve an effectively operating Leninist political structure, to remold society, and to construct an efficient centrally planned economy.

Of the fifteen regimes rated, no regime had the near perfect score that would represent an economically prosperous Leninist system genuinely supported by the people. Only four had a score below ten, which would indicate the absence of a state of crisis. Five, however, achieved a score of twenty or above, which means a condition of grave crisis. Moreover, of the relatively more "successful" four, the most important one, China, has avoided a condition of crisis largely by diluting on a wide front its communist praxis. This has enabled the regime to generate some social attraction and optimism, but at the cost of parting with some of the central tenets of communist doctrine. The other three—East Germany, Bulgaria, and North Korea—have proven more effective both in the maintenance of social repression and in the management of the statist economy. They have also encountered less resistance from society in the process of communist transformation. All the other Communist regimes are in various stages of crisis. Their efforts to create a new system have not resulted in innovative and productive economies and have generated increasing social and in some cases even political disaffection.

Thus, given the aggravating general crisis of communism, it is appropriate to formulate a final historical diagnosis of communism's performance and a prognosis of its prospects into the next century.

CHAPTER 22

The Historical Record

Communism's general crisis is deeply rooted in its deficient historical record. Its initial appeal was largely derived from the fact that in the early stages of the twentieth century many of the existing systems—even democratic ones—were unresponsive to the pains and injustices of the early capitalist phase of industrial development. It is also a fact, however, that no Communist regime ever took power as a result of the freely expressed will of the people. No Communist ruling elite—even after decades in power—has been willing to seek political legitimacy by permitting its people to exercise a free choice on the continuation of communism. This unwillingness to submit communism to the democratic test results partly from the Manichaean and self-appointed sense of mission inherent in the Marxist-Leninist doctrine and partly from the knowledge that communism in power has not succeeded in satisfying the social desire for material well-being and for personal happiness. To this day, no cases exist of significant flights *to* communist systems by people attracted by its way of life, whereas the desire to abandon communism is as evident in the case of the seventy-year-old Soviet system as it is in those of the forty-year-old system in Poland and of the fifteen-year-old system in Vietnam.

Moreover, communism's historical performance as a system of social organization has involved a painful disproportion between the massive human sacrifice forcibly exacted from the people and some of the undeniable socioeconomic benefits thereby achieved. Comparisons of Communist and non-Communist countries at similar stages of socioeconomic development—such as East Germany and Czechoslovakia with West Germany, Poland with Spain, Hungary and Yugoslavia with Austria and Italy, and China with India—indicate that virtually no Communist regime improved its standing vis-à-vis its comparable rival, in terms of GNP, trade in competitive world mar-

236

kets, or domestic standard of living. (See Appendix.) Only China advanced over India, which was itself a victim of an overly bureaucratized and quasi-socialist economic system, but only after Beijing initiated its retreat from Marxist-Leninist orthodoxy. The Soviet Union has fallen further behind not only the United States but also Japan. Between 1960 and 1988, with a population less than half that of the Soviet Union, Japan essentially caught up in GNP after trailing by more than a three-to-one ratio at the outset.

Communist economies are even further behind in terms of global competitiveness. In 1985, while total U.S. and Japanese trade in competitive markets stood at $576 billion and $308 billion respectively, the Soviet equivalent was $66 billion. In addition, Moscow's trade profile resembled that of a Third World country. Almost three-quarters of its exports came from extractive industries, with fuels accounting for 49 percent, gold for 18 percent, timber for 4 percent, and diamonds for 2 percent. Communist countries—with roughly one-third of the world's population—accounted for only 10 percent of global exports, a mere 3 percent of technological innovations, and just 1 percent of economic assistance to the developing countries. All of Eastern Europe exported less machinery to the industrialized democracies than did Singapore.

Communism's deficient record is also reflected in the domestic standards of living. Forty years after World War II, the Soviet government still rations meat and has recently started to ration sugar. According to the Soviet weekly magazine *Nedelya* of June 27–July 3, 1988, residents of the Sverdlovsk city and region have been issued "pale yellow coupons of food ration cards. There is an authorized person on every block to distribute them. Some 800 grams of boiled sausage each month . . . 400 grams of butter. And 2 kg. of meat a year—for the May and October holidays. Some Sundays there are not even noodles or groats to be had." *Nedelya* added, "For the time being it is better not to talk to these people about *perestroika*."

Official Soviet statistics released in the era of *glasnost* indicate that approximately 40 percent of the entire population and 79 percent of the elderly live in poverty. According to Soviet writer N. M. Rimashevstaya, only one-third of Soviet households have hot running water and another one-third do not even have cold running water. Also, *Izvestia* has reported, on January 26, 1986, that an unskilled worker's family of four typically has to live for more than eight years in a single eight-by-eight-foot room before somewhat better accommodations become available. It is, therefore, no exaggeration to state that the West's poor live on the same material level as the Soviet Union's middle class.

Car ownership statistics—modernity's rough indicator of the availability of consumer goods—tell a similar story. Western countries have almost reached a saturation point in automobile consumption. In 1983, there was one car for every 1.8 Americans, 4.4 Japanese, 2.5 Germans, and 2.8 Italians, but one for every 14.2 Soviets, 5.8 Czechs, and 10.8 Poles. It is a startling fact that blacks own more cars per capita in South Africa than do citizens in the Soviet Union.

Compounding these economic shortcomings is the growing ecological crisis in a number of Communist states. In Eastern Europe, the situation has become particularly dramatic in large parts of Poland and some sections of East Germany and Czechoslovakia. In the Soviet Union, industrial regions in general have become badly polluted, with the problem reported to be especially grave in Armenia, where highly toxic industrial wastes are routinely dumped into rivers. All Communist states, with their obsession with rapid industrial growth, have been grossly negligent in failing to take even minimal steps to protect the environment and have been woefully slow to respond to the mounting crisis. Ecological deterioration, coupled with inferior public health facilities, has doubtless contributed to some alarming increases in the death rates in all age groups and in all the countries of the Soviet bloc. A boy born today in the Soviet Union has—according to comparative studies by Nick Eberstadt of Harvard's Center for Population Studies—a life expectancy shorter than one born in Mexico.

None of the foregoing denies the fact that Communist states have made strides particularly in the development of heavy industry and —particularly in the initial phases of its rule—in social welfare and in education. However, the progress thereby achieved was purchased at a staggering human cost. No experiment in social reconstruction in all of human history has entailed a higher price in human terms —or has been as wasteful—as humanity's encounter with communism during the twentieth century. No one can measure precisely the overall cost because these regimes exacted the physical toll under largely secretive conditions and because the associated intangible psychological and cultural damage does not lend itself to quantitative estimates. Nonetheless, a rough estimate is possible of the specific categories of human suffering inflicted by Marxist-Leninist regimes in the process of the communist transformation of societies. Current Soviet and Chinese denunciations of past excesses—all of which have yielded much additional data on the human costs of the communist experiment in social engineering—facilitate this task and render its conclusions more credible to skeptical Westerners.

The human cost included:

1. *Summary executions in the process of taking power.* Without counting combat deaths in revolutionary or civil warfare, it can be estimated that such executions accounted for at least a million people in the Soviet Union, several million in China, about 100,000 in Eastern Europe, and at least 150,000 in Vietnam.

2. *Executions of political opponents and resisters after the acquisition of power.* These killings usually took place over a period of several years while the Communists consolidated their grip over the country. A rough estimate must place these figures at about the same level as those in the first category, yielding a combined and conservative death toll for the first two categories of about 5 million.

3. *Extermination of all people belonging to various social categories deemed to be potentially hostile, irrespective of the actual attitudes of the victims.* These groups typically included former military officers, government officials, aristocrats, landowners, priests, and capitalists. Some were executed, and others placed in labor camps, where most perished. While estimates for this category must be wide-ranging, even recent Soviet, East European, and Chinese disclosures indicate that the tolls were substantial, certainly not fewer than 3 million to 5 million people.

4. *Liquidation of the independent peasantry.* This category was typified by the physical elimination of the kulak class in the Soviet Union through executions and deaths in labor camps. With Soviet and Chinese figures in the multiples of millions and with those of Vietnam and North Korea in the low hundreds of thousands, a minimum estimate of fatalities in this category must be over 10 million people.

5. *Fatalities associated with mass deportations and forced resettlement.* These policies, which figured prominently in the collectivization drives in the Soviet Union, Eastern Europe, and especially in China during the anti-landlord campaign and in the establishment of the peasant communes during the Great Leap Forward, produced mas-

sive famines, epidemics, and other disasters. Any estimate should also take into account the Soviet policy of deporting suspect non-Russian peoples, such as many Latvians, Lithuanians, and Estonians from the Baltic republics, Poles from the western regions of the Soviet Union, Tatars from the Crimea, and others, to the remote areas of Siberia. Recent Soviet estimates put the number of victims in the range of 7 million to 10 million for the Soviet Union alone, while some estimates for China have placed its total at about 27 million. A cautious, yet still appalling, sum would be at least 30 million victims.

6. *Executions or deaths in labor camps of purged Communists.* In the Soviet Union, the number of Communists displaced in the course of power struggles and various purges and then liquidated from 1936 to 1938 can be safely estimated at more than a million. In Eastern Europe in the late 1940s and early 1950s, tens of thousands of Communists were killed or imprisoned. In China—particularly in the Cultural Revolution—several million suffered a similar fate.

7. *Physical and psychological scars from prolonged imprisonment and forced labor.* In the Soviet Union, the amnesties of the mid-1950s prompted the release of several million people who in some cases had spent as many as twenty years incarcerated under most severe conditions. Similar amnesties took place in Eastern Europe following Khrushchev's denunciation of Stalin in 1956, and in China after the end of the Cultural Revolution in the early 1970s.

8. *Persecution of the families of the regime's victims.* In the Soviet Union, the families of those who fell into the first six categories were subject to punishments ranging from execution to imprisonment to deportation to discrimination in housing and employment.

9. *A socially pervasive climate of fear and of personal and political isolation.* Entire social categories—other than workers or poor peasants—were exposed to manifestations of ideological hostility on the part of the officialdom during much of the era of forcible communist social reconstruction.

These social costs—which include at a minimum about 50 million fatalities—represent without a doubt the most extravagant and wasteful experiment in social engineering ever attempted. Given the current inclination of Communist regimes to acknowledge that much of their past involves a failure rooted in "errors and excesses" and that a significant change in their policies is necessary, the human tragedy becomes greater still. In other words, Soviet, Chinese, and some East European rulers have conceded that past Communist "excesses" were socioeconomically unproductive, in addition to having been ethically repugnant.

Communism's grand failure has thus involved, in summary form, the wasteful destruction of much social talent and the suppression of society's creative political life; excessively high human costs for the economic gains actually achieved and an eventual decline in economic productivity because of statist overcentralization; a progressive deterioration in the overly bureaucratized social welfare system which represented initially the principal benefit of Communist rule; and the stunting through dogmatic controls of society's scientific and artistic growth.

That historic failure, now explicitly acknowledged by the Communist leaders advocating reforms, has deeper roots than the "errors and excesses" finally regretted. It stemmed from the operational, institutional, and philosophical shortcomings of the communist experiment. Indeed, it was deeply embedded in the very nature of the Marxist-Leninist praxis.

On the operational level, the style of Marxist-Leninist decision making contributed to an atmosphere of paranoia and to an increasing reliance on force for the resolution of social and political problems. All the top Communist leaders—Lenin, Stalin, Mao, or their imitative counterparts in Eastern Europe or the Third World—comported themselves as if they were a conspiracy in power, a secretive priesthood, whose deliberations had to be shielded from a hostile world. Mystery and secrecy surrounded their doings, their personalities, and even their families. At the same time, since they perceived themselves to be endowed with a unique insight into human history and thus entitled to reshape mankind's future by force if necessary, they mistrusted profoundly anyone who did not share their peculiar perspective. The injunction "who is not with us is against us" bred an operational style that translated criticism into hostility, difficulties into sabotage, and alternative viewpoints into treason. In that context, the correction of policy could only occur after catastrophic calamities.

Institutional shortcomings magnified this operational deformity. The communist operational style helped to produce political systems that contained no safety valves or early warning mechanisms. Signs of malaise were inherently delayed in reaching the top; self-serving misinformation flowed upward more rapidly; fear inhibited open soul-searching. A leader held on to political power as long as he could physically and politically survive, and his replacement emerged normally through a debilitating political conflict, which maximized the Manichaean tendencies already noted. The absence of mechanisms for changing rulers who performed poorly made the effective control of power, and not the success or failure of policy, the key criterion for enduring leadership.

More fundamental still were the philosophical roots of the failure. In the final analysis, Marxist-Leninist policies were derived from a basic misjudgment of history and from a fatal misconception of human nature. Ultimately, communism's failure is thus intellectual. It failed to take into account the basic human craving for individual freedom, for artistic or spiritual self-expression, and increasingly—in the age of literacy and mass communications—for political choice. It also neglected the organic connection between economic productivity and innovation on the one hand, and the individual craving for personal material well-being on the other. Communism thus stifled social creativity even as it presented itself as the most creative and innovative social system.

That intellectual failure also afflicted communism on the international level. Marxism-Leninism did not anticipate or comprehend the basic forces that have shaped the twentieth century's international affairs. It underestimated the roles of ethnicity and nationalism, with the result that inter-Communist national conflicts came as a shock. Those conflicts, in turn, were intensified by the resulting inclination of the Communist sides to view each other as doctrinal heretics. This was the case in the ideologically destructive Soviet-Yugoslav and the Sino-Soviet disputes. Communism also misread the appeal of religion and was thus unprepared for the resistance based on the Roman Catholic religion in Poland or for the revival of Islam within the Soviet Union itself. Last but not least, the technetronic revolution, which so transformed the nature of the distribution of power and of the social structure within the advanced capitalist societies, found Marxist-Leninists still clinging to outdated concepts derived from the early phases of the industrial revolution.

Cumulatively, these operational, institutional, and philosophical factors contributed to policies that eventually not only had to result in the general crisis of communism but also had to prompt growing uncertainty about its future.

CHAPTER 23

Future Prospects

In the year 2017, one hundred years after the Bolshevik Revolution, scaffolding is covering the Lenin Mausoleum on the former Red Square, now renamed Freedom Square. The scaffolding is masking the reconstruction of the mausoleum into the entrance to an underground parking garage designed to accommodate the masses of tourists visiting the recently opened permanent exhibit in the Kremlin entitled "One Hundred Wasted Years—Fifty Million Wasted Lives."

The above is not quite as farfetched as it may first seem. Indeed, this imaginary news story from Moscow in the year 2017 is almost as probable as the notion that the present system will endure until then largely unchanged and that on the centenary of the Bolshevik Revolution yet another Soviet leader will be promising prosperity to the Soviet people while blaming his predecessors—including by then Gorbachev as well as Brezhnev and Stalin—for ongoing shortcomings.

Gorbachev has unleashed forces that make historical discontinuity more likely than continuity. Any analysis of the future of communism in the Soviet Union depends, therefore, on the answer to one question: Is Gorbachev's policy a signal of the renewal or attrition of communism? Despite Gorbachev's rhetoric about communism's vitality, the answer to the question must point toward attrition and not renewal. To the extent that his *perestroika* has so far involved any tangible changes, such changes have been away from the tenets of Marxism-Leninism, in terms of both theory and practice. In Eastern Europe and in China, where tangible reforms have been both bolder and more pragmatic, this trend is even more pronounced.

243

The general thrust within contemporary communism, including in the Soviet Union, is to abandon what once was held to be essential. On the economic plane, state or social ownership in agriculture, in the service sector, and even in industry is being jettisoned or compromised in varying degrees. Central planning and pricing are also under attack, with hesitant movement toward some form of the market-mechanism. On the political plane, total Communist control over the means of communications is breaking down. Ideological indoctrination is giving way to ideological retrenchment against "alien" influences. The single party's domination of the society's political dialogue is increasingly under assault in several Communist states. Only the Communist monopoly of the levers of political power still remains essentially unscathed.

Moreover, the communist ideology is being discredited not only by practical experience but also by the Communist rulers themselves. Engaging in a form of historical striptease, they have been repudiating—stripping off, so to speak—layer after layer of their own doctrinal past. True believers must be beginning to wonder what is left of the legacy as they hear twenty years of Brezhnevism denounced as the era of stagnation and corruption; as they learn that Khrushchev, previously denounced for his decade of "hare-brained schemes," was in fact a premature precursor of *perestroika*; as they witness the branding of a quarter of a century of Stalinism as unmitigated criminality; and as some of them whisper that Gorbachev's revisionism involves the beginnings of the de facto rejection of Leninism. Similarly, in China, once hallowed Maoism is being critically reassessed, while in Eastern Europe most of the early Communist leaders have been posthumously stigmatized as Stalinists. All of that strips Marxism-Leninism-Stalinism to the bare bones of Marxism—and nineteenth-century Marxism can hardly provide the needed guidelines for coping with the problems of the world on the eve of the twenty-first century.

Communism is thus on a historical retreat. Will that retreat yield economically more productive and politically more pluralistic systems? Here, the answer varies from country to country. Regarding the Soviet Union, skepticism is in order. For the reasons developed in the first two chapters, the chances are remote that Gorbachev's policies will produce a globally competitive economy and a political system in which the people practice self-government under the benign tutelage of a somewhat disengaged Communist party. The anti-democratic Leninist legacy, the multinational character of the state, and the deeply embedded centralist traditions all conspire to undercut social receptivity to the effective devolution of political and managerial responsibilities and thus to prevent such a positive development.

Successful pluralization of the Soviet Union is less likely than four alternative outcomes. The first is a protracted and inconclusive systemic crisis, lasting without any clear-cut resolution for more than a decade and periodically punctuated by outbreaks of social turbulence on the part of the increasingly economically dissatisfied urban masses and especially on the part of the politically more restless non-Russian peoples. The second possibility is renewed stagnation as the turmoil eventually subsides and the centralist traditions inherent in the Russian past reassert themselves. At some point, this could lead to the third possibility, a coup by the military and the KGB (perhaps even in conjunction with Gorbachev's untimely death), publicly justified by emotional appeals to Great Russian nationalism. The fourth potential outcome—at this stage a much more remote possibility—involves the eventual transformation of the protracted crisis into an outright and explicit overthrow of the Communist regime, precipitating the fanciful scenario outlined at the beginning of this section. The last outcome could involve also the fragmentation of the Soviet Union as a single state, inevitably prompting large-scale internal national and ethnic violence.

The most probable alternative—a protracted and inconclusive systemic crisis which might eventually subside into a renewed period of stagnation—would further deepen the general crisis of communism, contribute to increased diversity among the Communist states, and accelerate the process of ideological dissolution. It would also inevitably intensify national tensions within the Soviet Union, while strengthening separatist aspirations. In any case, by unleashing social passions in the context of an ideological vacuum produced by the discrediting of the official doctrine, Gorbachev has created an opening not only for the revival of Great Russian nationalism but especially for the self-assertion of the non-Russian nationalisms. As a result, Gorbachev has unintentionally placed on history's agenda the possibility of the actual dismantling of the Soviet Union.

The longer *perestroika* lasts, the more the non-Russian national

aspirations will mount. It is only a question of time—and perhaps
even of a relatively short time—before national ferment on behalf of
greater devolution of authority from Moscow to the republican capitals is transformed into explicit demands for national sovereignty.
This has already started to happen in recently conquered Estonia,
Latvia, and Lithuania, and is also beginning to happen in religiously
and culturally diverse Armenia, Azerbaijan, and Georgia. Before long,
it is also likely to occur not only in predominantly Islamic Tadjikistan,
Turkmenstan, Uzbekistan, and Kazakhstan, but also—most dangerously from Moscow's point of view—in the Slavic Ukraine and
eventually Byelorussia (despite the latter's advanced Russification).
Of these, the Ukraine—with its large population and rich natural
resources—poses the potentially gravest threat to the very survival
of the Soviet Union. It is thus quite possible that by the first decades
of the twenty-first century the largest region in the world beset by
intense nationalist conflicts will be the Soviet Union—a development
that would represent the final victory of the appeal of nationalism
over communism.

The only constructive solution for the nationally intensifying Soviet
disunion that is compatible with the professed goals of *perestroika*—
i.e., economic decentralization and political pluralism—is not a
coercive return to the imperial Soviet "Union" but movement toward
a genuine Soviet Confederation. However, a truly voluntary confederation may no longer be a practical option, given the aroused
national emotions of the non-Russians. Moreover, in any case, the
devolution of real control from Moscow, both economic and political,
would mean the practical end of the Muscovite empire and of Russia
as a world power—a prospect certainly not relished by the Great
Russians.

A military-police coup designed to terminate the protracted crisis
and to restore centralized domination would also contribute to, and
perhaps even accelerate, the global fading of communism. Under the
existing circumstances of a largely ritualized ideology and of increasingly assertive non-Russian nationalisms, a coup aiming at the restoration of more effective central control, even if justified formally
in doctrinal terms, would have to draw on Great Russian nationalist
sentiments for its political legitimation. This might provide the center
with the needed popular base for the repression of the non-Russian

nationalisms. But it is doubtful that, short of a return to Stalinist methods, such nationalisms can any longer be fully extirpated. Nationalist passions have been released from Pandora's box. In the age of nationalism, the lid can no longer be tightly shut.

In the meantime, *glasnost* has already helped to stimulate more extreme public manifestations of Great Russian nationalism. Some verge on rabid chauvinism. *Pamyat*, the surprisingly active and influential Russian public society, has capitalized on the fact that the gradual discrediting of the official ideology has left a vacuum which nationalism can most easily fill. As a result, *Pamyat* has struck a responsive chord among the Great Russians, who are increasingly resentful of the damage done to their national heritage by seventy years of communism (which *Pamyat* ascribes to Zionist and Masonic influences) and also increasingly fearful that a protracted crisis could prompt the dismantling of their empire.

While a flower arrangement at the Soviet border outpost on the railroad from Helsinki to Leningrad still spells out an optimistic slogan—"We are living in an age in which all roads lead to Communism"—all future variants for the Soviet Union portend a retreat from communism. Success for *perestroika* would entail a significant dilution of the communist praxis. Protracted turmoil would signal the political system's incapacity to effect a stable transfer of authority to a more dynamic and self-governing society. Renewed stagnation would mean that communism cannot creatively grow. A repressive coup based on nationalism and ideology would discredit the Soviet Union internationally, while fragmentation would represent a historical defeat. Thus, inherent in the uncertain future of the Soviet Union are social and political dynamics inimical to communism's prestige and global prospects.

Political and social changes in Eastern Europe are also likely to intensify communism's general crisis. These changes will differ from state to state, and they will be driven both by nationalist impulses and by a new sense of supranational collectivity. The former might intensify traditional conflicts—such as the Hungarian–Romanian dispute over Transylvania—while the latter is likely to result in the replacement of the last lingering vestiges of Communist internationalism by the mounting appeal of an increasingly *united* Europe. As Western Europe marches toward more genuine and organic economic unity, and as its political unity emerges in the wake of economic unification, the historical and cultural attraction of Europe to the East Europeans will dramatically increase. This will be reinforced by the economic self-interest of the East Europeans in becoming more closely identified with Europe. A progressively more united Europe, economically dynamic and culturally appealing, will stand in dramatic, and magnetic, contrast to either a turbulent or a stagnant Soviet Union.

As a unifying concept and as a model of social development, communism is thus no longer relevant to Eastern Europe. As a concept, it has no remaining intellectual appeal. As a model, it is discredited, even among the ruling elites. Two pertinent questions arise. First, how will the process of dismantling the existing Communist institutions occur? Second, will it lead to systems more akin to Western democracies or to nationalist dictatorships?

The picture is likely to be very mixed. Almost all of the East European states will seek closer links with Western Europe, with the lead probably maintained by Hungary and Poland. These two countries will most likely also sustain their status as leaders in the progressive dismantling of the Soviet-imposed institutional arrangements. In both, the emergence of an autonomous civil society, not subject to effective Communist control, will continue to narrow the scope of arbitrary political power and prompt the resurrection of an authentic political life. Both are thus likely to reach, ahead of the other East European states, the pivotal dividing line between a defensive, retreating, increasingly tolerant, yet still—in terms of political power—monopolistic Communist regime and the appearance of a genuine pluralistic democracy with true freedom of political choice.

Crossing that line will be difficult. No Communist regime has yet traversed peacefully across that invisible divide. Hungary is the best candidate for a peaceful transition. It is smaller and geopolitically less neuralgic to the Soviets, which means Moscow is less likely to engage in disruptive interference in the country's internal evolution. Its political elite is wiser and feels somewhat more secure than that of Poland's. All of that might permit the progressive transformation of the emerging Hungarian civil society into a political society, with genuinely pluralistic characteristics. In Poland, despite the fact that its society has asserted its political self-emancipation more vigorously than Hungary's, the prospects for a fully peaceful transition may not be quite as good. The very vigor of Polish national sentiments and the ultimate weakness of the Communist rulers suggest that a phase of turbulence may be the unavoidable concomitant of communism's demise—though much depends, of course, on the degree of Soviet acquiescence to this process.

Elsewhere, the pattern is likely to be more mixed. East Germany has become a Communist Prussia, disciplined, motivated, and productive. It may remain so for quite a while, especially since West Germany generously contributes to its economic well-being. However, its success is likely to become associated more with its distinctive national and cultural traditions than with communism as such. Czechoslovakia is likely to follow the Hungarian–Polish model in progressively dismantling Soviet-derived institutions and in seeking closer links with Europe. Any protracted internal Soviet turbulence will help to revive the sentiments that once motivated the Prague Spring, thus prompting a new period of political ferment. Romania and Bulgaria will probably be the laggards in the process, but with both relying increasingly on nationalist impulses in defining their domestic policies.

The nature of the Soviet response to political change in Eastern Europe will significantly influence the pace and extent of change within the Soviet Union itself. A Soviet Union that tolerates change in Eastern Europe is more likely to be a Soviet Union that engages in a prolonged, perhaps elusive, and almost certainly turbulent quest for its domestic *perestroika*. A Soviet Union that tries to crack down hard on change in Eastern Europe is likely to be a Soviet Union that is itself diluting and slowing down its reforms. Indeed, the effective end to Gorbachev's *perestroika* might be the price to be paid for the preservation of the external empire. In either case—whether actively seeking to join a larger Europe or again subjected to Soviet-sponsored repression—Eastern Europe will likely be a detriment to communism's global standing.

Only in China do the current developments seem to signal the renewal of communism's vitality. But even here the case may not ultimately be credible. As already indicated, the Chinese regime is more likely to succeed than to fail in its current efforts to stimulate China's rapid entry into the prosperous Pacific rim region. It will do so, however, by policies that have increasingly less to do with the Marxist-Leninist doctrine and more in common with the economically successful policies pursued by some of China's non-Communist neighbors, including the emphasis on foreign trade as the source of stimulus for internal growth. Commercial, and also partially corrupted, communism may attain high economic growth rates but at rather low levels of ideological orthodoxy. Any economic success in China will argue for the further abandonment of doctrine and serve as an example for other Communist states, like Vietnam or North Korea. Doctrinal orthodoxy will thereby be further undermined.

It does not follow that setbacks in China's economic programs would somehow revitalize or relegitimate the ideology. On the contrary, any such failure is likely to be viewed by many Chinese as further proof that economic success is not possible in a quasi-communist setting and can be achieved only by a comprehensive abandonment of all traditional Marxist-Leninist restraints on political freedom. Thus, in time, the political dimensions of change are likely to become increasingly important. China is almost inevitably fated to experience intensifying political tensions.

Indeed, it is impossible to envisage a long-term process of increasing economic pluralism without the appearance of a civil society in China that eventually begins to assert its political aspirations. That is likely to produce a difficult, potentially even stormy, confrontation. Thus, at some point, the economic success of China could be the catalyst for a political crisis that in turn could even place in jeopardy such economic success. China's leaders cannot indefinitely avoid facing the fact that ultimately no halfway house exists between centralized communism and a decentralized and self-managing society.

Outside of the existing Communist regimes, the opportunities for the spread of communism, either by revolution or by the ballot box, appear to be very limited. With the fragmentation of the Marxist-Leninist ideology, it is increasingly likely that revolutionary activities, particularly in the Third World, will be driven primarily by indigenous causes and motivated by hybrid doctrines that combine some elements of Marxism with more localized sources of emotional and intellectual appeal. The Shining Path in Peru or liberation theology in Latin America provide examples of such adaptations. Additional forms—especially imbued with some religious content—are likely to manifest themselves in those parts of the world where despair and frustration lead to political violence.

Some elements of Marxism are bound to be part of any residual doctrines of violent revolution and of coercive and rapid social reconstruction. The Marxist view of history is part of the world's intellectual heritage, and any radical leader will deliberately or subconsciously assimilate some Marxist notions into his revolutionary manifesto. But such elements will no longer be presented as an integrated whole that must be accepted in toto. Marxism-Leninism has lost its historical legitimacy as a comprehensive dogma.

Moreover, even within Communist ranks, a broad tendency has arisen toward a philosophical ecumenism somewhat reminiscent of what has manifested itself in recent years in organized religion. A good example of such "relativistic" thinking is the growing inclination of Soviet commentators to concede that the building of communism in the Soviet Union involved dogmatic distortions that deprive the Soviet experience of any universal validity. Intellectual pragmatism and syncretism may be welcome indicators of heightened tolerance, but they are also indices of growing doctrinal—or religious—indifferentism. Such indifferentism is the first phase in the progressive dissipation of core beliefs. It involves an inherent transition from absolutism to relativism, from dogma to mere opinion. That transition is the agony of communism.

CHAPTER 24

Post-Communism

A new phenomenon—post-Communism—is now appearing. While the twentieth century did not become the age of the triumph of communism, it was a century dominated by its challenge. That challenge is rapidly receding as communism itself fades. The paradox of the future is that communism's "success" is increasingly being measured by its ability to move in the direction of greater free enterprise and to dismantle direct party control over the society's political life.

Accordingly, a post-Communist system will be one in which the withering away of communism has advanced to the point that neither Marxist theory nor past Communist practice dictate much—if any —of ongoing public policy. Post-Communism, very simply, will be a system in which self-declared "Communists" just do not treat communist doctrine seriously as the guide to social policy: neither those who profess it as the source of legitimacy for their power while their system stagnates under it, nor those who profess to practice it while in fact successfully diluting its essence, nor those who reject it without any longer fearing to do so publicly. In varying degrees, the Soviet Union, China, and Eastern Europe can all be said to be approaching such a post-Communist phase.

The ongoing historical process of the emergence of post-Communism gives particular salience to two critical questions:

1. Will the transition from Marxist-Leninist dictatorships gradually lead to pluralist democracy or to some form of nationalistic authoritarianism?
2. What will be viewed as the political and intellectual legacy of the twentieth century's communism?

Indeed, the problem of post-Communist transition is likely to become intellectually the most interesting and politically the most central issue pertaining to what is today still called the Communist world. It will in all likelihood be the dominant dilemma confronting that world over the next several decades, and it poses not only analytical but also practical issues. Beyond pure prognosis, it begs for a Western strategy deliberately designed to enhance the prospects of a post-Communist transition to democracy.

In broad terms, two fundamental long-range alternatives exist for Communist regimes in the wake of communism's grand failure. The first is to evolve into increasingly pluralistic societies. This would mean initially involving various degrees of mixed state and private economic sectors, legitimated by increasingly social democratic phraseology, which would thereby create in some cases the eventual point of departure for a popularly determined turn toward a pre-dominantly free enterprise system. The second is to stagnate under largely existing institutional arrangements, with those in power tinkering at the margins but preserving dictatorial power through a military-police coalition that increasingly relies on appeals to nationalism—rather than on ritualized doctrine—as the main source of political legitimacy. In both cases, the subsidiary but related question is whether movement in either direction is likely to be evolutionary or will entail some violent upheavals.

So far, the historical record does not offer much encouragement for the first alternative. The case is different from the fascist regimes in Spain and Portugal, which made evolutionary change possible by permitting the existence of autonomous clusters of social and economic activity that at the critical juncture could be transformed into pluralistic sources of political activity. Soviet-type regimes, however, created a totalitarian mode of social organization that precluded such potential political pluralism. Even in relatively nontotalitarian Yugoslavia, the monopolistic Communist tradition—rooted specifically in Leninism—has worked against the emergence of alternative sources of political leadership and has so far stymied the progressive transformation of the country into something approximating a social democracy.

Moreover, as already noted, with the fading of the ideology, Communist elites are everywhere tempted to reinforce and legitimize their power by increasingly strident nationalistic appeals. This has happened already in Communist Poland, where a military leadership has been superimposed on the party leadership. It has been occurring somewhat less overtly in the Soviet Union, but this tendency is also likely to intensify with growing doctrinal disillusionment. Strong nationalism is certainly manifest among the Chinese leaders. While this may work against the continued vitality of the communist doctrine, the appeal to nationalism does have the effect of strengthening authoritarian impulses. It reinforces those institutions of power that can most effectively translate nationalist symbols into dictatorial rule, thereby inhibiting a democratic evolution.

It would be wrong, however, to exclude altogether the possibility of a post-Communist transition in the more democratic direction. In some Communist states, social self-emancipation and the resulting emergence of a civil society that coexists with but is no longer dominated by the political system augur the possibility of progressive transformation into more genuinely pluralistic forms. The impact of novel means of mass communications is especially important, because it not only breaks down the Communist monopoly over the society's political dialogue but makes possible the articulation of alternative political viewpoints.

The chart on the following page not only delineates the probable stages of the retreat from communism but also notes some of the uncertainties in the potential sequence of political change within the existing Communist regimes. As the earlier analysis suggests, the critical but perhaps necessary stage in that retreat is phase two—Communist authoritarianism—from which a regime can evolve in four alternative directions. As noted, the most likely evolution is to phase three—post-Communist authoritarianism—with the less probable options involving fragmentation, an attempted return to the totalitarian phase, or a direct evolution into a pluralist democracy.

In any case, in that process of change the loss of Communist monopoly over mass communications is the key to the breakdown of Communist totalitarianism. Under the conditions of communism and particularly in the setting of its intense and monopolistic indoctrination, the following processes take place. An ideologically alienated mass is created, eager to ingest alternative information. It thus seizes upon new techniques of mass communications—such as foreign radio, television, video cassettes, underground press—to forge a dissenting if vague political outlook. Economic failures enable politically active intellectuals to transform that outlook into demands not only for

PHASES IN THE RETREAT FROM COMMUNISM	*HISTORICAL STATUS*
Phase 1: Communist Totalitarianism Communist party controls political system. Political system controls society and economy. *Transition* to Phase 2: by succession struggles which divide ruling Communist party and increase societal pressures for socioeconomic concessions.	Albania North Korea Vietnam East Germany Romania Cuba Czechoslovakia
Phase 2: Communist Authoritarianism Communist party controls political system but emerging civil society contests it; political supremacy in the economy on the defensive. *Transition* to Phase 3: most likely by top-level coup in response to regime fears of rising social pressures; in some exceptional cases, directly to Phase 4; alternatively, if change blocked, systemic fragmentation or repressive attempt to return to Phase 1.	Soviet Union China Nicaragua Hungary Poland
Phase 3: Post-Communist Authoritarianism Authoritarian regime based largely on nationalist appeal; ideology ritualized; civil society becomes political society; political supremacy over economy in broad retreat. *Transition* to Phase 4: most likely turbulent in final stage of Phase 3, though peaceful evolution in some exceptional cases may be possible; alternatively, if change blocked, systemic fragmentation.	Yugoslavia
Phase 4: Post-Communist Pluralism Political and socioeconomic systems become pluralistic.	

socioeconomic but also for political pluralism and for the rule of law. Belated Communist economic reforms, involving concessions and decentralization, unintentionally contribute to the progressive institutionalization of such economic and political changes, cumulatively producing a social assault on the totalitarian dictatorship.

These processes, which are already deeply affecting some parts of the Communist world, can be encouraged by a far-sighted Western strategy for the promotion of post-Communist democratization. In that strategy, the nationalist authoritarian phase of post-Communist transition may be viewed, perhaps even in the majority of cases, as an unavoidable stage in the progressive dismantling of the Marxist-Leninist systems. However, it is certainly in the interest of democracy that any such authoritarian stage be brief, especially since—in the context of economic deprivation and of popular resentment against Communist rule—popular impatience could easily explode into large-scale and historically premature rebellion, in turn provoking a repressive and more assertive Communist reaction. There is, therefore, some historical urgency to the promotion of a strategy of progressive post-Communist democratization.

The powerful impact of the appeal of human rights is particularly significant in accelerating the processes of communism's fading. Human rights is the single most magnetic political idea of the contemporary time. Its evocation by the West has already placed all Communist regimes on the defensive. Its appeal is responsive to the emergence of increasingly literate and politically conscious masses who can no longer be so easily isolated and indoctrinated. Post-Communist authoritarian regimes are likely to be especially vulnerable to the appeal of human rights because of their lack of a comprehensive, credible, and compelling ideology. They will thus be doctrinally porous and politically brittle.

The evocation of human rights has not only placed the existing Communist regimes on the defensive, but in the global perception it has also served to divorce communism from democracy. By focusing global attention on the denial of freedom of choice, on the violation of individual rights, on the absence of the rule of law, and on the political monopoly both of mass communications and of economic life under communism, the connection between a multiparty system, a market economy, and genuine democracy has been more sharply established. Pluralism is now widely viewed as the antidote to totalitarianism. The result has been the widespread acceptance, now even within Communist states, of the proposition that a democratic communism is an oxymoron.

The active propagation of human rights also provides the philosophical legitimacy for more direct democratic engagement designed to nurture increasingly independent and politically assertive civil societies under existing Communist regimes. The appearance of an autonomous civil society is the point of departure for the eventual self-emancipation of society from Communist control. Independent groups are already springing up quite spontaneously in several Communist states, even in the Soviet Union, taking advantage of the new technical means for the dissemination of mass information. The autonomous political dialogue thereby surfacing can contribute to the emergence of a democratic consensus regarding needed socioeconomic changes, and thus to the transformation of dissent into actual political opposition capable at some point either of negotiating a peaceful transfer of power or of politically exploiting the degeneration of assertive Communist totalitarianism into a defensive post-Communist authoritarianism.

Indeed, some of the currently existing East European Communist regimes, after passing—perhaps with some terminal violence—through the post-Communist phase, eventually are likely to become fully integrated into the world community. Growing scientific exchanges, intellectual contacts, and even economic relations with the Communist states can thus also contribute to the process of democratizing change, especially if they coincide with efforts to enhance the emergence of genuinely autonomous civil societies under the existing Communist regimes. The bitter but also hopeful irony of history may, therefore, be that for some communism will come to be ultimately viewed as an inadvertent, and costly, transition stage from preindustrial society to a socially developed pluralistic democracy.

Such eventual absorption of some Communist states into a broader global community may be enhanced by the fact that in this century pluralistic democracies will have assimilated into their own systems some of the more benign and even constructive aspects of Marxism's quest for a perfect society. With social democracy providing much of the impulse in the West for public programs designed to enhance social well-being, recent decades have seen the incorporation even into those democratic systems that are most inclined to cherish free enterprise of a variety of state-sponsored initiatives in the areas of welfare, equal opportunity for personal enhancement, progressive taxation to reduce social inequality, access to the educational system for the less privileged, and provision of minimum medical services to the masses. Pluralistic and free enterprise democracy thereby acquired also a more developed social consciousness.

The infusion of social consciousness into the processes of political democracy has served to underline even more strongly the proposition that communism no longer has a historical mission. Democracy's heightened sense of social responsibility wedded to genuine political freedom of choice—a formula in which the state is not exalted but used as a limited tool for the enhancement of social and individual self-expression—has created a superior mechanism for the satisfaction of human needs as well as for the protection of human rights. The growing worldwide emphasis on individual initiative and on politically in-dependent social solidarity reflects the widened realization that human-kind's most soaring dreams can be turned into a nightmare if a dogmatic and all-powerful state is worshiped as history's central instrument.

Humanity's catastrophic encounter with communism during the twentieth century has thus provided a painful but critically important lesson: Utopian social engineering is fundamentally in conflict with the complexity of the human condition, and social creativity blossoms best when political power is restrained. That basic lesson makes it all the more likely that democracy—and not communism—will dom-inate the twenty-first century.

Appendix: Tables

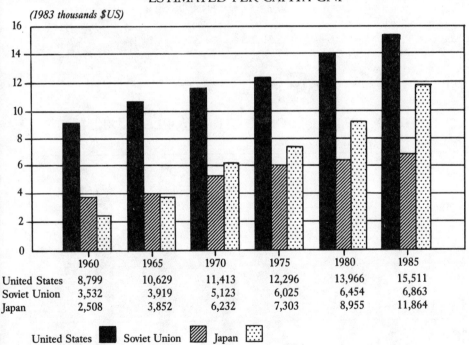

ESTIMATED PER CAPITA GNP

(1983 thousands $US)

	1960	1965	1970	1975	1980	1985
United States	8,799	10,629	11,413	12,296	13,966	15,511
Soviet Union	3,532	3,919	5,123	6,025	6,454	6,863
Japan	2,508	3,852	6,232	7,303	8,955	11,864

United States ■ Soviet Union ▨ Japan ▦

(Source: CIA)

TOTAL TRADE* IN COMPETITIVE WORLD MARKETS

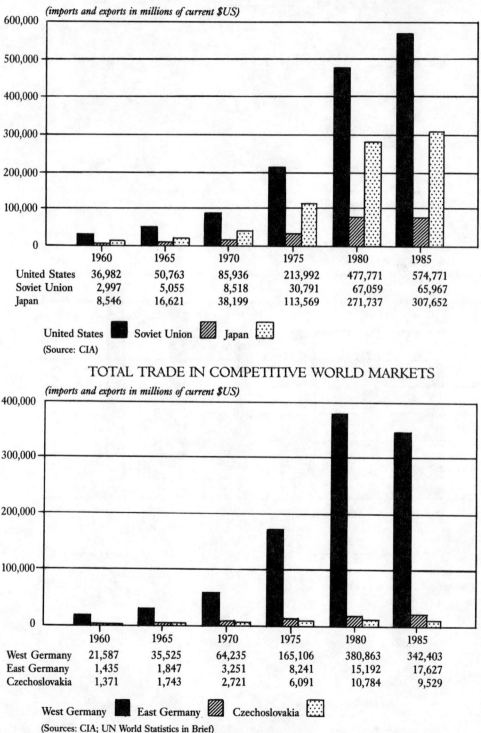

(imports and exports in millions of current $US)

	1960	1965	1970	1975	1980	1985
United States	36,982	50,763	85,936	213,992	477,771	574,771
Soviet Union	2,997	5,055	8,518	30,791	67,059	65,967
Japan	8,546	16,621	38,199	113,569	271,737	307,652

United States ■   Soviet Union ▨   Japan ▦
(Source: CIA)

TOTAL TRADE IN COMPETITIVE WORLD MARKETS

(imports and exports in millions of current $US)

	1960	1965	1970	1975	1980	1985
West Germany	21,587	35,525	64,235	165,106	380,863	342,403
East Germany	1,435	1,847	3,251	8,241	15,192	17,627
Czechoslovakia	1,371	1,743	2,721	6,091	10,784	9,529

West Germany ■   East Germany ▨   Czechoslovakia ▦
(Sources: CIA; UN World Statistics in Brief)

*The trade figures include only those transactions that take place in free markets and exclude those transpiring within state-controlled transnational organizations, such as COMECON.

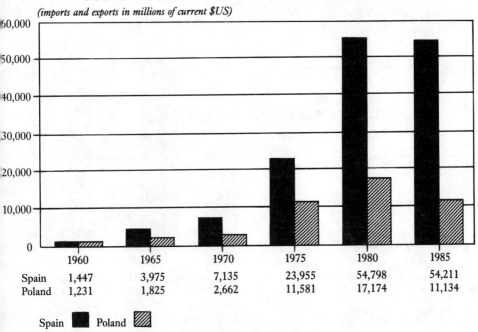

TOTAL TRADE IN COMPETITIVE WORLD MARKETS
(imports and exports in millions of current $US)

	1960	1965	1970	1975	1980	1985
Spain	1,447	3,975	7,135	23,955	54,798	54,211
Poland	1,231	1,825	2,662	11,581	17,174	11,134

Spain ■   Poland ▨

(Sources: CIA; UN World Statistics in Brief)

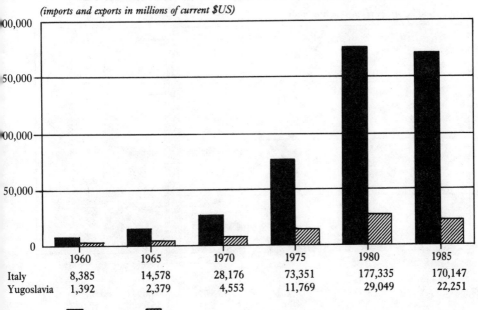

TOTAL TRADE IN COMPETITIVE WORLD MARKETS
(imports and exports in millions of current $US)

	1960	1965	1970	1975	1980	1985
Italy	8,385	14,578	28,176	73,351	177,335	170,147
Yugoslavia	1,392	2,379	4,553	11,769	29,049	22,251

Italy ■   Yugoslavia ▨

(Sources: CIA; UN World Statistics in Brief)

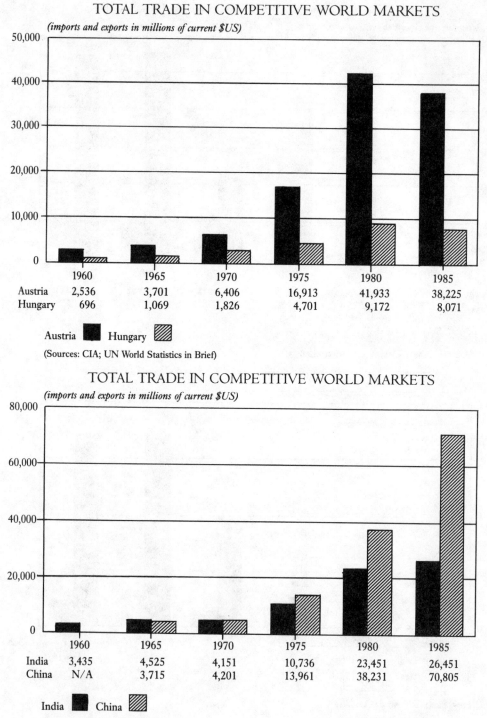

TOTAL TRADE IN COMPETITIVE WORLD MARKETS
(imports and exports in millions of current $US)

	1960	1965	1970	1975	1980	1985
Austria	2,536	3,701	6,406	16,913	41,933	38,225
Hungary	696	1,069	1,826	4,701	9,172	8,071

Austria ■   Hungary ▨

(Sources: CIA; UN World Statistics in Brief)

TOTAL TRADE IN COMPETITIVE WORLD MARKETS
(imports and exports in millions of current $US)

	1960	1965	1970	1975	1980	1985
India	3,435	4,525	4,151	10,736	23,451	26,451
China	N/A	3,715	4,201	13,961	38,231	70,805

India ■   China ▨

(Sources: CIA; UN World Statistics in Brief)

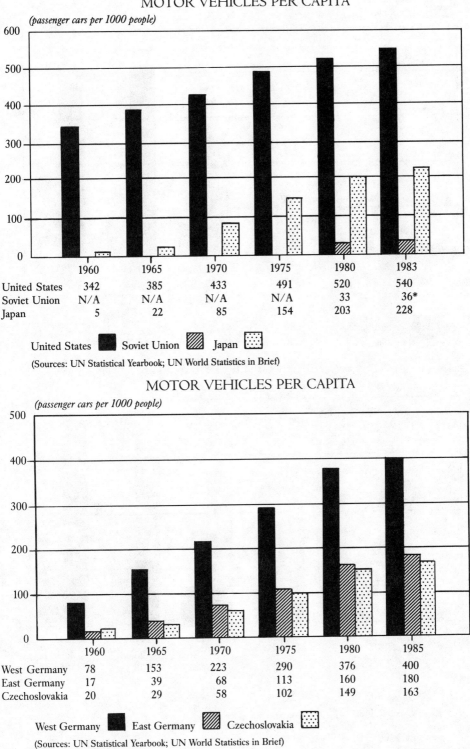

MOTOR VEHICLES PER CAPITA

(passenger cars per 1000 people)

	1960	1965	1970	1975	1980	1983
United States	342	385	433	491	520	540
Soviet Union	N/A	N/A	N/A	N/A	33	36*
Japan	5	22	85	154	203	228

United States ■   Soviet Union ▨   Japan ▦

(Sources: UN Statistical Yearbook; UN World Statistics in Brief)

MOTOR VEHICLES PER CAPITA

(passenger cars per 1000 people)

	1960	1965	1970	1975	1980	1985
West Germany	78	153	223	290	376	400
East Germany	17	39	68	113	160	180
Czechoslovakia	20	29	58	102	149	163

West Germany ■   East Germany ▨   Czechoslovakia ▦

(Sources: UN Statistical Yearbook; UN World Statistics in Brief)

*Closest available year.

MOTOR VEHICLES PER CAPITA

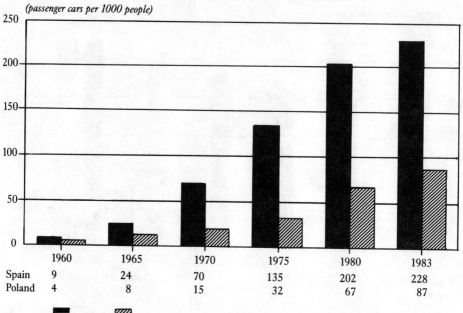

(passenger cars per 1000 people)

	1960	1965	1970	1975	1980	1983
Spain	9	24	70	135	202	228
Poland	4	8	15	32	67	87

Spain ■   Poland ▨

(Sources: UN Statistical Yearbook: UN World Statistics in Brief)

MOTOR VEHICLES PER CAPITA

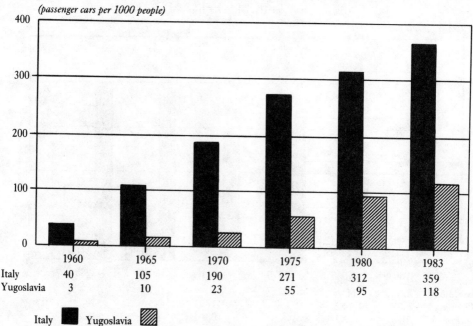

(passenger cars per 1000 people)

	1960	1965	1970	1975	1980	1983
Italy	40	105	190	271	312	359
Yugoslavia	3	10	23	55	95	118

Italy ■   Yugoslavia ▨

(Sources: UN Statistical Yearbook; UN World Statistics in Brief)

MOTOR VEHICLES PER CAPITA

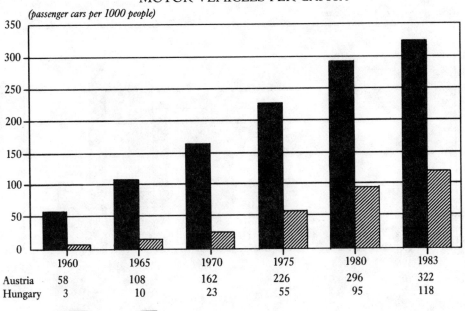

(passenger cars per 1000 people)

	1960	1965	1970	1975	1980	1983
Austria	58	108	162	226	296	322
Hungary	3	10	23	55	95	118

Austria ■ Hungary ▨

(Sources: UN Statistical Yearbook; UN World Statistics in Brief)

TELEPHONES PER CAPITA

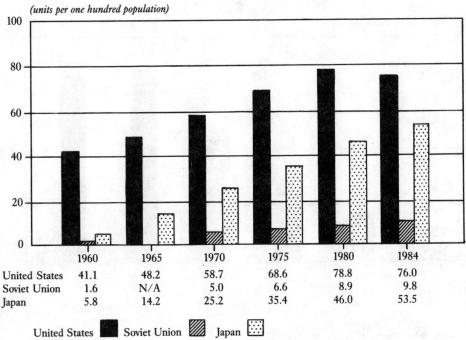

(units per one hundred population)

	1960	1965	1970	1975	1980	1984
United States	41.1	48.2	58.7	68.6	78.8	76.0
Soviet Union	1.6	N/A	5.0	6.6	8.9	9.8
Japan	5.8	14.2	25.2	35.4	46.0	53.5

United States ■ Soviet Union ▨ Japan ▦

(Source: UN Statistical Yearbook)

TELEPHONES PER CAPITA

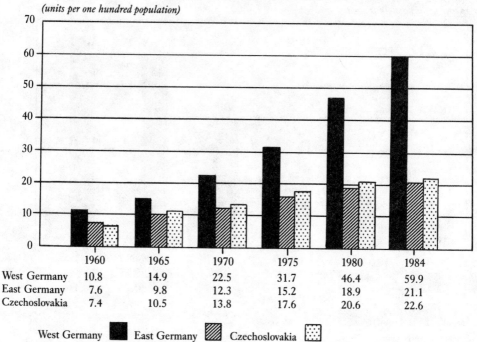

West Germany █   East Germany ▨   Czechoslovakia ▦
(Source: UN Statistical Yearbook)

TELEPHONES PER CAPITA

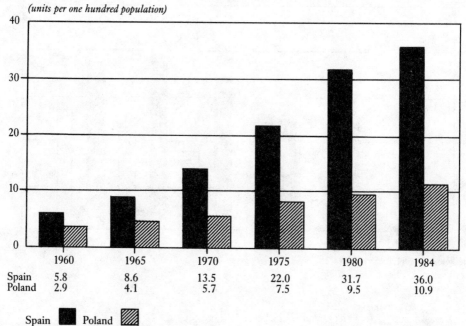

Spain █   Poland ▨
(Source: UN Statistical Yearbook)

TELEPHONES PER CAPITA

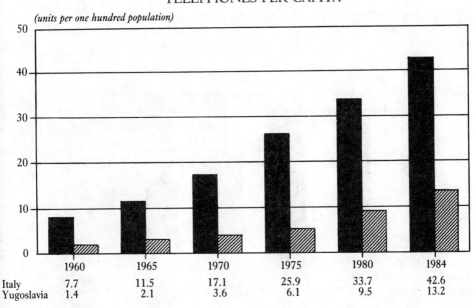

(units per one hundred population)

	1960	1965	1970	1975	1980	1984
Italy	7.7	11.5	17.1	25.9	33.7	42.6
Yugoslavia	1.4	2.1	3.6	6.1	9.5	13.2

Italy ■ Yugoslavia ▨

(Source: UN Statistical Yearbook)

TELEPHONES PER CAPITA

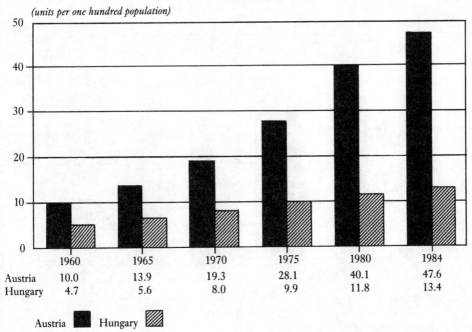

(units per one hundred population)

	1960	1965	1970	1975	1980	1984
Austria	10.0	13.9	19.3	28.1	40.1	47.6
Hungary	4.7	5.6	8.0	9.9	11.8	13.4

Austria ■ Hungary ▨

(Source: UN Statistical Yearbook)

INFANT MORTALITY
(deaths in first year per 1000 births)

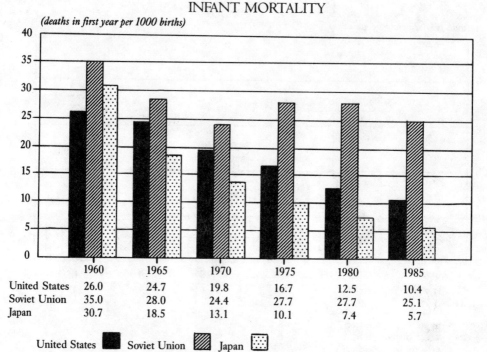

	1960	1965	1970	1975	1980	1985
United States	26.0	24.7	19.8	16.7	12.5	10.4
Soviet Union	35.0	28.0	24.4	27.7	27.7	25.1
Japan	30.7	18.5	13.1	10.1	7.4	5.7

United States ■ Soviet Union ▨ Japan ⬚

(Sources: UN Demographic Yearbook; UN Statistical Yearbook)

INFANT MORTALITY
(deaths in first year per 1000 live births)

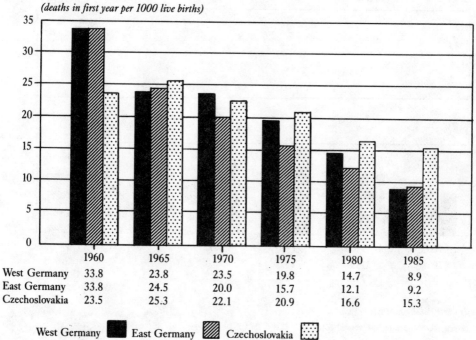

	1960	1965	1970	1975	1980	1985
West Germany	33.8	23.8	23.5	19.8	14.7	8.9
East Germany	33.8	24.5	20.0	15.7	12.1	9.2
Czechoslovakia	23.5	25.3	22.1	20.9	16.6	15.3

West Germany ■ East Germany ▨ Czechoslovakia ⬚

(Sources: UN Demographic Yearbook; UN Statistical Yearbook)

Appendix **269**

INFANT MORTALITY

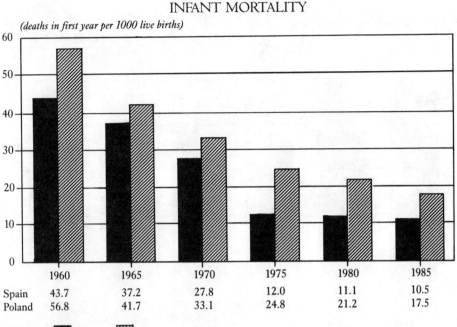

(deaths in first year per 1000 live births)

	1960	1965	1970	1975	1980	1985
Spain	43.7	37.2	27.8	12.0	11.1	10.5
Poland	56.8	41.7	33.1	24.8	21.2	17.5

Spain ■ Poland ▨

(Sources: UN Demographic Yearbook; UN Statistical Yearbook)

INFANT MORTALITY

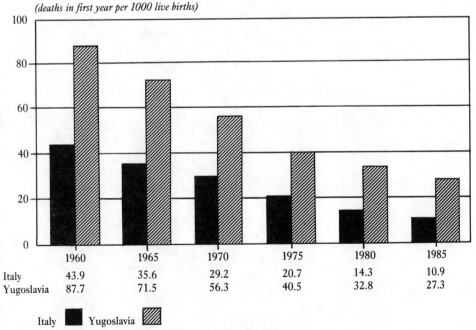

(deaths in first year per 1000 live births)

	1960	1965	1970	1975	1980	1985
Italy	43.9	35.6	29.2	20.7	14.3	10.9
Yugoslavia	87.7	71.5	56.3	40.5	32.8	27.3

Italy ■ Yugoslavia ▨

(Sources: UN Demographic Yearbook; UN Statistical Yearbook)

INFANT MORTALITY

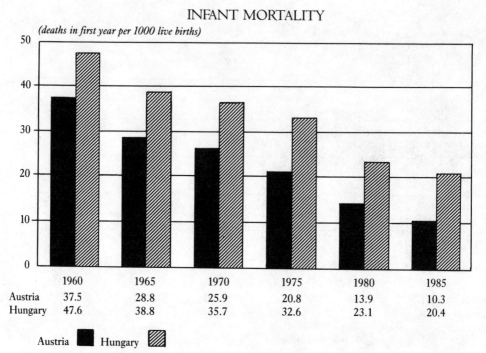

(deaths in first year per 1000 live births)

	1960	1965	1970	1975	1980	1985
Austria	37.5	28.8	25.9	20.8	13.9	10.3
Hungary	47.6	38.8	35.7	32.6	23.1	20.4

Austria ■   Hungary ▨

(Sources: UN Demographic Yearbook; UN Statistical Yearbook)

Index

Abalkin, L. I., 66–67
Abolition of property, 1–2
"Action Program," 57, 62
Afanasyev, Yevgeniy, 38
Afghanistan, 91–92
Africa, 212–215
Aganbegyan, Abel, 66, 88
Agricultural decollectivization, Chinese, 165
Agriculture, collectivized, 66, 68
Aitmatov, Chingiz, 80
Alcoholism, 37
Algeria, 212, 213
American capitalism, 217–218
American prosperity, 3–4
Andropov, Yuri, 42
Angola, 212, 213, 214, 215
    index of crisis level in, 234
Anti-American perspective, 217
Argentina, 219, 224
Armenians, 90, 246
Asia, 214
Atheism, 81, 82
    in Poland, 124
Authoritarianism, Communist and
    post-Communist, 255
Autonomous civil society, 256–257
Autonomy, political, 102
Azerbaijanis, 90, 246

Ballot, secret, 76
Batkin, Leonid, 34
Beijing University, 168
Bell, Daniel, 174
Benin, 212, 214
Between Two Ages, vii
Bierut, Boleslaw, 195
Black, Cyril, 31
Bogomolov, A. I., 25–26
Bogomolov, O., 92
Bolivia, 217
Bolshevik Revolution, 15, 17
Bolshevism, 56
Bonino, José Miguez, 218
Bourgeois policy, 200
Bovin, Aleksandr, 92, 140, 198, 201–202

Brazil, 219
Brezhnev, Leonid, 32, 33
Brezhnev doctrine, 112, 197
Brezhnev legacy, 41
Bribery, 169
Britain, see England
Brovikov, Vladimir, 142
Brzezinski, Zbigniew, vii–viii, 160
Bulgaria
    future prospects in, 249
    index of crisis level in, 234
Bureaucratic conservatism, 164
Bureaucratic opposition, 67–68
Bureaucratization, 111
Burlatskiy, Fedor, 49, 176–177
Buying, panic, 66
Byelorussia, 246

Cambodia, 214
Canada, 202
Cape Verde, 212
Capitalism
    American, 217–218
    crisis of, 200
    general crisis of, 233
Capitalist industrialization, 204–205
Car ownership statistics, 238
Castro, Fidel, 199, 221
Catholic religion, Roman, 114–116
Ceauşescu, Nicolae, 134–135
Central America, communism in, 223–224
Central Europe, 139
Centralism, democratic, 162, 227
Chebrikov, Viktor M., 19, 72–73
Chernenko, Konstantin, 42
Chiang Kai-shek, 151–152
China, 151
    coastal strategy of modernization of, 179,
        180, 183
    Cultural Revolution in, 61, 155
    future prospects in, 249–250
    index of crisis level in, 234
    Soviet Union rift with, 227
    Soviet Union versus, 175–183
Chinese agricultural decollectivization, 165

271

Chinese communism, 150–156
    reform of, 147–149
Chinese industrialization, 166
Chinese People's Communes, 154
Chinese reforms, 1, 163–174
Chow, G. C., 155
Chu Teh, 148
Church, Russian Orthodox, 81–82
Ciosek, Stanisław, 11–12
Civil society, autonomous, 256–257
Class struggle, 2, 108–109
Coastal strategy of China's modernization,
    179, 180, 183
Cold War, 10, 195
Collectivized agriculture, 66, 68
Cominform, 190, 195
Comintern, 190, 192–193
Commercial communism, 178
Communes, Chinese People's, 154
Communications, 7
    mass, 254
Communism, 6, 164
    African, 212–215
    agony of, 251
    approaching end of, 191
    in Britain, 209
    in Central America, 223–224
    Chinese, see Chinese communism
    commercial, 178
    contemporary, 244
    death of, 53, 54
    discrediting, 94
    doctrinal eclipse of, 64
    doctrinal obsolescence of, 201
    in Eastern Europe, 107–113
    Eurocommunism, 205
    French, 206–207
    full, 53
    future prospects of, 243–251
    general crisis of, 232–235
    historical record of, 236–242
    on Iberian peninsula, 207–209
    ideological crisis of, 225
    Indonesian, 212
    institutional shortcomings of, 241–242
    Italian, 205–206
    in Japan, 202–204
    in Latin America, 215–222
    long-range alternatives for, 253
    in Mexico, 223–224
    operational level of failure of, 241
    oppression and, 231
    overthrow of, 245
    phases in retreat from, 255
    philosophical roots of failure of, 242
    Polish, 114–119
    Portuguese, 208–209
    post-communism, 252–258
    prospects for, 95–102

rejection of, by Eastern Europe, 106
    rise of, 6
    Soviet-style, 189
    Spanish, 208
    spread of, 8–9, 11
    terminal crisis of, 1
    in Western Europe, 204–209
    world, 199, 233
Communist authoritarianism, 255
Communist doctrine, 2
Communist Information Bureau, 190, 195
Communist International, 190, 192–193
Communist party, reform in, 75–77
Communist totalitarianism, 255
Competitiveness, global, 237
Computers, 36
Confederation, Soviet, 246
Congo, 212, 214
Conquest, Robert, 27
Conservatism, bureaucratic, 164
Conspiracy in power, 241
Conspiratorial resistance, 114
Consumer goods, 69
Cooperatives, small-scale, 66
Corruption, 169
Coup, military-police, 246
Creative intelligentsia, 78–79
Crisis, ecological, 238
Crisis level, index of, 234
Cuba, 199, 215, 218–222
    index of crisis level in, 234
Cultural Revolution in China, 61, 155
Cultural self-confidence, 183
Cultural superiority, 105
Culture, political, 43–44
Czechoslovakia, 137–139
    future prospects in, 249
    index of crisis level in, 234

De Custine, Astolphe, 44, 65
Debate(s)
    intellectual, 93–94
    internal Soviet, 65–66
Decentralization, economic, 96, 169–170
"Decision of the Central Committee of the
    Communist Party of China on Reform of
    the Economic Structure," 166–167
Decollectivization, Chinese agricultural, 165
Decolonization, 210
Defense, imperial, 140–144
Defense policy, 92
Democracy, 4
    fear of, 61
    social, 15, 55–56
    Western-style, 63
"Democracy Wall," 158
Democratic centralism, 162, 227
"Democratic dictatorship, people's," 174
"Democratic pluralism," 128

Democratic socialism, 9
Democratization, 44, 45–46
  political, 70–75
  post-Communist, 255–256
Demokratizatsiia, 58–59, 63
  backlash against, 99
Deng Xiaoping, 147–148, 155, 157–159, 162
Deportations, mass, 239–240
Despotism, 44
Deutscher, Isaac, 31
Dictatorship
  definitiion of, 20
  military, 100, 102
  "people's democratic," 174
  of the proletariat, 17
Dimitrov, Georgi, 194
Dissent, 135
Dmowski, Roman, 121
Dobrynin, Anatoly, 190–191
Doctrinal infallibility, 63
Doctrinal obsolescence of communism, 201
Doctrinal purity and doctrinal unity, choice
  between, 225–228
Domestic standards of living, 237
Dubček, Alexander, 57, 62, 134, 137,
  138–139
Dzerzhinskiy, Feliks, 72

East Germany, 57
  future prospects in, 249
  index of crisis level in, 234
Eastern Europe, 93, 105–106, 132, 139
  changes in, 247–248
  communism in, 107–113
  rejection of communism by, 106
  terror in, 110–111
Eberstadt, Nick, 238
Ecological crisis, 238
Economic decentralization, 96, 169–170
Economic failure, political stability and, 102
Economic hierarchy, global, 40
Economic pragmatism, 12
Economic reform, 66–68
Economic zones
  "free," 88
  special Chinese, 167
Economics, 36
Ecumenism, philosophical, 251
El Salvador, 218, 222
Emptiness, spiritual, 80
Energy per unit of production, 36
England, 4–5
  communism in, 209
Enhanced responsibility, system of, 66
Entrepreneurial initiative, 167
Estonians, 88, 246
Ethiopia, 212, 213, 215
  index of crisis level in, 234
Ethnicity, 242

Eurocommunism, 205
Europe, 139
  Central, 139
  Eastern, *see* Eastern Europe
  non-Communist, 209
  united, 247–248
  Western, communism in, 204–209
European Community, 209
Executions, 239–240

Fairbank, J. K., 185
Fang Lizhi, 181–182
Farms, household, 169
Fascism, 6, 30
Fegnalli, Jandira, 219
Feuchtwanger, Lion, 9
Food rationing, 37
Forced resettlement, 239–240
Ford Foundation, 116
Foreign policy, 92
France, 5
  Marxism in, 207
Franco, Francisco, 208
"Free economic zones," 88
French Communist party (PCF), 206–207

Gang of Four, 159
Gelman, Aleksandr, 45–46
Georgians, 90, 246
Gerasimov, Gennadi, 134
Germany, 5
  East, *see* East Germany
Ghana, 214
Gierek, Edward, 126
Gillin, J. L., 10
Glasnost (overtness) campaign, 43, 54, 58, 247
Global competitiveness, 237
Global economic hierarchy, 40
Global modernization, 203–204
GNP (gross national product), 35, 39–40, 53
Gomułka, Władysław, 56–57, 195
Gorbachev, Mikhail, 21, 30, 42–45, 53–54,
  175–176, 227
  revisionism and, 55, 57–64
Gottwald, Klement, 195
Grain imports, 37
Gramsci, Antonio, 128
Granin, Daniil, 80
Great Britain, *see* England
Great Depression, 202
Great Leap Forward, 153–155, 196
Great Russian nationalism, 245
Gromova, Valentina Zinovevna, 25–27
Gross national product (GNP), 35, 39–40, 53
Grosz, Karoly, 137
Guatemala, 222
Guevara, Che, 217
Guinea, 211, 213
Guinea-Bissau, 212

GULAG, 24
Gutiérrez, Gustavo, 218
Guyana, 219

Harding, Harry, 180
Harvard University, 168
Havel, Vaclav, 111
"Hegemonism," 203
Hindus, Maurice, 10
Historical dialectic, 2
Historical record of communism, 236–242
Hitler, Adolf, 7–8
Hodgkin, Henry, 9–10
Hollander, Paul, 9
Honduras, 222
Hong Kong, 183–184
Hong-qi (Red Flag) journal, 174
Household farms, 169
Hu Qili, 12, 174
Hu Yaobang, 159–163
Hua Guofeng, 157, 158
Human rights, 256
Human suffering, 239–240
Hungary, 56, 133, 136–137
    future prospects in, 248
    index of crisis level in, 234

Iberian peninsula, communism on, 207–209
Imperial defense, 140–144
Imperialism, 200
Import, grain, 37
Index of crisis level in Communist states, 234
India, 211–212
Indifferentism, 251
Indonesia, 211–212
Industrial robots, 36
Industrialism, 6
Industrialization, 29–30, 108
    capitalist, 204–205
    Chinese, 166
Infallibility, doctrinal, 63
Infant mortality, 37
Inflation, reforms and, 179–180
"Informal groups," 73–74
Initiative, private, 167
Institutional reform, 71
Institutional Revolutionary Party (PRI), 223
Intellectual debate, 93–94
Intelligentsia, creative, 78–79
International trade, 167–168
Ionin, L. G., 85
Islam, 89
Italian communism, 205–206

Japan, 35–36, 237
    communism in, 202–204
Jaruzelski, Wojciech, 123, 126
John Paul II, 220

Kádár, János, 133
Katyń Massacre, 84, 131
Kazakhstan, 246
Kennedy, Paul, 151
Kenya, 213
Kerensky, Aleksandr, 18
KGB, 71, 72
Khrushchev, Nikita, 32, 34–35, 53, 196,
    210–211
KOR (Workers' Defense Committee), 121
Kuklinski, Ryszard, 141
Kuomintang, 152
Kurile Islands chain, 203

Land, private ownership of, 165–166
Languages, Russification of, 88
Laos, 214
Laski, Harold, 10, 212
Latin America, communism in, 215–222
Latvians, 88, 246
Leftism, 10
Lendvai, Paul, 110
Lenin, Vladimir Ilyich, 7, 17–21, 193
Lenin Mausoleum, 243
Leninism, 8
    redefining, 47–50
    Stalinism and, 86–87
Leninist era, 18–19
Leninist legacy, 41, 55
    centrality of, 96
Li Peng, 162–163, 179
Liberalization, 45–46
    political, 170
Liberation theology, 218, 220
Libya, 212, 213
Ligachev, Yegor, 45, 46, 78–79
Limits on tenure of office, 176
Lithuanians, 88, 246
Living, domestic standards of, 237

MacFarquhar, Roderick, 185
Madagascar, 212
Malenkov, Georgyi, 82
Manuilsky, Dimitry, 194
Mao Zedong, 148, 151, 152–156
Mao Zedong thought, 153
Market-mechanism, 96, 126
Martial law, 119, 120
Marxism, 2, 6, 15, 105
    in China, 161
    in France, 207
    perversion of, 201
Marxism-Leninism, 61
    in China, 157
Marxism-Leninism-Stalinism, 105
Marxist-Leninist doctrine, 35
Marxist-Leninist "praxis," 189, 199
Marxist-Leninist theory, 196
Mass communications, 254

Mass deportations, 239–240
Mass media, Soviet, 79
Mass murders, 7, 27
Mass terror, 20
Mensheviks, 56
Mexico, communism in, 223–224
Military dictatorship, 100, 102
Military-police coup, 246
Miłosz, Czesław, 107
"Mitteleuropa," 139
Moczar, Mieczysław, 107
Modernization
    China's, coastal strategy of, 179, 180, 183
    global, 203–204
"Modernizations, four," 156, 158
Monopoly of power, 50
Morality, socialist, 80–81
Moslems, 89
Mozambique, 212, 213
    index of crisis level in, 234
Murders, mass, 7, 27
Musiyenko, Oleksa, 89
Mussolini, Benito, 7

Nagy, Imre, 56
National Democratic Front, 223
National Fronts, 76–77
National unity, Soviet, 87–91
Nationalism, 242
    Great Russian, 245
    growing, 98–99
    resurgence of, vii
Nationalist manifestations, 87–90
Nationalist separatism, 130
Nazism, 6
NEP (New Economic Policy), 18–19
New Deal, 202
New Economic Policy (NEP), 18–19
Nicaragua, 199, 215, 218–222
Nineteenth Special Party Conference, 58–59
Nomenklatura, 19, 33, 42
North Korea, index of crisis level in, 234

Office, limits on tenure of, 176
Oksenberg, Michel, 180
Oppression, communism and, 231
Orthodox church, Russian, 81–82
Ownership, private
    car, statistics, 238
    of land, 165–166

Paetzke, Hans-Henning, 109
Pamyat (memory) group, 74, 247
Panama, 222
Panic buying, 66
Passivity, 62
PCE (Spanish Communist party), 208
PCF (French Communist party), 206–207
PCI (Communist party in Italy), 205

People's Communes, Chinese, 154
"People's democratic dictatorship," 174
Perestroika (restructuring), 43, 53, 58, 245, 247
    obstacles to, 48
    options to, 100
    professed goals of, 246
    second political stage of, 60
Perestroika (Gorbachev book), 62
Personalism, 122
    "socialist," 125
Peru, 219, 224
Peshketov, Vasiliy Petrovich, 28
Philosophical ecumenism, 251
Planning, social, 11
Plimak, E., 201
Pluralism, 124, 256
    "democratic," 128
    political, 126–127, 181
    post-Communist, 255
    "socialist," 127–128
    socioeconomic, 181
Pluralistic political framework, 96
Poland, 56–57
    future prospects in, 248–249
    index of crisis level in, 234
Police, secret, 19, 72
Polish communism, 114–119
Polish-Czechoslovak statement, 131
Polish political life, 121–125
Polish Socialist party (PPS), 116, 121
Polish underground press, 120–121
Political autonomy, 102
Political culture, 43–44
Political democratization, 70–75
Political framework, pluralistic, 96
Political liberalization, 170
Political life, Polish, 121–125
Political pluralism, 126–127, 181
Political power, 3
Political reform, 58, 96
Political stability, economic failure and, 102
Politics, 34
"Polycentrism," 195, 206
Popular Fronts, 76–77
Population growth rates, 97
Portuguese communism, 208–209
Post-communism, 252–258
Post-Communist authoritarianism, 255
Post-Communist pluralism, 255
Poverty, 237–238
Power, 7
    conspiracy in, 241
    monopoly of, 50
    political, 3
    state, 23
Pozsgay, Imre, 136, 137
PPS (Polish Socialist party), 116, 121
Pragmatism, economic, 12

Prague Spring, 57, 110, 112
"Praxis," Marxist-Leninist, 189, 199
Press, Polish underground, 120–121
PRI (Institutional Revolutionary Party), 223
Price reform, 171
Pricing system, 169
Prigogine, Ilya, 174
Primakov, Ye., 92
"Primary stage of socialism," 172–173
"Principles, four," 157
Private enterprise, 171
Private initiative, 167
Private ownership, see Ownership, private
Privatization, 214
Privileges, special, 69–70, 127
Proletariat, 17
Property, abolition of, 1–2
Prosperity, American, 3–4
Public opinion polls, Radio Free Europe, 138
Purity, doctrinal, and doctrinal unity,
      225–228

Qin dynasty, 153
Quotas, 39

Radio Free Europe public opinion polls, 138
Rajk, Laszlo, 109
Rakosi, Matyas, 195
Rationing, food, 37
Reactionary repression, 100
Receptivity, social, to reform, 97
Red Flag journal, 174
Red Square, 243
Reform
    boundaries of, 41–45
    Chinese, 1, 163–174
    of Chinese communism, 147–149
    in Communist party, 75–77
    drive for, 54
    economic, 66–68
    inflation and, 179–180
    institutional, 71
    need for, 46–50
    political, 58, 96
    price, 171
    social receptivity to, 97
    urgency of, 59–60
Religion(s), 2
    appeal of, 242
    revival of, 81–82
    Roman Catholic, 114–116
Repression, reactionary, 100
Resentment, social, 38
Resettlement, forced, 239–240
Resistance, conspiratorial, 114
Responsibility, system of enhanced, 66
Revisionism, 54, 55

Gorbachev and, 55, 57–64
    manifestations of, 56
Revolution, socialist, 200
Revolutionary situation, 101
Robots, industrial, 36
Roman Catholic religion, 114–116
Romania, 134–135, 137
    index of crisis level in, 234
Roosevelt, Theodore, 4
Russia, see Soviet Union
Russian Orthodox church, 81–82
Russian Revolution, 15, 17
Russification of languages, 88

Sakharov, Andrei, 130
Sandinistas, 199
São Tomé and Principe, 212, 214
Sartre, Jean-Paul, 198
Scherer, J. L., 166
Schuldfrage, term, 85
Secret ballot, 76
Secret police, 19, 72
Self-confidence, cultural, 183
Selyunin, V., 49
Separatism, nationalist, 130
Separatist attitudes, 97–98
Seychelles, 212
Shaw, George Bernard, 10
Shmelyov, Nikolai, 67
Siberia, 24
Singapore, 132
Sino-American cooperation, 167–168, 199
Sino-Soviet split, 196–197
Slavic Ukraine, 246
Small-scale cooperatives, 66
Soares, Mário, 208
Social change, 48
Social democracy, 15, 55–56
Social engineering, utopian, 258
Social planning, 11
Social priorities, 68–70
Social receptivity to reform, 97
Social resentment, 38
Socialism, 5, 15, 211
    dawn of, 18
    democratic, 9
    "in one country," 22
    "primary stage of," 172–173
    state, 9
    understanding, 9
Socialist morality, 80–81
"Socialist personalism," 125
"Socialist pluralism," 127–128
Socialist revolution, 200
Society, 21
    autonomous civil, 256–257
    politicized, 34
    subordination of, to state, 136

Socioeconomic pluralism, 181
Solidarity, 117–119
Solzhenitsyn, Aleksandr, 31, 101
South Africa, 212
Soviet Bloc: Unity and Conflict, vii
Soviet Confederation, 246
Soviet debates, internal, 65–66
Soviet failure, 15
Soviet High Command, 141
Soviet mass media, 79
Soviet national unity, 87–91
Soviet-style communism, 189
Soviet Union, 194; *see also* Russian *entries*
    alternative outcomes in, 245–247
    China versus, 175–183
    failure of, 199
    index of crisis level in, 234
    rift with China, 227
Sovietization, 108–109, 141–142
Spanish Communist party (PCE), 208
Special Party Conference, Nineteenth, 58–59
Spiritual emptiness, 80
Sputnik, 34
Stagnation, 34–35
    renewed period of, 245
Stalin, Joseph, 7–8, 21–24, 27–32, 194
Stalinism, 33–34
    dismantling of, 47
    issue of, 82–87
    Leninism and, 86–87
Stalinist legacy, 41
Standards of living, domestic, 237
Starvation, Ukrainian, 24
State power, 23
State socialism, 9, 211
State, the, 7
    centrality of, 21
    subordination of society to, 136
State violence, 22–24
Statism, flight from, 12
Steel, per unit of production, 36
Suffering, human, 239–240
Sun Yatsen, 151–152
Superiority, cultural, 105

Tadjikistan, 246
Taiwan, 167, 184
Tanzania, 212, 213, 214
Tatu, Michel, 92
Tenure of office, limits on, 176
Terror
    in Eastern Europe, 110–111
    mass, 20
    reliance on, 19–20
Thailand, 214
Theology, liberation, 218, 220
Third World, 210–224
    future prospects in, 250–251

Tito, Marshal, 195
Toffler, Alvin, 174
Togliatti, Palmiro, 195
Toranska, Teresa, 115
Totalitarianism, 7–8, 41, 111
    abandonment of, 96
    communist, 255
Touré, Sékou, 211, 213
Trade, international, 167–168
Transylvanian Hungarians, 135
Trotsky, Leon, 22, 192, 193
Tukhachevskiy, Marshal, 84
Turkmenstan, 246
Twitchett, Denis, 185

Ukrainian starvation, 24
Ukrainians, 98, 246
Ulbricht, Walter, 195
Underground press, Polish, 120–121
Unemployment, 68
United Europe, 247–248
United Front, 152
United States, 202
Unity
    doctrinal, and doctrinal purity, 225–228
    Soviet national, 87–91
Urgency of reform, 59–60
Uruguay, 224
USSR, *see* Soviet Union
Utopian social engineering, 258
Uzbekistan, 246

Valladares, Armando, 222
Vanguard party, 17
Video cassette recorders (VCRs), 138
Vietnam, 199, 214
    index of crisis level in, 234
Violence
    justification of, 2
    state, 22–24
Voznesensky, A. A., 23

Wage-leveling, 63
Walesa, Lech, 117
Warsaw Pact, 106, 141
Webb, Sidney and Beatrice, 10
Wei Jingsheng, 158–159
Welfare state, 9
Western Europe, communism in, 204–209
Western-style democracy, 63
Wilson, Edmund, 10
Winiecki, Jan, 36
Witos, Wincenty, 121
Workers' Defense Committee (KOR), 121
World communism, 199, 233
World Marxist Review, 190
World War I, 6

World War II, 8, 107–108
Wyszyński, Stefan Cardinal, 116

Yakovlev, Aleksandr, 11
Yeltsin, Boris, 69–70
Yugoslavia, 56
  index of crisis level in, 234

Zambia, 212
Zhao Ziyang, 159, 162, 163, 170–175,
  181–182
Zhivkov, Todor, 132
Zhou Enlai, 148, 155, 162–163
Zinoviev, Grigori, 192, 193